PRAISE FOR *THE BLOOD OF PATRIOTS*

"Endlessly entertaining and as timely as it gets. This reads like an Elmore Leonard yarn and wakes you up like a Jon Stewart bit."
—Thom Hartmann, *New York Times* bestselling author
and internationally syndicated radio host

"*The Blood of Patriots* is one hell of a read. It's a page-turner that combines the thrilling elements of a Richard North Patterson novel with the hard-hitting gonzo reportage of the late Hunter S. Thompson. Its publication couldn't be more timely. I salute Bill Fulton. This book taught me what patriotism really means."
—Jason Leopold, investigative reporter for BuzzFeed
and Emmy-nominated journalist

"A crazy book, but good crazy. If this were a novel, you'd love the rocking read. But it's for real, and that really makes it rattle your cage. A brilliant, quirky keyhole into the armed and dangerous brains of America's fringe—which is no longer fringe."
—Greg Palast, *New York Times* bestselling author of
The Best Democracy Money Can Buy

"Knowing Bill Fulton during the timeframe presented in this book, I can attest that saying 'Bill took one for the team' is an understatement. His humor and constant redirection of credit away from himself, does nothing to change the stress and real danger that he and his family went through. True to Bill's character; he found a problem, analyzed the problem and possible solutions, intervened to fix the problem and prevent even greater problems, and then faced the backlash without reward. Today, there are innocent people still alive because Bill Fulton wasn't just willing to do the right thing, but also because Bill Fulton was willing to be prepared to do the right thing.

Jeanne Devon is the perfect person to collaborate with Bill Fulton on this story. She seeks experiences that are contrary to her nature to write about. Jeanne can easily present both sides of a story to find the underlying truth and significance of any opinion or event. Even though she may play a part in a story, she presents it as if the reader were the actual observer. Much like Bill, Jeanne will only allow herself to be recognized for a fraction of what she deserves credit for."

—Kenneth Blaylock, lieutenant colonel (retired) and martial arts instructor

THE BLOOD
OF PATRIOTS

THE BLOOD OF PATRIOTS

HOW I **TOOK DOWN** AN ANTI-GOVERNMENT **MILITIA** WITH **BEER, BOUNTY HUNTING,** AND **BADASSERY**

BILL FULTON

AND JEANNE DEVON

BenBella Books, Inc.

Dallas, TX

BenBella

BenBella Books, Inc.
10440 North Central Expressway, Suite 800
Dallas, Texas 75231
www.benbellabooks.com
Send feedback to feedback@benbellabooks.com

Printed in the United States of America
10 9 8 7 6 5 4 3 2 1

Library of Congress Cataloging in Publication
Names: Fulton, Bill (Undercover operative), author. | Devon, Jeanne, author.
Title: The blood of patriots : how I took down an anti-government militia with beer, bounty hunting, and badassery / by Bill Fulton and Jeanne Devon.
Description: Dallas, TX : BenBella Books, Inc., 2017. | Includes bibliographical references and index.
Identifiers: LCCN 2016052704 (print) | LCCN 2017005658 (ebook) | ISBN 9781944648077 (trade cloth : alk. paper) | ISBN 9781944648084 (electronic)
Subjects: LCSH: Fulton, Bill (Undercover operative) | Informers—Alaska—Biography. | Undercover operations—Alaska. | Militia movements—Alaska. | Terrorism—United States. | United States. Federal Bureau of Investigation.
Classification: LCC HV7911.F85 F85 2017 (print) | LCC HV7911.F85 (ebook) | DDC 364.1/31—dc23
LC record available at https://lccn.loc.gov/2016052704

Editing by Vy Tran
Copyediting by Brian J. Buchanan
Proofreading by Erica Harmon and Cape Cod Compositors, Inc.

Cover design by Ty Nowicki
Jacket design by Sarah Avinger
Text design and composition by Aaron Edmiston
Printed by Lake Book Manufacturing

Distributed by Perseus Distribution
www.perseusdistribution.com

To place orders through Perseus Distribution:
Tel: (800) 343-4499
Fax: (800) 351-5073
E-mail: orderentry@perseusbooks.com

Special discounts for bulk sales (minimum of 25 copies) are available.
Please contact Aida Herrera at aida@benbellabooks.com.

"The tree of liberty must be refreshed from time to time
with the blood of patriots and tyrants."
—**Thomas Jefferson**
—**Timothy McVeigh's T-shirt**

CHAPTER 1

★ ★ ★ ★ ★

NORTHERN MIGRATION

"There are strange things done in the midnight sun . . ."
—**Robert Service,** *The Cremation of Sam McGee*

The rat in the back seat of the U-Haul gave birth somewhere in the Yukon. White-knuckling the wheel through icy mountain passes, trying to corral two basset hounds and a fat orange cat with seventeen plastic bags of my prized and pampered tropical fish stacked across the dashboard heater, I was oblivious to the miracle of life happening two feet behind me. The cat bore witness alone. He'd managed to get his paw between the bars of the cage and enjoyed the fresh, warm snack delivery. He'd finished off all but two before he either got full or mama rat went into defense mode. Life was brutal on the open road, as it tended to be everywhere.

My new wife Stacey's mortal fear of flying was what you might call a "newlywed discovery." We'd had lots of those considering we married only thirty days after we met at a strip club. That sounds like the beginning of a "What was I thinking?" story, but it was really more of a "What was *she* thinking?" story. I could tell she didn't want to be there. She looked like a fish out of water. And no, I did not save her from a seedy life on stage taking off her clothes for a bunch of jackass drunk guys. I was the one on stage, and she saved me. I thought it might be fun, so I was moonlighting from the Army and making a few extra bucks on the side. So while the other women at the bachelorette party were stuffing my G-string with bills and shrieking, all I could see was this beautiful, awkward, uncomfortable girl with a sweet face and dark hair who looked like she wanted to be any-where else on the face of the earth than in a strip club with her rowdy co-workers. I tried to talk to her after the show. She wanted nothing to do with me. At all. But luckily for me she had gotten a ride to the club and the driver had no intention of leaving early. She finally talked to me, and I was thunderstruck. Like in the movies. I absolutely had to marry this girl, and all I had to do was convince her she had to marry me too.

I don't want to call what ensued "stalking," per se. But it did involve a lot of roast beef and cheddar sandwiches from the Arby's where she was the night manager, and flowers, and pouring out my heart over the counter. And whatever I did, it worked. She said she'd go on a date. And then another. And then she said yes. I didn't want to question my unbelievable luck, but I swore I was going to do everything in my power not to fuck this up. I would go to the ends of the earth for this woman. And her terror of flying meant that I'd be going to the ends of the earth in a rental van. And so we left my Army post at Fort Stewart, Georgia, and headed out for Fort Richardson, Alaska. Nothing says "I love you" like a cross-continental drive with a traveling zoo. That's the way I thought of it, anyway.

The simultaneous launch of our marriage and the 4,000-mile odyssey into the unpaved and unpopulated arctic took place in December. Don't believe anyone in Georgia who tells you a vehicle has been "fully weath-erized" for a road trip to Alaska in the winter, because they're full of shit.

The U-Haul truck that would be our home on wheels belonged to a fleet with one of fifty designs painted on the sides—a different illustration for each state of the Union. We'd be sporting the gigantic blue horseshoe crab, touting the unique and magical marine ecosystem of Delaware.

Turned out the horseshoe crab was not a fan of the northern tier, and daily breakdowns of one kind or another had already turned our seven-day trip into a twelve-day trip, and probably took at least that much time off the end of my life. Christmas Day was supposed to be enjoyed in the bosom of my new wife's family in Prince Rupert, B.C. Instead, we woke that morning in a Super-8 motel in Vancouver, nine bags of fish on the motel heater; litter box, rat cage, and dog breath replacing the oxygen in the tiny room; and Stacey, on our first Christmas as husband and wife, looking tragically unmerry.

We packed up the animals to spend Christmas Day on the road. We'd be a day late, which was better than two. I revved up the truck to make sure it was warm before the daily ritual transfer of the fish. The heat was slow coming up. Really slow. Really, really, way too goddamn slow. After half an hour, I knew it wasn't coming. We'd be stranded at the Super-8 for another night unless we could fix the heat.

U-Haul. Those bastards . . . As I sat in the meat locker of a truck, fuming, it occurred to me that for quite some time I'd been directing my mental rage directly at a U-Haul logo. It was the sign across the street—a U-Haul rental place right there, with several trucks just like mine, fifty feet away. My thick frozen fingers stabbed at the tiny buttons on my Blackberry until I got the number right, and a Gwendolyn picked up the phone. After a "Merry Christmas" and a "Can I help you?" and my explanation of exactly how she *could* help me, I began to get a regretful legal review of why U-Haul America and U-Haul Canada aren't really the same entity, technically, and that she'd definitely call the US entity on the 27th, because tomorrow was Boxing Day in Canada and, of course, they wouldn't be open. Surely I understood.

"Hello, sir? Are you there?"

"OK, here's what we're going to do, Gwendolyn. I'm sitting here right now, looking at a truck in your lot that's just like my truck. I'm betting it's got the same defroster. You're going to send a guy over here to help me get the heater out of *your* truck. And then I'm going to leave you the heater from *my* truck. And then we're going to put *your* heater in *my* truck, and I'm going to drive away this afternoon in my newly winterized vehicle that your people promised me in Georgia, more than five breakdowns ago. And then the U-Haul international family can get together and figure this all out after Boxing Day, and have a big group hug. OK? So that's what's going to happen now."

"Sir, I'm sorry but we simply can't do that. U-Haul Canada is not affiliated . . ."

Forty-five minutes later Gwendolyn got another call.

"Hi, Gwendolyn. It's me again. I'm over here in your lot, and I'm holding this heating unit I've managed to pry out of my van. I'd really appreciate a little help before I move on to your van. Is that possible? . . . His name is what? Jerry? OK, I'll keep an eye out for him. Thank you, Gwendolyn. Merry Christmas to you too. And Happy Boxing Day."

Sometimes confidence and balls will get you places that good manners will not. The key is knowing when to employ each strategy.

I knew exactly what to expect when we got to Alaska—big sky, big mountains, lots of open space. I was raised on a Montana ranch. Been there, lived there, done that. But a land mass that could swallow four-and-a-half Montanas, with lush rainforest, barren tundra, fjords, mountains so numerous most didn't even have names, three species of bears, most towns (including the state capital) inaccessible by road, one person per square mile, and four lakes for every human being, redefined my notion of big. Alaskans like to taunt swaggering Texas tourists by informing them that if they cut Alaska in half, Texas would be the third-largest state. "Everything's bigger in Texas," my ass.

Alaska didn't take much time proving to me my own lack of knowledge. They even had a word for people like me. A "cheechako" is a newcomer, a greenhorn completely ignorant of the land, the wildlife, the culture, the people, the terrain, the weather, the driving conditions, and basic arctic survival skills. After seven years, if you make it that long, you get to lose the "cheechako" moniker and become an honorary "sourdough." After fifteen years, they start to take you seriously. After thirty, it's as good as it's ever going to get without the ultimate badge of honor: "I was born here."

Once we made it through Canada, after our delayed holiday visit, and crossed the border back into the US, where the local license plates were stamped blue on gold with "ALASKA—The Last Frontier," the mercury sank to twenty below zero, and the rumbling metal horseshoe crab took even a second of my inattention to make a suicidal beeline for the guard rail or skitter toward the ditch across a patch of invisible black ice. The entire steering process felt more like a suggestion than a command, and I'd spend hours on end with the copper taste of adrenaline in my mouth.

Although we were now technically back in the United States, a feeling of familiarity never came. This was an alien land. The twenty hours of frigid darkness pressed down like a weight, my nose hair crystallized into needles with every inhalation, and when I went outside to piss, I swore it would freeze before it hit the ground. We'd planned our trip segments between off-season motel and off-season motel, connecting the only dots we could find in the travel guide. Polyester bedspreads, watercolors of wolves and mountains bolted to the wall, rust-stained sink drains, bad paneling, tiny crappy coffee makers with tiny crappy Styrofoam cups began to blend into the same never-ending room. Every morning that the engine of our truck groaned to life with metallic cries of protest felt like a victory. Again and again, Stacey and I would begin our sleepy ritual in the dark, feeling our body heat dissipating into the biting air. She scraped the thick frost from the inside of the windows where the moisture from our breath and yesterday's coffee had condensed and frozen, and I got the outside. One foot on the front tire, my body stretched reaching over the windshield, I shoved the plastic ice scraper across the glass.

"Hey, babe? Did you know that 'Alaska' is actually an ancient Eskimo word for 'Fuck you'?" She looked up just in time for her face to meet a cascade of streaming frost from my scraper that settled on her eyelashes and the dark brown fringe of hair that peeked out from under the tight knit red cap that framed her heart-shaped face.

"Alaska," she said with a half-smile, holding up the middle finger of her Gore-Tex glove as she rubbed her wet cheeks. I loved that woman.

The first ray of the sun had just peeped up over distant mountains like a single-pointed yellow laser. Four and a half hours later, after a half-hearted journey skimming the treetops, it blinked out. My eyes, dry and burning and losing focus, had finally had enough and started playing tricks. The blackness began to pulsate and flicker, and the snow looked almost green at times. Clearly I'd spent too many hours of my life in the eerie, two-dimensional greenish glow of night-vision goggles, and now I was paying for it.

"Oh, my God!" Stacey had her cheek pressed against the passenger-side window and was looking straight up. Her hand shot out and she tapped my upper arm, never breaking her gaze at the sky.

"Pull over!"

It wasn't my eyes. The aurora borealis—the northern lights—were out to play. We got out. Even this frozen piece of meat, this sunlight-starved, grumpy U-Haul chauffeur who was counting the miles until the next cheap motel bed and dribbling shower, stood speechless. It didn't matter that my analytical brain knew that molecules in the upper atmosphere were becoming excited as solar particles from a magnetic eruption on the sun reached Earth. Standing under these pulsing ribbons of light that stretched from the mountaintops to the right, over our heads and across the open tundra to the left—green, and red, and pink—rippling across the blackness, moving like a thought, in and out of existence, crackling with a sound that took up the whole sky and came from nowhere, could make you believe you were witnessing magic.

"Oh my God . . . oh my God . . ." Stacey's whispered mantra rode on frozen puffs of breath over the rumble of the engine we dared not shut off in case it would never start again. Only genuine fear of frostbite eventually got us back inside. Alaska was not going to be ordinary. Message received.

Anchorage, the state's largest city, was our final destination. It's thought of as "Seattle Lite" by the rest of the state, but that's not meant to be a compliment. In a uniquely Alaskan brand of reverse elitism, only "the frontier," made up of rural areas, many in the vast and isolated interior, is considered the "real Alaska." Bragging rights in the forty-ninth state come from hardship, from endurance, from making do and living off the land, from knowing how to handle yourself, from near misses, from survival. Go to Alaska as a tourist and expect to impress anyone with your expensive shoes, or your Italian sunglasses, or your Rolex watch, and prepare to be branded a complete and total douchebag. You're the weak member of the herd. You're the one they'd eat first in an emergency. Nobody has to outrun the bear; they just have to outrun you.

Despite the mockery Anchorageites endure from the rest of the state for living a comparatively coddled, out-of-touch city life, it's a place most of the country would consider rugged wilderness. Residents regularly deal with a half-ton bull moose in the driveway or bears rummaging through the trash; they can go fishing for all five species of Pacific salmon, backpack or bike remote mountain trails, ogle the tallest peak in North America on the morning commute, and ski world-class runs, all from inside the city limits. And even though half the state's residents call Anchorage home, its population is only 300,000 people. The rest are scattered across a land mass that, if superimposed on a map of the lower forty-eight states, would see San Francisco mark the end of the Aleutian Island chain; Jacksonville, Florida, the tip of the southeast panhandle; central Minnesota would overlap Barrow, Alaska's northernmost settlement; and Anchorage would be somewhere in Texas. And the Anchorageites wouldn't like that at all.

The strategic geography and readily available space means a large military presence in the state, with nine bases. The civilian population is a strange mix of oil-field workers, adventurers, commercial fishermen, federal employees, naturalists, bush pilots, environmentalists, hardscrabble wilderness survivors, entrepreneurs, those looking for second chances, those fleeing the law, and a large indigenous Native population of 229 federally recognized tribes whose history spans 10,000 years. It is a tug-of-war between those who want to develop and those who want to preserve; those who want to find themselves and those who don't want to be found.

In a state that has leaned politically at various times in its history to the left and to the right, a strong libertarian streak unites both sides of the aisle. Alaskans don't need anyone telling them what to do or how to do it. "We don't care how they do it Outside" is an almost trite expression. And "Outside" is always capitalized. This is a land where Democrats carry guns. Because Democrats also don't want to be eaten by bears, and do want to eat moose. Firearms are an elemental part of a world that is quite literally "eat or be eaten," and where defense of home and property often falls to the owner, especially in remote areas.

Those in the "Lower 48" may be accustomed to federal regulations and programs designed for urban dwellers who possess modern conveniences and infrastructure, and can't fathom a world where a working generator, the right extra pair of boots in the back of the truck, a bear gun at the ready, or remembering to file a flight plan when you go moose hunting can mean the difference between life and death. They don't understand only being able to travel to the state capital by boat or plane; or rural schools hundreds of miles apart from the nearest neighboring school; or needing to know how to fix an engine, or a heater, or a generator, because there's no one around to call to fix or replace things that get broken. Alaska may as well be a series of small, sparsely populated islands—geographically, politically, and sociologically. And to most Americans, it may as well be another planet—one that nobody in his right mind would ever want to live on. And that's OK, because Alaskans don't want you to live there, anyway. They're happy the wildness weeds people out. They'd just as soon keep the place to themselves.

As the big blue horseshoe crab and its menagerie thrummed up the snow-packed highway, north and north and north, all I knew was that this was my assignment. This is where my country told me to go. And there were only five bags left on the dashboard, so I'd better get there fast or it was going to be a complete fish genocide. As the miles passed, the idea of being in the Army in Alaska began to feel real, and I found myself smiling out of the blue—like a kid anticipating a grand adventure.

The Alaskan Highway. Photo by Zach D. Roberts.

I'd been a soldier in my heart since I was ten years old but had to wait the longest seven years of my life to enlist. The story wasn't an unusual one—Dad leaves, Mom remarries abusive alcoholic asshole, kid escapes by joining the military. It may have been the day he broke my brother's legs with a two-by-four, but there was a point where something clicked in my head, and I made a decision. The choice is either you repeat the cycle or you fight it with everything you have.

The eight-by-ten, black-and-white glossy photo of my grandfather in his Army uniform on the mantel in our Montana ranch was always present, overseeing the disaster, his eyes filled with purpose and strength. I wanted to be like *him*. I did not want to grow up to be that fucker asleep on my mom's couch holding a bottle in the hand that was swollen from beating the shit out of her. I was going to be the good guy—the one who got the enemy, the one who risked himself to save his buddies, and nothing, not even fate, was going to tell me how my life would end up. Fuck fate.

To help me become the man I wanted to be, I insisted that I sleep on a regulation Army cot and stored my sharp-folded clothes in a military footlocker. A rare trip to the Army surplus store in the big city of Helena even got me my own scratchy green wool blanket bought with saved allowance I'd jammed into my pocket. I'd throw that blanket off at 4 a.m., shivering in the chill morning air before my alarm went off, and get chores done before school because I wanted to prove I could. I read every piece of military history I could get my hands on. I watched every movie made about World War II and Vietnam. I played Army in the caves up in the hills across the river with my friends.

Even *playing* Army was an escape from home. My friends Dave and Timmy and I would pack provisions, throw rifles over our shoulders, and head for the caves. Dave and I were about the same size and each of us could have fit in one of Timmy's pant legs. One weekend campout in the summer, we discovered to our horror that Timmy had eaten all our food for the entire weekend by the first night. He suggested we could just go home early. I suggested he could shut the fuck up and do what I was going to do for food. He wasn't happy about roasting frogs and chipmunks on a spit over a coffee can fire, but that was too fucking bad. I wasn't going home a minute before I had to.

I counted the days until the Army got to be real.

I had seven more years to wait. Seven more years of working on my parents' ranch, seven more years of going to school, seven more years of playing soldier in the caves in the mountains with Dave and Timmy. Seven more years of church youth-group trips to Helena, where I'd get to eat McDonald's and Cynthia Douglas would let me feel her up on the bus. Seven more years of pulling pranks.

"Oh, man!" Dave would sit on a fence rail like he always did, like he was riding a horse. His forehead was sweaty, his right index finger coated in Cheeto-colored spray paint. He tossed the can next to my empty one on the ground. It bounced off with a little clank and landed in the grass. "Can you imagine what Mr. Foster's gonna say when he sees this shit?" His fit of laughter bent him over like he was going to throw up. There had to have been thirty cows in all, brown ones, white ones, black ones, spotted ones, but they all had one distinguishing mark in common now. Each cow stood in the sun, tail twitching, serious, chewing its cud, with the same message painted in orange block letters on its flank—"F U C K."

"And everyone who drives by!" I added. For me and Dave, the herd of FUCK cows was some seriously funny shit.

The Ranchers' Association kept us busy too. They put a five-dollar bounty on coyotes to keep the predator population down. I became Sheriff Pat Garrett and every coyote was Billy the Kid. We'd pool our bounty money and give it to Dave's older brother, who kept a cut and bought us beer. Everyone was happy.

I submitted my enlistment paperwork a year early, hoping that they wouldn't notice that whole "date of birth" part. They did, but I figured it was worth a shot. Low risk, high reward. Everything to gain, nothing to lose.

When I got to Fort Benning, Georgia, a year later, in December 1992, I loved the Army as much as I thought I would. While the other new recruits were crumbling before the mental battery of basic training, I was like a pig in shit. "Drop and give me twenty" was music to my ears, and every time I succeeded, I loved it more. I loved it to the marrow of my frozen bones that were now rattling around in this fucking horseshoe-crab-billboard-piece-of-shit U-Haul in the middle of goddamn nowhere with no cell reception, no lights on the road, not even a building for dozens of miles in any direction. All that was out there was lonesome darkness covering the spinal ridge of mountains to the left and the flat, windblown tundra on the right. When the sun rose at whatever afternoon hour it felt like getting up, it would reveal some combination of mountain and flatness, and some combination of white and grey, and some combination of cold and unbelievably goddamn cold.

Something in me liked Alaska already. It didn't fuck around. It was clear that Alaska had no patience for incompetence and was brutally unforgiving to those who underestimated it. It gave you something to push against, something to measure yourself by. Nothing was a given, no safety nets. It was a place where there would be a cost to exist, an effort to survive, but where the rewards and challenges of living at the top of the world would be incredible. There aren't many road trips where a flat tire can mean life or death, and we were on one. Alaska could kill you pretty easily. I could tell that already. I just needed to get my crew somewhere they'd be safe and warm, and then let me at it. This was basic training of a different kind, and I was ready for it.

I don't know what I would have done if I'd known then that when I eventually left Alaska, it would be against my will, that I'd no longer be a soldier, that I'd have risked my life, lost my livelihood and my home, deceived my men and my family, jeopardized my marriage, and risked everything I had that was dear to me. I would leave Alaska as an outcast, despised by my city, a traitor to those I had befriended, escorted by a fleet of black SUVs to the airport for my own protection. I like to think I would have found comfort in the fact that I didn't betray my country, and I did not say no when I was called. I'd like to think I would do it all again.

CHAPTER 2

★ ★ ★ ★ ★

THE DROP ZONE

"The highest obligation and privilege of citizenship is that of
bearing arms for one's country."
—Gen. George S. Patton Jr.

On the morning of my seventeenth birthday, I grabbed the duffel bag
that was packed and sitting by the door, headed for the military
entrance process station in Spokane, Washington, and didn't look
back. I was somewhere in the middle of a family with eight kids, and some
had already left the shit show we called "home." There was no great fanfare,
no tears, no goodbye party; I didn't have to break the news to anyone. My
departure was expected and inevitable, and my mom knew my trajectory
by the time I was thirteen. When I left she had divorced my stepdad for the
third and final time, so I didn't have to worry anyone was going to die without my presence. I was *out*, out in the wide world, and my heart pounded
with anticipation.

Don't cut your hair before going to basic training. That's some free
advice if you're going to enlist. It didn't take me long to realize that half
the function of basic was for them to break your head, and the other half
was to glue it back together again how they wanted it. It makes sense that

after decades in the business of brainwashing soldiers the US military has perfected this art. The military loves to reprogram new recruits. They don't want you to *want* to be there. They want your chin to quiver, they want you to piss your pants, they want you to miss your mommy. Like Samson in the Bible, they want to cut your hair to take your power, then dole it back piece by piece the way they want to. And they want you to hate it. They do not want you to show up from Montana with a brand new buzz cut and a big dopey smile on your face like this is the greatest day of your life.

If they couldn't get the psychological effect they wanted by shaving my head, they would try to get it a different way.

"Get off the fucking bus you fucking piece of shit motherfucker!" It was beautiful. I'd never been allowed to cuss at home. I said "fuck" in the kitchen once while my mom was making biscuits and she hit me with a rolling pin. I don't even think she really meant to hit me. It was just instantaneous reflex. Fuck. Rolling pin. Whack.

A metal bunk with a scratchy wool blanket? Nobody else used that blanket; they fucking hated that blanket, but for me it was just like the one at home. Dump my footlocker and make me fold and stack my clothes again? I could do that with my eyes closed. Up at four? That meant I got to sleep in for two extra minutes. I'd been a horse at the starting gate my whole life, and despite being property of the United States government, I felt utterly and completely free. Nobody was beating the shit out of me or anyone I loved. And that was enough. Basic training and infantry school were some of the best days of my life.

At breakfast on my first morning I stood in the chow line with a metal tray and got handed a plate—powdered eggs, greasy potatoes, and then . . . something I'd never tried before. Something utterly forbidden in my house. But there it was. The smell wafted like a delicious ribbon and curled around my nostrils like in a Bugs Bunny cartoon. Bacon. Sweet Jesus. The skies opened. The angels sang. Sun rays streamed down on my plate. It wasn't long after that that I discovered processed American cheese. And then shrimp, which there aren't a lot of in rural Montana, and which the Bible and my mother called an abomination. There had also been a vending machine during "reception" when I arrived that had a dozen different packages of things containing refined sugar and preservatives. It was Satan's snack food, according to Mom, and I stuffed Ho Hos into my Ho Ho hole until I thought I was going to hurl. And then I ate more Ho Hos and washed them down with a sugary carbonated beverage in a can. I shoved quarters into that machine like I was playing slots and winning every time. I emptied it of Ho Hos and crammed my pockets with them.

My intent was to save them—to ration this orgasmic sweetness so it would last me through basic. But it wasn't to be. I ended up having to throw my treasure trove into the "amnesty box," along with everyone else, who dumped cigarettes, chocolate bars, weed, and porn. Anyone who gave his contraband up at the start wouldn't get into trouble. Smuggle it in and get caught later? Your dick was in the wringer.

After four or five weeks, those who couldn't cut it were gone, and those of us left pretty much looked and acted the same. We were olive-drab androids who marched to the range, marched with guns, marched twenty miles with thirty-five-pound rucksacks, and marched back to the barracks. When we weren't marching, we were learning how to make explosive devices, start fires, stay fed, find water, and take apart and put together our rifles in the dark. I also tried to keep my big mouth shut and go unnoticed, which was harder for me than that other stuff.

Success in basic means not being special. The goal is to get all the way through without their knowing your name. The second they know your name it's over, because that means you made an impression. The Army doesn't like impressions. The Army smacks down impressions like a hammer on the head of a crooked nail.

Drill Sergeant Russ Mitchell was a hard-core bastard with a pregnant wife. He was a Ranger instructor, and he came over to our unit as a fill-in drill sergeant until the baby was born. To be an Army Ranger instructor, you had to be the best of the best. And I was convinced that Russ Mitchell was the best of the best of the best. All of four feet, eleven inches tall, he was like a concrete brick and at the top of his game. He looked like a kid off the high school football team but with a voice that could crack paint. He was one badass motherfucker, and we all wanted to be him.

It didn't matter what he said, what we heard was, "I will fucking kill you."

But not even the unspoken threat of being fucking killed by Drill Sergeant Mitchell was enough to squash my budding entrepreneurial spirit, also known as desire for contraband. Within the first three weeks, I'd established a relationship with a certain enterprising cab driver I'd meet behind the chapel every Wednesday night. I'd hop into the cab with orders and money, and we'd head to town where I'd buy smokes, booze, *Penthouse*, and Snickers bars. I was always careful, and soon enough, I'd created a ninja network of lookouts and a lucrative side business. And I got my goddamn Ho Hos. Take that, asshole with the amnesty box.

Russ Mitchell made soldiers—hard-assed, desensitized, ice-cold, professional soldiers. Drill sergeants were allowed to do that back then. In today's new touchy-feely Army, drill sergeants have different rules. They can't even use profanity, for fuck's sake. And they must always be "sensitive" to the emotional needs of the recruits. And if they're too mean to little Jimmy, his parents can call his congressman and complain. Somewhere along the line, somebody forgot the whole purpose of basic is *to train people how to kill other people*—seek out, meet with, and destroy the enemy. ISIS doesn't give a fuck about little Jimmy's emotional needs. During my training, Drill Sergeant Mitchell made damn sure that all the little Jimmies who couldn't hack it didn't actually make it out into the real world to endanger themselves or their units. Tough love at the start prevented soldiers from entering combat who really shouldn't be there. And in turn, there weren't as many broken soldiers coming back.

Drill Sergeant Mitchell left when his son was born. At the end of training he came back and pinned a blue cord on me. Then he took me out for a beer and told me I wasn't as fucking smart as I thought I was, and that he knew all the shit I'd been doing—smoking and selling cigarettes, trafficking in Ho Hos. He didn't want me to walk away thinking I'd pulled one over on him. But he did want me to leave knowing that he thought I was resourceful and that he believed in my abilities.

"You're smart, but you're not that goddamn smart," he said with the hint of a smile. "You're not smarter than me, you little fuck."

"No, drill sergeant," I said, and I meant it.

"That was some stupid shit you pulled. But you never know when that shit will serve you. You learned leadership doing that, you learned logistics, you learned covert operations. Just don't land your ass in jail. You use that for good, you hear me? You use that to bust some punk-ass motherfucker who's out to hurt people."

"Yes, drill sergeant."

"I want you to remember something, Fulton," he said, his voice getting slightly deeper and more serious. "You took an oath to serve this country. To protect this country from all enemies, foreign and domestic."

"Yes, drill sergeant."

"That oath did not just expire today when I pinned that cord on you, soldier. And it will not expire tomorrow, or next year, or the year after that. Or when you leave the Army. You took that oath for the rest of your god-damn life, do you understand me?"

"Yes, drill sergeant."

"I'm proud of you, soldier," he said and put his hand on my shoulder.

"Thank you, drill sergeant." We clinked beers, and even though Drill Sergeant Mitchell was only ten or twelve years older than me, I thought that this might be sort of what it felt like to have a dad.

The next six years were spent marching, and digging holes, and jumping out of planes. After marching and digging holes in the US, I got to march and dig holes in Asia and Africa and Europe. It wasn't glamorous, but it wasn't Montana. Somewhere between Asia and Africa I got an unex-pected contact from Drill Sergeant Mitchell. He had a "proposition," he told me, an "offer" to come to the aid of my country, to test myself. It was unorthodox, and I wouldn't be able to talk about it, but he'd recommended me. As much as I loved marching and digging holes and jumping out of planes, I couldn't say no. I'd have done anything for Russ Mitchell, and the challenge was irresistible. I remember telling Stacey that I had to go, but I couldn't tell her where or I'd have to kill her. That went over about as well as you'd imagine. But I went, and I had the crap scared out of me in ways that were hard to explain, and I saw things that made me learn to love and appreciate my country to the marrow of my bones. I also learned to know myself, the things I was capable of doing, the things I could overcome, the fragility of life. I'd love to write a chapter on it, but I'd have to kill you.

After my "dark time," it was back to business as usual. My whole life felt like man versus gravity, up hills, out of planes. Gravity always won, even off the job.

I remember trying to learn Kendo from the Old Man. That's what I called him, although he was only ten or twelve years older than me. He was my commanding officer in Alaska, but we'd become close on a much deeper level than CO and private. He'd taken me under his wing for reasons I never fully understood. We talked about philosophy, and alien abduction, and chess, and psychic intuition, and history, and organic farming, and how to kill people.

I remember looking up into his face from the floor of the gym after a particularly hard landing. He looked calm and vaguely amused, as he often did, staring down and studying me through his little wire-rimmed glasses as I lay on my back panting.

"I do not think you are ready," he said, holding his giant bamboo stick. He was a Kendo master and had wanted to teach me.

"You 'do not think I am ready'? What are you, fucking Yoda?"

"I'm not Yoda," he said with a chuckle. "But ready . . . you are not." He extended a hand, pulled me up, and gave me a pat on the shoulder. "We'll try again another time."

I thought about my stepdad, and I thought about Russ Mitchell, and I thought about the Old Man as I sat in the semi-dark of my living room wearing boxers and socks, draining my sixth beer after the Army dumped me. Yes, they dumped me and it was worse than any broken heart I'd ever had.

It turns out the human body isn't designed for marching with heavy weight or jumping out of airplanes. I guess it's not so much the jumping part as the landing part. The curse of the airborne infantry had done me in. My knees and ankles were pretty well destroyed, and my back was trying to catch up. Along with nine years' worth of frayed tendons and wrecked joints went my Army career. "Involuntary medical discharge," they called it. Damn right it was involuntary. I fought them tooth and nail, like I was fighting for my life, because in a way I was—the only life I had ever wanted. I had more to do, more to give. It wasn't supposed to end like this. This was not the plan.

The Army had been everything to me—my childhood dream, my adolescent salvation, and my family. I had even gotten involved with CID, the Army's Criminal Investigation Command. No one was going to bring shame on my house or harm to my fellow soldiers. Not on my watch. I did use those skills I'd learned in my black market days in basic training for good, just like Drill Sergeant Mitchell wanted. I volunteered throughout my Army career to help bring down assholes dealing drugs, doing backdoor weapons sales, and sexually assaulting their fellow troops. I had made myself useful. I had used my skills, however sketchy, to serve. I had kept my oath.

And in the end, after I'd seen doctor after doctor, the Army handed me a giant bottle of industrial-strength Motrin and kicked my ass out the door. I kept calling the VA, and they kept giving me more drugs, more powerful drugs, until I stopped calling. It was an effective method of dealing with it for them. Keep medicating this asshole until he shuts up and leaves us alone. But finally, after I sat on the couch for three weeks drooling and staring at the TV, Stacey said I had to stop taking what they gave me and figure out a way of dealing with life. Somewhere inside I knew she was right, but that place inside was in denial. I sank into a dark place. I drank too much—way too much. I had no Plan B and nothing directing me. I felt useless, worthless, I didn't sleep enough, and I argued about almost anything with anybody I could find. I couldn't stand myself, and I don't know how Stacey did. There was a hole in my life. I had skills in counter-terrorism training, combat weaponry, ranching, and smuggling. And I had to find something to do with my life that wouldn't land my ass in prison.

As I sat alone in the darkness of my third Alaskan winter, I got a call from the Old Man. He had some kind of sixth sense about when I was having an existential crisis. That Yoda thing he had. He asked how I was doing—and he was rewarded over the next hour with a big pile of my guts on the table.

"Do you remember when you and I talked about the sheepdog?" he asked.

"What sheepdog?"

"There are three kinds of people," he said, and it started coming back to me. "There are sheep, there are wolves, and there are sheepdogs. Most people are sheep—they are gentle, and kind, and just want to live in peace. They are oblivious to anything outside their sheep world. They eat grass. They see that the other sheep are nice, and they don't worry. Then there are the wolves that prey on the sheep—they see weakness, gullibility, pacifism, an inability to fight. They exploit the weakness of the sheep, they hurt, they kill. These are the criminals, the terrorists, the sociopaths, the psychopaths, the criminally insane. But then there are the sheepdogs. The sheep are nervous of the sheep dogs. The sheepdogs are always on alert, on patrol, they think differently, they move differently. Their brains are wired to constantly watch for threats the sheep are unaware of, that they can't even imagine. The sheepdogs' eyes are always open, and their energy frightens the sheep. The sheep get annoyed. Until there is a wolf. Then the sheep understand what the sheepdog is for, that he will lay down his life for the sheep, that he will face the wolf and keep them safe or die where he stands. You and I, we are sheepdogs, Bill. And we are much more like the wolves than the sheep. That's the interesting part."

"Yeah, well now I'm a goddamn sheep. A sheep with busted ankles."

"Who you are doesn't just change. You *are* a sheepdog. You have always been one, and you will always be one. You took an oath to serve. But you know you don't have to be a soldier to serve and protect your country and your countrymen," he said, his voice piercing the fog of the six-pack I'd just downed. "There are other ways. You will find one."

The Old Man was speaking in riddles as far as I was concerned, but I had to do something to make money and keep busy so Stacey wouldn't put a pillow over my face in my sleep. I began buying and reselling outdoor survival gear and military surplus items on eBay. I made a few bucks, and I could work while drinking beer in my underwear, and feel sorry for myself all at the same time. I also took some security gigs at concerts and events, watching the door and making drunk people take a cab. I hired Chuck, a friend of mine from the Army who needed a job, to help me out. Chuck, a born-again Christian and former Marine, had kept his "high and tight" haircut because he actually liked it, and wore a big ol' cross around his neck. We should never have gotten along, but we did.

I wanted us to do things right, so I read up on all the legal restrictions and codes of conduct and ethics of being a bouncer. There are more than you think. The last thing I needed was to get sued by some drunk for assault or by a bar owner for violating some obscure rule I didn't know about. Knowledge is power, and I became a self-taught bouncing specialist, and passed on to Chuck what I'd learned. We had forms requiring signatures, and guidelines, and waivers, and a license, and everything required to be a legit business.

Then we hired some other vets and officially became our own little security company. Like so many, our new recruits were having problems transitioning back to civilian life, and it felt good to call them and say, "Hey, I need you to work this weekend." It gave them focus and a reason to get up. I knew what it felt like not to have one and it sucked. Seeing them feeling useful, and the impact it had on their outlook on life and self-worth, made me feel useful too. And I realized as the months passed that the business was about more than just making some money. It was about having a purpose. I had people depending on me, and they had someone depending on them. It was good for them and good for me. I'd stuck a Band-Aid on a bullet wound, but it was something.

Meanwhile, my eBay business got derailed when Stacey came home from work one night through the front door instead of straight from the garage.

"You know it's February, right?" she said, stomping her fur-lined boots on the mat, leaving a little pile of snow. "And you know we live in Alaska, right?" She was slightly breathless from the cold.

"Yeah . . ."

"And we have a two-car garage. That's one of the reasons we bought this house, remember?" She shook the snow off her hat and hung it on the peg.

"Yeah." I braced myself because I knew where this was headed.

"Well, it would be really nice in the middle of February in Alaska, if we still *had* that garage, and not some kind of military surplus store taking up my parking space so I have to park outside."

Two months later I opened Drop Zone, a military surplus store, in a former Chinese restaurant, right across the street from an abandoned cinder-block strip club in the seedy Anchorage neighborhood of Spenard. The drop zone in military speak is a designated area where troops or supplies are dropped by parachute. The drop zone literally ended my last career, and Drop Zone would be where my next one started.

Stacey was thrilled. So were my security-team buds I hired to help me run it. It meant more work and more money for them, and, more important, a place to hang out. Drop Zone became our tree house, the clubhouse of every man-child's dreams, the caves with Dave and Timmy, a fortress and a sanctuary. We brewed our own beer in the office, and set up some cots where we could sleep it off. The office served double duty for any-one whose wife or girlfriend had kicked them out, or just as an escape when the world closed in. We filled the retail space with a bunch of badass toys and tactical gear, and we built a fire pit in the parking lot because we needed a place to drink and smoke and talk, and in Alaska nobody gives a shit if you build a fire pit in your parking lot.

I'd started teaching "What you need to know to be a bouncer" classes too. I went over the fine points of the law, how to get drunk people to leave without touching them, and, if all else failed, how to legally arrest them. Once hands were on, arrest was *mandatory*. I drove that home more than anything else. Unlike in the movies, bouncers can't just pick people up by the back of their shirts and toss them onto the sidewalk. That would have made my life a lot simpler. Nowadays, that's a lawsuit waiting to happen. So once your subject makes physical contact with you or someone else, or you make physical contact with them, they have to be arrested for their own safety. You cuff them, sit them down in a chair, and wait for the cops. And it's your responsibility to keep them from hurting themselves. They belong to you until the cops show, and you protect them.

You'd be surprised at the diversity of bouncers. There were college kids, former cops, taxi drivers, tech guys, teachers, and one time a former bounty hunter from California. He said he was done with those days—a little too exciting after a while. But I picked his brain. He'd contact local bail bondsmen whose clients had jumped bail and become fugitives. Then he tracked them down. Alaska would be the perfect place to do it, he said. Not many people, only two roads out, and nowhere to hide.

"Everybody knows everybody here," he said. "This place is a fugitive's worst nightmare."

My brain was spinning. I couldn't think of anything I wanted to do more than literally hunt bad guys in Alaska. I couldn't believe I hadn't thought of it. It didn't sound like "easy money," but it sounded like "fun as hell" money. I called Chuck immediately and ran the idea by him.

"Are you serious, man? Of course I'm in! Why didn't we think of this before?"

So we decided to expand the business and began doing freelance fugitive-recovery work. There was no way this was not going to happen. Expanding the business to this level would mean putting guns in our hands, and that would be a game-changer for anyone we brought in with us. In the Army, your weapon is more than a tool—it's your companion, a source of security and meaning that defines who you are. We could literally take them apart and put them together in the dark. For most of the men, the heavy, solid feel of that weapon was a reunion with a faithful friend. It was like handing a carpenter his hammer. Chuck was uncontrollably excited, and so were the other guys.

"This is going to be killer, dude! I can't wait to go kick in some doors!" Chuck had been called "Suicide" in the Marines because of his "act first and think later" mentality. He had titanium balls and zero flight response. Ever. That cross around his neck must have been serious, because there's no way he did the shit he did if he didn't believe in Heaven.

Stacey did not share Chuck's or my enthusiasm for this plan. She thought her days of worrying about me were over. The idea of her husband with a loaded AR-15 and a pistol on his hip, out in the middle of the night arresting bad guys, did not jibe with her idea of peaceful, post-military life.

"What the hell is wrong with you? Why do you want to go play soldier if you don't have to?" she wanted to know. "You don't have to do this! And it doesn't just affect *you* now. You have me, you have Emma! We are your family! Don't we count?"

I suddenly felt like kind of a shithead. And I understood her worry. She and our new daughter in her arms were the most important things in the world to me, hands down. And I don't know why, but it didn't change things. What good would I be to them if I turned back into that angry, beer-drinking, mopey asshole again?

"It's not playing, babe. It's not a game to me." I kissed her forehead and wrapped my arms around my girls. "It's who I am. I'm just wired this way, and when something is what you are, it doesn't change. Look at me." I held her face in my hands. "I'm very good at what I do. And I promise I'll be careful. I'll be fine. And there are other people out there who will be fine because of me and my guys. There are people who need protecting, and there are people who need to be off the street, and we're able to do that. We have an obligation to use what we've got to help people."

And so Drop Zone fugitive recovery went forward full steam. I've done this since I was a kid, I kept telling myself, thinking about the coyotes no longer plaguing ranchers because of me. Only this time, the coyotes might have guns too. And hopefully I'd be making more than five dollars a head.

Alaska has some weird laws, and one that worked to our advantage is that anyone can arrest anyone for breaking the law. This tradition stemmed from a time when only a handful of law enforcement officers inhabited a giant landmass full of ornery gun-slinging frontiersmen that stretched the width of the continental United States. The law couldn't do it all and had to rely on regular citizens to help keep the peace so the place wouldn't fall into anarchy.

Maybe it was the dark, or the cold, or the isolation, but Alaska provided a never-ending stream of violent felons, meth cookers, heroin dealers, thieves, and bail jumpers who all thought they were above the law. We reminded them they weren't, and we lived for it. Busting down doors was like mainlining adrenaline, and we loved adrenaline. It was way better than Motrin.

We developed our skills over time and became a highly effective unit, sometimes making five or six arrests a day. We blew the cops' minds. Nobody got rich, but we got the rush, we got to play with guns, and we got to be the good guys who took dangerous people off the streets. We'd have done it for free. I felt like I was back in the Army. And for my guys it was a hell of a lot more therapeutic than lying on some couch talking about their feelings, plus we all got to go home at night.

Soldiers may complain about rules but deep down they like them. They want and need to know their parameters, and I spelled it all out in black and white, right on the office door at Drop Zone: *Fulton's Rules.* Some were straight-up military:

- ★ Be the best you can be. There's always somebody better and he may be trying to kill you.
- ★ Trust your squad mates. They will save your life.
- ★ Communicate with your leaders weekly. If we don't know what's going on, we can't help when you're fucked up—and you will be fucked up.

Some I couldn't believe we even needed until someone decided to prove we did:

- ★ No drinking before noon. No drinking at all if you're going to be armed within the next twenty-four hours.
- ★ **Keep your wives and/or girlfriends away from the shop and the unit**—somebody other than you will fuck them.
- ★ If you have a dispute you can't settle verbally, you get one fight. ONE. Then man up, shake hands, and move on. We have no room for Drama Queens, and one of you will have to go if you can't settle it.
- ★ Do not be a bigot. Bigots are assholes. Racist, homophobic language, etc., will not be tolerated from anyone—you or customers. Nobody needs that bullshit.

And then, the most important one:

- ★ Remember we are soldiers. There is no greater honor, nor larger burden. Do not dishonor yourselves or the men who will give their lives for you.

We *were* soldiers, even if not in the conventional sense anymore. Our allegiance was sworn to each other. We didn't use our real names—we each went with a handle given by the group. Nobody got to pick their own; they got named by someone else, and we all knew when a handle had been born.

Chuck would keep his moniker, "Suicide." Stacey directed her unhappiness at him and blamed him for talking me into "becoming a goddamn bounty hunter," and thought he was a "horse's ass," but that was one of the other reasons no wives or girlfriends were allowed in the shop. That firewall kept things simpler.

The other reason was Clay Aiken. He got his country-singer handle from his Southern drawl. We loved Clay and trusted him with our lives—but not our women. He was better at getting women in bed than he was at arresting people—and he was pretty damn good at arresting people.

The ironically named and always mopey Sunshine spread his Eeyore vibe wherever he went. He was sort of loveable in his way. Sherlock was our brainiac, complete with little round glasses and an encyclopedic knowledge of government and the military—a walking military Google.

And while the vast majority of Drop Zone employees were active duty or former military, we did have a few civilians filter through. And by civilians, we meant hippies, and we called them that. Hippie Alpha grew up at his parents' fly-in Alaskan hunting-and-fishing lodge. He was an unbelievable sharpshooter and an expert tracker. He could sniff a twig and say "bear" and you'd believe him. Hippie Omega was our peacenik—the dreadlocked bleeding-heart liberal. He devoted himself to taking troubled kids out into the woods for "wilderness therapy," which sounded suspiciously tree-huggy, but which I also actually understood. He was an accomplished medic. And this hippie healer turned into a total badass once he found out he liked breaking down doors and carrying an AR-15. You just never know with people.

My handle was Foxfire, which is also my actual middle name. My parents named me after the eerie green glow in the woods caused by some kind of weird fungus. They were also apparently tripping balls on acid when I was conceived. Stacey said that explained a lot, but I really didn't want to think about it.

We were a ragtag team, but we were a team—a company. And we had each other's backs.

Drop Zone sales counter and a couple of the guys.

Outside the Drop Zone.

CHAPTER 3

★ ★ ★ ★ ★

BEARS AND DANES

"What doesn't kill you makes you stronger, except for
bears. Bears will kill you."
—**Anonymous**

Bear security? What the fuck is that?" asked Sunshine. "We supposed
to guard a bear?"

"Um, bears don't really need guards, dude. We have to guard
people *from* bears. There's a crew filming a commercial out by Matanuska
Glacier. They want us."

"Bears? Fuck that, man. Did you hear about that guy out in Katmai last
fall who was filming them? They fucking ate him, man. ATE him. Him and
his girlfriend. Fuck bears. No way, I'm not doing it."

"Timothy Treadwell? They ate him because he was a dumbass from
California who was trying to be friends with them," I said. "He didn't
have a gun. He didn't even have bear spray for fuck's sake. We're not out
there to hug them. If one gives us trouble, we shoot it."

Sunshine wasn't finished. "AND . . . Do you know that pilot's name?
The one that flew out there to pick them up, and then found the guy's head

at the campsite?" He raised his eyebrows and stared at my face. "His name is William Fulton, man. I shit you not. Bad juju, don't do it."

"Look, we get to spend the day outside, we get to carry guns, and they're paying us three hundred bucks each. It's not always the worst-case scenario that happens."

"Three hundred dollars? Damn . . . fine. I'll go, I guess, but don't say I didn't warn you. Fucking bears . . ."

"That was seriously his name?"

"Yes!"

"I'm ready to pay," said a man who had been listening to our conversation as he wandered around the store. He had two Drop Zone T-shirts on the counter. In a rare moment of artistic creativity, I'd done the logo myself—a skull, handcuffs, and Army jump wings. Triple badassery. Black was the only color option.

"Do you take American money?"

"Umm. Yeah," I said.

"Well, you know . . . with that NAFTA trade thing, I wasn't sure."

"You do know Alaska is part of America, right?"

He stared blankly. The stupid was strong.

"We're a *state*. The forty-ninth *state*. As in the 'United *States*.' We've been a state since 1959, man. Catch up."

Sometimes I felt like I was leading a tourist-education program. No, we don't live in igloos. No, there aren't six months of total darkness and then six months of total light. Yes, my English is very good. No, we don't train the moose to cross at the "Moose Xing" signs. No, chicks don't wear much makeup here, and most of them could kick your ass and out-fish you blindfolded. We kind of like that. And yes, people are friendly, and strangers will help you—you'll just have to get used to it. That last one killed me. "Why are people so friendly here?" tourists would ask, as if these sneaky Alaskans were up to something. It's because we're all basically on a big isolated island (no, not like in that box on the map next to Mexico) and you help people out, because next time it'll be you that slides off the road and into the ditch, and you'll need somebody. And because we don't like tourists doing dumb shit like trying to commune with bears and getting themselves killed; it makes us look bad. Alaska plays by the unwritten "pay it forward" rule: always do something nice for strangers.

The day of the commercial shoot was perfect for filming. The air was crisp and clear, cobalt sky, and golden autumn leaves on the birches and aspen. I could feel my blood pressure dropping as we sped north on the Glenn Highway out of Anchorage. The traffic thinned, the sky got bigger, and the world felt at peace.

"I have a bad feeling about this," Sunshine said.

"You have a bad feeling about puppies and ice cream," I said.

We pulled into the parking area next to the mighty Matanuska, Alaska's most famous drive-up glacier, and saw our group milling around a large white van full of camera equipment.

"Jorgen Skov," the producer introduced himself to me with a very serious handshake and a thick Scandinavian accent. This wasn't just any commercial; this was a Danish bottled water commercial, filmed and produced by actual Danes who had flown in for the occasion. I was pretty sure there were glaciers a lot closer to Denmark than this, but I wasn't here to question—I was just here to smile, hold a big gun, and collect my paycheck.

"This are the photographers, Jens Gregerson and Bent Bang," he said, gesturing toward two twenty-something scruffy blonds unloading the gear.

"Bent Bang" sounded like some kind of horrible accident at the shooting range, and I may have laughed a little. Clearly his parents didn't speak English.

"Good to meet you," I shook their hands. "I'm Bill, and this is my associate. You can call him Sunshine, because he's very happy all the time—a real optimist. We're here to keep you alive."

Two pairs of blue eyes got wide, as they scanned us standing in all our gear, mirrored sunglasses, head-to-toe camo, 1911 pistols strapped to our thighs, and Mossberg twelve-gauge shotguns slung on our backs. Ready to rumble. We were the crazy gun-totin' Americans they'd tell their turtleneck-wearing, skinny-jeaned friends about over a warm beer when they got home. But like most people who are freaked out by guns—the sheep—they're awfully glad to have you when they need you. And they needed us now, or at least they thought they did. That was all that mattered.

Jorgen Skov spent the morning trying to find the perfect spot to film, where the light would be best to capture the deep blue of the towering four-mile-wide river of ice that made its slow-motion journey between the mountains, stacking up shards like vertical knife blades, melting into a clear, icy river that someone somewhere was to believe came from Denmark and ended up in their water bottle.

Sunshine and I set up a large open field tent so they'd have somewhere to keep gear and belongings. Bent and Jens nodded vigorously and smiled in thanks for a safe, clean spot for their camera equipment. I looked to make sure Jorgen was happy, but he was nowhere in sight. When I asked, Jens pointed, indicating he'd gone down a narrow trail that turned to the left out of sight around a granite outcropping and a large stand of birch trees. I trotted off after him, leaving Sunshine to watch camp. Despite Sunshine's "bad feeling," it was highly unlikely we'd have a bear encounter. Bears usually avoid people if they can. But I didn't want Jorgen wandering off in the woods and getting disoriented. It would be bad for business if we lost a client, and the nights were getting cold. I stopped periodically to see if I could hear him. Hopefully he hadn't wandered off the trail. After a few minutes I started to get concerned.

"Jorgen!" Nothing. "Jorgen!" Nothing. "JORRRRGEN!"

"Ya?" He had gotten farther down the trail than I thought.

"You can't just walk off like that! You need to let me know where you are!" I called in the direction of his voice.

"OK, ya. Look what I found here!"

"What?" I asked as I crossed the hundred remaining feet between us.

"Well, I don't know but it's a very big animal, and buried in the ground."

It was way too early for hibernating bears, and the only animals I knew that lived in the ground were marmots, Alaska's version of a groundhog.

"It has big . . . how do you say them? Hoofs?"

"Oh, FUCK. OK, Jorgen? You need to back away slowly," I called, enunciating all my words. "Back up *now*."

To his credit, Jorgen seemed to understand I wasn't joking around, and even though he didn't understand what was happening or why, he did what I said. He held his hands up like he was getting robbed at a bank and backed up slowly and carefully, step by step, while I unslung my twelve-gauge, which was already loaded with slugs and 00 shot, and turned a full 360 degrees scanning for the bear. I side-stepped my way over to Jorgen, skirting the kill as much as possible. The thing was starting to stink—a huge oblong mound of moss and dirt with three big moose legs sticking up in the air at odd angles. The area to one side of the kill had been torn to shreds to bury it, and there were deep claw impressions trenched in the ground. Grizzly for sure.

I made it to Jorgen's side.

"You can put your hands down," I said. "This is bear food," I explained. "A bear did this, which means it's coming back."

We began to pick our way back along the trail toward the outcropping. We'd see camp from there.

"MMMMMPH." We heard a low rumble. Leaves rustled and small twigs snapped behind us.

"Dammit." Sure enough, the grizzly was lumbering down the trail.

"Do what I do!" I told Jorgen, and raised my arms up waving them back and forth and bellowing as loudly and deeply as I could. The first rule of bear defense is to be scary and look as big as possible. I had the gun if I needed it, but I really wasn't into unnecessary bear shooting. And even when you shoot a bear, it doesn't drop right away, and making it even more angry is a real possibility. I unslung the Mossberg and cocked it just in case. Jorgen tried to imitate me, but the noise he made sounded like someone making a slightly-louder-than-conversational "aaaaaaaaaaa" sound as he slow-motion marched in place pulling his knees up high, and moving his arms over his head. It would have been hilarious if there wasn't a fucking 1,000-pound bear fifty feet away. But there *was* a fucking 1,000-pound bear fifty feet away.

The rule with bears is that you never know with bears. Some are playful, some are mellow and laid back, some are high-strung, some are curious, some are skittish and afraid, and some are crazy-ass killing machines. They're kind of like people.

The grizzly stopped and watched us, as we continued our intimidation efforts. "MRRRaaaAAAAhhhhmph," it bellowed, curling its lips back and revealing teeth as long as my fingers that could have crushed our skulls like vice grips on eggs. It opened its mouth and let out a wall of sound that

I'm pretty sure made Jorgen piss his pants. Then it shook its massive head like a dog shaking off water, turned around, took a giant steaming black shit on the path, and headed back to its lunch. We lucked out, and so did the bear.

We headed back, pounding hearts, shaky thighs, and quick steps. At the tent, I could see Jens sitting in a camp chair leaning with his head tipped way back. Bent Bang was holding Sunshine's camelback water pouch over his head, and Sunshine was pouring water from the nozzle into Jens's eyes. This couldn't be good.

"Bear spray," Sunshine answered my question before I asked it.

The odds seemed astronomical that we both had a bear encounter in the same half hour. Maybe it was the same bear? If the wind was wrong and you hit a bear with bear spray it sometimes drifted into your eyes.

"They thought it was bear *repellent*. So they were spraying themselves to keep bears away." Sunshine shot me a look of disbelief.

"There's no such thing as bear repellent," I said to the Danes. "And there's a safety clip on the can!"

"Apparently they were smart enough to figure out how to get it off," he said.

Jens's eyes were inflamed and impossibly red. I took off my camelback so they could use that water too. Bear spray is like mace on steroids. It's designed to spray at a charging, angry, 700-pound carnivore and be painful enough to stop him in his tracks. It is not Deep Woods Off for Scandinavian photographers.

Most people who visit Alaska are either too afraid or not afraid enough. Jens was the first type, and Jorgen was the latter. But after he almost became bear bait, he stuck close and managed to get his footage from a new camp we set up, far away in the opposite direction.

Sunshine and I headed back south to town in the late evening sun, checks in hand, and I knew I'd get the obligatory "I told you so" lecture about bears, and his "bad feeling."

"You fucking mocked me, man. But I had a bad feeling. I even said it."

"Yes, you did."

"You're lucky you weren't eaten," he said.

"I probably would have tasted pretty bland since I didn't douse myself in pepper spray." We knew we'd be laughing about this for years.

"So get this," he went on. "In Denmark, you have to have a special license for a gun and you have to give a 'valid reason' why you want one, like for hunting or because you're a collector or some shit. There's only like 20,000 people licensed in the whole country."

"I figured it was something like that. Did you see the way they looked at us when we got out of the Hummer? Fucking hilarious. They looked like they were gonna piss themselves."

"I know, right?" he said. "These people used to be Vikings, man. What the fuck happened? I'll tell you what happened: The Vikings had no Second Amendment."

Second Amendment issues were always a hot topic of conversation in the store and out. The hard-right libertarian love of guns combined with Alaska's mostly rural lifestyle fed off each other, creating a culture of necessity for guns and worship of them. Just over half of Anchorage residents own guns. The Fairbanks area has the highest percentage of gun ownership in the nation at 59.1 percent. It's not only because Alaskans hunt. It's because if the government knows there is an armed citizenry, it's more likely to stay in line. And if it doesn't stay in line, wherever that "line" is, then violence directed against the government and its agents is always a possibility. Alaskans feared government overreach before fearing government overreach was cool. Anti-government sentiment brews hot in Alaska, and savvy politicians have seized upon it, from Gov. Sarah Palin to Congressman Don Young, notorious for his anti-government rhetoric. He despises the Bureau of Land Management, the Department of Education, and the Department of the Interior, but reserves special venom for the Environmental Protection Agency. He called environmentalists "a socialist group of individuals that are the tool of the Democrat Party" and said, "I'm proud to say that they are my enemy. They are not Americans, never have been Americans, never will be Americans."

"Yeah," Sunshine said. "Europe is just totally fucked up about guns. You'd think after World War II they'd get it. Arm the people, man. Then the government doesn't fuck with you and round you up in the train cars."

"Switzerland isn't fucked up about it," I said.

"Dude, all they have is those little red pocket knives. What do they do? 'Hold still while I shove this corkscrew into your head.' 'Wait, I'm almost through your artery with my tiny fucking scissors.'"

"No, seriously. The Swiss love guns. They start shooting really young. Like little kids, ten years old. They teach it in school so people know what the fuck they're doing. Men between twenty and thirty report for training and get issued military weapons, and they keep them at home. That's why the fucking Nazis didn't go there. They all have guns. The Swiss just don't go out and shoot everyone, like our dumb asses do. Americans have to look badass, and they don't know what the fuck they're doing. They think it makes them cool. It's a fucking tool, man. I mean, yeah it's a cool, badass tool, but you need to know how to use it and respect it. They tried once to regulate guns in Switzerland and make people keep the military-issued ones in armories, and people were like, fuck that."

"Shit, I had no idea. The government gives everyone guns. Maybe that's how they put all the fucking holes in their cheese, man. Target practice!"

I laughed. We drove in silence then, watching the color of the rocky mountain peaks as the late night sun turned everything the color of honey.

"I would totally shoot a fucking cheese," said Sunshine as he looked out the window. "Hey, you don't want to be my roommate, do you?"

"Roommate? Dude, I have a wife and a kid! No, I don't want to be your fucking roommate."

"Well, I need one or I'm going to have to move soon," he said. "Or I'm gonna end up on that cot in your office. So let me know if you hear of anybody. And speaking of your office, how are the new security cameras doing?" he asked. "You work the bugs out?"

"Oh, yeah. They're working just fine." I started laughing.

"What? Why is that funny?"

"Ask me how I know," I said.

"How do you know?"

"Because the first goddamn thing I see in the morning when I review the tape is Clay banging some chick on that pile of tents in the office."

"Oh, shit! No way!" Sunshine laughed. "Oh, my God, he's such a whore."

"Yeah, this means a new rule."

"Aw, fuck, man, no!"

"In case the 'No wives or girlfriends in the store' rule wasn't quite clear enough for those motherfuckers, we now have a 'No fucking in the office' rule."

"New rule, courtesy of Clay Aiken," he said, shaking his head.

CHAPTER 4

★ ★ ★ ★ ★

THE DEATHBOT, THE BIG MEXICAN, AND THINGS THAT GO "BOOM!"

"When I was a child I was afraid of ghosts. As I grew up I
realized people are more scary."
—Sushan R. Sharma

I began to understand why Alaskans always wanted to know how long
you've lived in the state. It took a while to get used to highway traffic
screeching to a halt so a moose and her calf could safely cross, or hearing someone say, "The lights were out last night!" and realizing they didn't
mean a power failure—they meant the aurora borealis. Alaskans never get
tired of moose. Or the aurora. No matter how many times they've seen
them, there's still a measure of awe. Even the landscapes of the most mun-
dane commute or the huge flakes of the hundredth snowfall of the year
made you look around and feel like you'd walked into a movie set. Usually
that movie was a *National Geographic* documentary like our glacier shoot.
Usually that movie was not *Mad Max*. But one day at Drop Zone, it was.

When Gunny walked into the shop, all six-foot-four brick shithouse of him, he created a solar eclipse in the doorway. He had thick, black, coiled tribal tattoos creeping up his neck from under the collar of his shirt and out the bottom of his black leather trench-coat sleeves. He was horrifying.

"I hear you guys do good work." His voice was gravel, and his eyes like coal; so dark you couldn't see the pupils. He locked eyes with me. "I work for you now."

We all stood frozen for what felt like a long time. Gunny didn't blink.

"Welcome aboard," I said, holding out my hand.

"I don't touch people," Gunny said.

He did work for us now, because I wasn't about to find out what happened if I told him he didn't.

Gunny was a former Marine who now worked for a three-letter government organization that he wouldn't specifically name. We pretty much ruled out the EPA or HUD.

Gunny was a closed book. He would disappear for long periods of time to places unknown. After he finished whatever black-ops mission he was on, he'd come back from wherever he went, and doing whatever the hell he did, and he'd fill our doorway. Then it was game on. He'd be around for a couple of months, kick in some doors, step on some heads, and then he'd vanish again, usually with no warning. The rest of us always needed a beer or three, and a few hours around the fire, to decompress from a day of arrests. But Gunny said that the fugitive recovery itself helped him blow off steam and relax from the stress of his *regular* job. We almost didn't want to know.

Sales were good at the shop, and Stacey was pleased for the most part. It had been about a year since we'd started fugitive recovery, and even though she wasn't thrilled about my hours, I was easier to live with, and she could tell I had my sense of purpose back. If I was happy, she was happy, and if she was happy, I was happy. We started our lives together on an adventure, and we never lost the sense that we were each other's emotional support. The guys were great, don't get me wrong—but going home at night to my girls was the highlight of my day. There were many uncertainties in life, but the one abiding thing I knew was that I had won the wife lottery, and I remembered it every single day.

Military folks were our most frequent customers at the shop. Soldiers would come in and sell off gear when their tour was over and would find reasonably priced replacements for things they'd lost. Cops and troopers were daily visitors too. And, living in Alaska, civilians also needed what we sold. You couldn't throw a rock without hitting a hunter or fisherman, or wilderness adventure guide, or mountain climber, or doomsday prepper who needed camo or a field medical kit or rubber inflatable "bunny boots" to keep his feet warm in subzero temperatures. Anyone who lived in Alaska was, by virtue of that fact, a survivalist of sorts, so our clientele was broad and deep.

I knew at the outset, from my experiences in the Army working with CID and from eBay, that some of my customers would be trying to hawk stolen goods. Some stuff would undoubtedly slip by me, but usually it was easy to tell. Sure enough, not long after the shop opened, a young soldier from Fort Richardson came in looking to buy an extra pair of boots and casually asked at the register if I'd be interested in some thirty-round magazines.

"Sure," I said. "How many you got?"

"A pallet."

A pallet? It didn't take a rocket scientist or a supply sergeant to figure out that nobody has an extra pallet of banana magazines just lying around. These were stolen from the base. I had a special kind of hatred for assholes who stole vital supplies our guys could need in Afghanistan or Iraq, just so they could make a quick buck.

"Awesome, man. I'll take all of 'em! Can you come by on Saturday?"

I set up the deal, got his license plate written down, called my contact at the base, and arranged for some guys from CID to be there "shopping" when he showed up with the goods. The CID guys were even nice enough to help the jackass unload the pallet and bring it into the store.

He thanked them. I took the magazines, he took my money. They arrested him.

"You fucked me!" he snarled, red-faced and pissed off as the cuffs zipped closed. "I hate a rat! I hate a fucking snitch."

"Listen you little shit," I got in his face. "You stole property from your fellow soldiers and from the country you vowed to serve. Remember that vow? I think the troops in harm's way need these more than you need your goddamn beer money. So fuck you."

It was a rush of satisfaction—one more bad guy stopped in his tracks. It was like watching all the bullshit he was ever going to do get erased from the future. I'd rather be a snitch than be responsible for whatever he was going to pull. I'd been called that plenty while I was weeding out the bad apples in my unit. You reap what you sow. And if you sow shit around me, I will make you reap it.

They hauled him out in cuffs just as Clay brought in a new Drop Zone recruit who swiveled his head around to make sure he was really seeing someone get dragged out in cuffs on the way to his interview. Clay introduced Raul and reminded me we'd talked about bringing him on.

"Remember I told you about him?" Clay said. "I served with him. He's still active duty . . . the big Mexican from East L.A.?"

"Oh, right! The big Mexican. I remember. Kind of a culture shock from East L.A. to Alaska," I said as I shook his hand.

"Yeah, just a little different," he said. "Not many low-riders with all the damn snow up here. I like messing around with cars. Kinda like the guy in the parking lot. But he likes messing with the insides, and I like the outsides."

Grease was out in the lot tending to the motor pool. When he was bored, he changed oil. If ever anyone was born to be a grease monkey, it was him. His dad was a mechanic and he'd practically grown up in his shop. Now he was an Army mechanic who liked hanging out with us on his off time. Nobody could imagine him with clean hands and not smelling like an engine.

"So, you're interested in working here?" I asked the Big Mexican.

Suddenly a huge boom from outside shook the walls, and a flash of orange light lit up the window. Everyone startled, and I ran outside to see Grease staggering toward the door, his face twisted in pain, clutching his hand. "Fuuuuuuck!"

"Should I call 911?" Clay asked in a mild panic.

"I don't need a fucking ambulance," Grease said through clenched teeth, gripping his thumb and putting pressure on the wound. "Hippie's here."

Hippie Omega grabbed the first-aid kit from the office, and we sat Grease down in the chair. The smell of burned hair filled my nostrils.

"What happened?" Hippie Omega asked as he cleaned the wound. He was our healer. The Omega—the final stop. He's where you went when you were done for the day.

"I tossed my butt and it landed in a puddle of diesel," Grease said, trying not to wince.

"I told you, man, smoking will kill you," Hippie Omega said as he pushed the needle through his skin. "But did you listen to me?"

"Very fucking funny."

Hippie Omega carefully stitched six tiny sutures on Grease's thumb, like delicate needlepoint, and then he wrapped the sterilized wound in gauze. No anesthesia. Well, unless you count beer.

"OK, I gotta go finish changing that oil," said Grease. "Thanks, man."

"No problem, brother," said Hippie Omega. "And try to keep that clean, at least for a little while!" he called out as the door shut. "He's not going to keep it clean . . ." he said, mostly to himself.

"Are things always this exciting around here?" asked the Big Mexican as he watched Grease head back to his patient in the parking lot.

"Is that going to be a problem?" I asked, handing him a Solo cup of home brew.

"No, man. I kinda like it," he said with a big smile.

The Big Mexican was going to fit in just fine.

CHAPTER 5

★ ★ ★ ★ ★

DOGS IN THE NIGHT

"If your attack is going too well, you're walking
into an ambush."
—Infantry Journal

Suicide was riding shotgun in my Hummer, drawing finger doodles of AR-15s with dashed lines coming out of the muzzles in the moisture that had condensed on the inside of the window.

"Where *is* this place?"

"We're almost there."

It was three in the morning, and we anticipated our target would be asleep. Even violent felons need some shut-eye, and when you kick their doors in, it's nice if they're not alert and thinking on their feet. Unfortunately, 3 a.m. seemed to have a sedative effect on everyone, including us, and we'd drained our twenty-ounce convenience-store coffees long ago.

We had two teams of eight guys, bouncing down the rutted, snow-covered highway that cut through downtown Wasilla. The caravan of three SUVs was filled with cigarette smoke, empty cups, and a bunch of weapons and gear. I was driving the lead vehicle, my inconspicuous candy-apple-red Hummer. Nobody bothers washing cars from November to April much, and when Suicide told me to "be respectable and wash that embarrassing piece of shit," I told him it was "road camo." Gunny and the Big Mexican followed, driving matching black Ford Expeditions with tinted windows. Gunny was tailgating me. Part of me wanted to tap the brake lights to make him back off. The other part of me thought that was a dumb idea.

The gentleman we'd be escorting to jail that night was wanted for breaking and entering, and known to have weapons. He'd jumped bail, so I went to the bar. If you're ever looking for a fugitive in small town Alaska, just remember—they will always go to the bar eventually.

"Yup, I know him." Nick the bartender poked the end of his thick index finger into the center of the mug shot and slid it back toward me. "That's Bobby Ray Watkins." The knotted-spruce bar was lacquered thick like a gym floor. "He's staying in Hanson's trailer, way up off the road down past the gravel pit. He's lookin' after his dogs while he's Outside. You know where it's at, right?"

I did, and it would mean two things. First, we'd need to park close to the road and hike in half a mile to get to the trailer so he wouldn't see us coming. Second, there were the dogs. When Nick said he was looking after the dogs, it didn't mean that Bobby Ray Watkins was pet-sitting—it meant there was a sled-dog kennel, likely with a dozen or two hyperactive young huskies who loved nothing more than barking and howling at noises they didn't recognize. This was also known as a really efficient biological audio-trigger security-alert system with auto backup. We were going to have to get sixteen guys past the enclosure of four-legged sentries undetected if we didn't want to tip off the target.

"Thank you, sir. It's a pleasure doing business with you, as always." I left a hundred-dollar bill under my empty beer glass and knocked twice on the bar as I swiveled and headed for the door. Nick and I had an understanding. Being generous was the least I could do since I kept arresting his customers.

I drove down the road and did a turnaround at the end of the driveway. A little reconnaissance work can go a long way. The next night we'd come to collect our prize. We rode a long wave of rolling green traffic lights through downtown Wasilla—passing the police department, car dealerships and big equipment-rental lots, strip malls with log cabin façades, the pawn

shop on the corner that offered gun loans, liquor stores, Taco Bell, the sec-
ondhand clothing store, and the Mat-Su Cinema. Wasilla itself wasn't much
to look at. Architecture wasn't really its thing, and building codes were nonexistent. It was an exercise in libertarian urban planning: "Nobody's gonna
tell me how to build my own damn house, or make us plant some trees
around this gigantic parking lot. You can't force *me* to make things look
nice!" In other words—a shithole. Beyond its appearance, it had a fairly
notorious reputation in the rest of Alaska for being home to a lot of good
ol' boys with baseball caps and guns and pickup trucks, pregnant teenagers,
hard-core evangelical churches, bars, and meth labs. The day the Wal-Mart
Superstore broke ground was practically a religious holiday.

But during the daylight, and facing outward, the sawtooth ridges of
the Talkeetna Mountains jut up into the sky and cradle the south side of
the sprawling 7,000-person town. The lower elevations of the slopes are
covered with spruce, birch, and aspen. The upper elevations soar past
the point where trees will grow and long vertical troughs carved by ava-
lanches descend from jagged grey peaks that are so steep they won't even
hold snow, and so high there's no plant life but lichen. On the other side of
town, broad, flat expanses of marshland and mudflats reach out from the
terminus of Cook Inlet, a 180-mile-long body of water extending up from
the Gulf of Alaska. In the summer, the inlet is a migration route for all
five species of Pacific salmon, which spawn in the rivers and creeks—the
Deshka, the Little Susitna, Wasilla Creek, Montana Creek, Sunshine Creek,
and dozens of others. Some will arrive at their birth river, spawn, and die,
their carcasses eaten by bears or eagles. Others will meet their fate with
cracked pepper on the grill or in the smoker. But right now, in February,
the sun wouldn't rise for another seven hours, and Wasilla was just a long
line of frozen crappy strip malls and a violent felon with our names on him.

We did lots of fugitive recovery work in Wasilla, which is only forty
miles north of Anchorage. It marks the beginning of the Idiot Zone, where
the not-too-bright would relocate themselves, thinking no one would ever
find them. They were still on the road system but figured they could flee
into the woods if they had to. At least that was their thinking. Most of
those dumbasses wouldn't last two days in the woods. And for some reason
they all think Wasilla is a great place to disappear—which, of course, made

it a great place to look. They were the kids who really sucked at hide-and-seek. And school.

"Aww, look who's sleeping!" drawled Clay, sitting in the back with Sunshine, who had slumped forward, nodding. "Wakey, wakey, little lady!" He reached over and tickled his ear.

"Fuck you. Go away." Sunshine snorted awake and gave Clay a half-hearted slug on the arm. "Asshole."

"We're almost there, so wake the fuck up and get your shit together," I said with a tinge of Drill Sergeant Mitchell.

"So where's Grease? Why doesn't he ever come out?"

"Thinks it's too dangerous," I said.

"Well, shit . . . I guess that's a good call coming from a guy who almost blew his thumb off changing the oil in a car."

"You OK, Scott?" I asked our newest recruit in the farthest back seat. "Yup."

He was a man of few words. He was probably nervous. He'd arrested someone with me who was too drunk to stand, but this was his first big mission.

"Hey, aren't we near Sarah's house?" Clay asked. A last name was unnecessary. Unless otherwise specified, "Sarah" was Sarah Palin, Alaska's new governor. She had once been the mayor of this picturesque shithole, and yes, she lived pretty much right across the highway from Mr. Bobby Ray Watkins, who was about to have a very bad night if all went according to plan. But that was Alaska—everyone thrown together in the same big icebox. There were no gated communities in Wasilla to separate the governor from the runaway felons.

Palin had stunned the state in a devastating upset in a three-way primary election. She took over 50 percent of the vote, crushing the incumbent Republican. Then she rode the populist wave and kicked the ass of former Democratic Gov. Tony Knowles in the general. Alaska was ready for a change, she said, and clearly she was right. The governor's seat in the forty-ninth state is always vulnerable to corruption and undue influence from the oil industry, and her predecessor, Frank Murkowski, had succumbed. Shady backdoor deals with oil companies altered Alaska's tax structure to give these large multinationals billions of dollars in tax giveaways, straight out of the state's coffers. And he hadn't even really bothered to cover it up very well.

"Heyyy, Guvner!" Clay drawled from the back seat, looking in the direction of Sarah's house, which was about fifty yards off the highway, hidden by trees, and sharing the shore of Lake Lucille with the local Best Western. "She's so fucking hot. I love that naughty librarian thing—the bun and the glasses . . . Dayum."

There was that too.

"OK, focus, gentlemen! You can't do recovery with a hard dick."

I clicked the right turn signal and eased off the road into a large parking lot. In the center of the lot was a tall light pole with a coffee shack in the middle of the pool of flickering orange light. There had to be at least a million of these little shacks in Alaska, with names like "Java Jive" and "Kodiak Kup" and "The Jittery Moose." Usually about sixteen by eight feet, with a drive-up window on each side, they serve espresso drinks to a population that consumes more coffee per capita than any state in the nation. I'm a regular gas-station coffee guy—definitely the exception to the rule. If I'm going to be a snob about a beverage, I'll save it for wine and beer. Coffee? As long as it's black and has caffeine, I don't give a shit. This little shack was the governor's stop for her daily skinny white chocolate mocha. If Alaskans need coffee and have to drive more than a mile without seeing a drive-up window, they start to get the DTs.

We all pulled into the back corner of the lot and exited our vehicles for the mission brief. The blast of dry, frigid air woke us up like a slap to the face. I unrolled a large map of the area I'd drawn on the hood of Gunny's Expedition and the guys huddled around.

"OK, we're parking here on the road," I said pointing my gloved finger on the spot. "We'll get snowshoes on and head up the left side of the driveway as far from the dog kennels as we can get, but not too close to this house here. Then we'll sweep around this way and approach the trailer from the north side. Hand signals only. No sound. We fall in, two lines, backs against the structure. Normal protocol. I'll lead, kick in the door, and we can introduce ourselves to Mr. Watkins. Questions?"

All eyes were glued to the map. No more laughing or joking around. We were on mission—hyper-vigilant, focused, and wide awake.

"Here's our bad guy. Take another look," I said, passing around a printed picture of Bobby Ray Watkins' mug shot. He was in his forties, thin stringy dark hair about shoulder length. His eyes were closely set, small, and angry, with dark circles under them. A thick Fu Manchu moustache exaggerated the natural downward curve of his mouth. His chin jutted slightly forward, defiant. The whole image was one of scorn and contempt for the photographer, law enforcement, and humanity in general. You couldn't make up a guy to look more like a scary dirtbag if you tried.

"This asshole's no joke. We know he's got weapons, and he's probably about as much fun as he looks. Don't get shot. You guys ready?"

"Yeah!"

"You good?" I asked Scott.

"You bet, Boss."

"OK, remember. Do not alert the dogs. Silent like ninjas. Got it?"

Gunny leaned in. "If they wake up, I can take care of 'em."

"No! Nobody is going to shoot or otherwise harm the fucking dogs." I didn't think I had to say that, but apparently I did. "Do not harm the animals, everyone understand?"

There were nods all around.

"All right. Let's go ruin this fucker's night."

The ritual began. My guys were trained well. A thorough check of equipment was first on the list—batteries in night-vision goggles, batteries in weapon scopes, batteries in flashlights, handcuff keys, load the weapons.

Then, the round count. Every man counted and recorded how many rounds of ammo he had. If shots were fired, the police would have to be called, and we'd need to know who had fired how many shots. We counted in and out religiously after every mission to make sure we left no ammo on the scene. It was imperative to collect all the brass on the ground. Anything left behind could be used to contaminate some other crime scene, which could be used against you. We never took chances.

Everyone was already suited up in combat boots, pants and shirts in MultiCam—a camo pattern designed to reduce the visual and infrared signature of the human body. MultiCam is hard to see with night-vision goggles, and the alpine pattern created for use in the snow meant that we'd be as close to ghosts as was technologically possible as we moved through the trees. Would this guy have night vision too? I'd sold enough goggles in the store to know that there were lots of them out there, and the guys hiding out in the woods were the ones most likely to own them.

Under our shirts was soft body armor, over our jackets were ballistic vests called plate carriers, with pouches in the front and back to hold large dense ceramic or metal plates to absorb and disrupt the impact of a bullet. Everyone had mag pouches filled with ammo, a radio, a first-aid kit, a couple pairs of handcuffs and keys, a helmet equipped with night vision, a camera, an infrared illuminator, and a flashlight if we needed it.

We all carried the same weapons—a 1911 .45 ACP semiautomatic handgun in a holster around the waist, and an AR-15 carbine semiautomatic rifle across our backs. These were the workhorses of the firearms world for a reason—solid, accurate, reliable.

By the time it was over, we'd all gained a quick forty-five pounds. We felt like hippos tramping through the snow, but we were used to it. Nobody had a death wish, not even Suicide, and that extra poundage wrapped around your body made you as secure as you'd ever feel. There were no guarantees, though—a direct shot to the face or an unlucky stray round from a ricochet that got up under your vest were real threats. A hit anywhere else would hurt like hell, but at least you'd be around to feel it afterwards.

Suited up for a mission.

I made sure everyone had the best gear possible. This wasn't play. Anyone who didn't have his own gear or weapon checked out whatever he wanted from Drop Zone's armory.

The act of putting on our gear got us mentally into our space, like actors getting into costume. We were different now—a highly focused team. We never knew what we'd find on the other side of a door. Adrenaline was pumping—reflexes on a hair trigger. We were ready for anything, but what we really hoped was that Bobby Ray Watkins and his kennel of dogs would be fast asleep when we kicked in his door, and it would be over quick and easy.

Our destination was about a mile down the road, and the only thing left to do was pull the brake light fuses on the rigs and make sure the headlights were off. We'd drive that final awkward mile in full gear using night-vision goggles only and arrive in the dark with nothing to give us away. The road was deserted.

I saw the marker I was looking for—a white stake with a little round plastic reflector on top. It marked the entrance to the long, unlit driveway that led up a slope and through the trees.

A low-hanging crescent moon was getting ready to sink behind the mountains. To our night vision, that sliver of moon was a floodlight, and its pale reflection off the snow was enough to turn our world into a bright, harsh landscape of flat, electric green. It was five degrees above zero, and the stars were out by the billions, even though we were only a few miles from the glow of downtown Wasilla that washed out part of the sky.

I killed the engine and rolled the dark Hummer to a full stop on the side of the road, leaving enough room for Gunny and the Big Mexican to pull in behind me. We moved quickly so no random motorist would see sixteen guys in camo holding rifles and pouring out of SUVs in the middle of the night and call the cops. But no vehicles passed as we unloaded and headed up the driveway.

The snow cover was about two feet deep, so we used snowshoes to cover the distance on foot. A far cry from the big tennis rackets made of sinew from the Alaska of history, these snowshoes were compact and sleek, aluminum tubing bent into an oval, with webbing and tough vinyl straps that slipped over combat boots. To keep them on your feet, forward momentum is required or they slip off. We'd all practiced hauling gear and done military exercises in snowshoes for enough hours to feel confident in situations like this. I made the hand signal for "follow me" and indicated the left-hand route into the trees that would keep us far away from the dogs.

Night vision is the most useful and hideous gear ever invented. Everything is flattened into two dimensions. Depth perception is nonexistent, and it feels like playing a first-person-shooter video game from inside the screen. The disorientation is predictable, but it never gets easier or feels normal. The sensation of walking into a flat plane tricks your brain and eyes into feeling like your body isn't really moving forward. We had to use the damn things. It was an incredible advantage at times like this, but you could count on a noticeable reduction in efficiency and effectiveness in other ways.

I started off—*shhh shhh shhh*—across the top of the snow. One by one I could hear the *shhh shhh shhh* of snowshoes behind me, and soon all sixteen of us were stepping in unison, synchronized stealth, winding through the trees, left, right, left, right, staying away from the spruce trunks where the snow dipped down in a natural depression that could throw us off balance. *Shhh shhh shhh* through the weird piercing green. My ears scanned. No dogs barking. No dogs barking. No dogs barking. Just a little further.

I caught the outline of the trailer through the trees. In the woods, the eye notices angles because they stand out against a natural background of soft irregular shapes. As we got within fifty feet, I knew we'd made it past the kennels. So far, so good. Forty feet, thirty feet, twenty feet. I gave the hand signal to stop. We were out of powder snow and standing on the packed driveway. It was time to ditch the snowshoes—definitely not the preferred footwear for a home invasion. I gave the forward signal again. We'd split into two teams and line up with our backs against the front of the structure, eight on one side of the door, eight on the other. I'd take the door down, and then it was showtime.

Something happens to snow when it gets really cold. The physics of it makes sense; snowflakes are flat, like plates, and when super-chilled and pressed together, they rub against each other. And when they rub against each other they make a noise. At temperatures close to zero, it sounds like a combination of squeaky shoes and rubbing a balloon. We moved forward and suddenly sounded like sixteen kids with rubber soles crossing the gym floor. This was bad, but we were committed. Ten feet to go.

Still no dogs. Gunny's team lined up shoulder to shoulder on the right, my team shoulder to shoulder on the left, our backs pressed against the trailer on each side of the door. No sound except my own breath, and pulse, and the breath of Suicide behind me. Hopefully we hadn't tipped off Watkins. All was quiet. I gave the hand signal indicating I was about to take out the door. I took a step forward and heard it. Unmistakable. *Cha-chunk.* A shotgun.

I recoiled instinctively. A concussive blast. My ears screamed. The metal door groaned and collapsed, blasted through the center where I'd been standing a fraction of a second before. We had to move now, before he got off another shot. We had to get in. Reflex and muscle memory pushed me through the door. The green glowing image of Bobby Ray Watkins stood in the flat plane, cocking his shotgun, and suddenly the world was literally upside down. My legs were gone from under me. My right shoulder and head slammed into the floor. The rest of me followed as I tumbled over something in the dark.

Cha-chunk.

A green face, eyes squinted, and the double barrels of a shotgun pointed into my face. Jesus. This was it.

Bobby Ray Watkins reeled sideways and hit the wall with a crunch and a cry of pain, his arms pinned, still clutching the shotgun in one hand against the wall. Suicide was smaller than him, but held him easily as Gunny wrenched the gun from his grip and unloaded it.

"On the floor, motherfucker! Hands behind your head! Don't you fucking move!" Suicide's voice was higher pitched than usual and he was panting. He knew what had just happened. A shotgun blast to the face and I'd have been done. If he'd been a fraction of a second later . . .

He pushed Watkins's face to the floor and the Big Mexican cuffed him from behind. I was standing, although I don't remember getting up. My legs were shaking from the adrenaline, and I finally saw what had done me in. A large flowered velvet couch had been shoved in front of the door as a barrier, and I'd been so fixated on getting to Watkins before the next blast that I'd missed it. Suicide had seen me go ass-over-teakettle and hurdled the couch before Watkins could blow my head off. It was times like that I was really glad Suicide lived up to that handle. No hesitation, no fear, just go.

"Good going, bro. Way to wake up the dogs," he said with a hand on my shoulder. I hadn't even noticed, but the kennel was now wild with howls and frantic barking.

"Thanks, man. I owe you big."

"Hell, yeah, you do!"

Scott, the new guy, rounded the corner from the kitchen on the other side of the wall.

"I do believe we got us a meth lab back here, gentlemen. Bonus points!" He stood, feet apart, arms crossed, victorious. A weird silence fell, and one by one, all pairs of eyes turned to Scott.

"What?" he said, looking from one face to the other, visibly uncomfortable.

Clay finally spoke, pointing.

"Dude. What the fuck is THAT? Please tell me for some fucked-up reason you pack your flashlight in your pants."

Scott looked down at his crotch in horror and pulled his feet together.

"I can't help it. It just happens in . . . exciting situations . . . like this."

"That's . . . uh . . . impressive," Suicide stared and shook his head in disbelief.

"Wow," said Bobby Ray Watkins from the floor—hands cuffed behind his back.

"What the fuck kind of banana hammock do you need for *that* thing?" asked Clay. "At least tuck it up under your belt or something. Jesus Christ! And hey, Boss," he said looking at me. "I believe you told us not too long ago that you cannot do recovery work with a hard dick. I think perhaps you were mistaken. Just saying."

Scott was now blushing furiously and retreated into the kitchen.

"Banana Hammock," Gunny said as he sat on the velvet sofa sharpening a small hunting knife on a whetstone. Scott had his handle.

The Wasilla Police Department dispatched two units to collect our target. We saw the lights, and with Clay at his left and Suicide at his right, Watkins was escorted out the door to his ride.

Then I noticed it. Something came hurtling out of the trailer. The tiniest, whitest woman I've ever seen in my life, dressed in nothing but an equally white bra and grandma panties, was running barefoot across the snow headed for our group. You could see her dark hair against the snow, but other than that, her camo rivaled ours—white on white. With a shriek like a banshee, she leapt up in the air and threw her arms around Gunny's neck. Yes, in a crowd of sixteen guys, most of normal human size, she went for Gunny. She locked her arms around his neck and wrapped her legs around his waist like a child getting a piggyback ride. Releasing a hand she began beating him on the top of the head with a tiny balled fist to the rhythm of her words.

"You. Give. Him. Back! You. Let. Him. Go!"

"Could someone please get this thing off me?" said Gunny as he kneeled down and the police officers peeled her off his massive frame. I was glad he didn't hurl her against a tree, but Gunny had his own set of rules for how to deal with things. Turns out Miss Elizabeth Grimes Calhoun also had an outstanding warrant for petty theft. Go figure.

There was a lot to talk about when we got back to the store. We recapped, and speculated, and recounted our stories one by one. We should have swept the trailer better. Where the fuck had she been hiding? Hell, she was so small she could have been in a cabinet. They all thought I was dead for sure. What was going to happen to the dogs? And one by one the guys drifted away to sleep it off. Suicide was the last to head out, and I followed him into the parking lot.

"OK, man. Take it easy. I'm outta here," he said, giving a little salute as he looked over his shoulder.

"Hey, man. Wait a second. Listen, I just wanted to say again I appreciate what you did up there." It wasn't every day I had to thank someone for saving my life, and I wasn't really quite sure what the protocol was. I opted for the awkward man hug. I grabbed him by the arm and did the traditional one-handed slap on the back.

"I owe you," I said. "Seriously."

"It was nothing, man. You'd have done the same for me. For any of us. We're brothers."

He smiled and walked off to his truck. He was right.

CHAPTER 6

★ ★ ★ ★ ★

PATRIOTS

"When they get home they wonder if there's something wrong with them because they find war repugnant but also thrilling. They hate it and miss it . . . The self-condemnation can be crippling."

—David Brooks

One out of every ten Alaskans is a veteran, a higher concentration than in any other state in the nation. Many are stationed at one of the nine military bases in the state at some point in their career, get bitten by the Alaska bug, and come back to settle down and retire there when their service is over. And along with the most veterans per capita comes the most military post-traumatic stress disorder, or PTSD. During the American Revolution, it was called "nostalgia." During the Civil War, it was known as "soldier's heart." During World War I, "shell shock"; during World War II, "battle fatigue"; during Korea, "gross stress reaction"; and during Vietnam, "Vietnam combat reaction." Whatever you call it, it's the same shit—flashbacks, avoidance of places or situations or people, hypervigilance, nightmares, reliving experiences, crippling anxiety, emotional numbness, alienation from family and friends, irritability, can't sleep, don't want to sleep, thoughts of suicide, and feeling like you're the only one living in that hell.

Our latest little adventure in the Sandbox has seen hundreds of thousands of men and women diagnosed with PTSD. The longest wartime in our history, with soldiers' exposure to life-threatening situations, and our expectation that they can somehow ricochet back and forth from stateside peace to desert warfare, has caused massive problems. In Alaska it's not even called PTSD anymore, but officially now "PTSI"—post-traumatic stress injury, to make it sound less like a mental illness and more like something that can be managed, and even cured, which it can be.

Suicide discovered Terry at a concert. He had come to have dinner at a local club with his wife, and Suicide was working the door. Terry handed Suicide his military ID to get in, and they struck up a conversation. He'd received an honorable discharge from the Air Force. He was back from his third tour in Iraq. He'd gotten a job at a lumber yard, but it didn't last. His boss said he was "unreliable." Terry had never been unreliable in his life, he said, but something had changed. Now he was out of work and had finally given up looking. He left the show early, after it got loud, and lights started flashing. Suicide gave him a business card as he and his wife hurried out and told him to call if he was interested in a job.

"He seems like a good guy, just kind of fucked up right now. He needs patience, and time, but he'll be good," Suicide said. If Terry was good enough for Suicide, that was all the recommendation I needed.

I'd forgotten about him when he showed up at the shop a full three weeks later, dressed in ratty jeans, hands jammed in the pockets of his hoodie. He pretended to be looking at merchandise for a long time.

"Can I help you? What are you looking for?" I asked.

"Nothing. Just looking," he said.

A long time went by as he kept taking things off pegs and reading packaging and looking at prices before he asked if I was Bill and told me who he was.

"What did you do in the Sandbox?" I asked after a handshake.

"Loaded bombs." He looked away from me. His face was gaunt, and his round dark eyes looked at the same time detached from our conversation and hyper-alert to his surroundings.

"You get a job after you got home?"

"I tried a couple things but it didn't really work out. For one reason or another."

"Are you having a tough time?"

He looked uncomfortable, like he didn't know how to answer the question. I'd seen guys going through this.

"I just . . . I don't really like to sleep," he said. "But plenty of guys had it rougher than I did," he added quickly. "I didn't have it the worst." He jingled the keys in his pocket.

PTSD normally manifests after you get out of the military. If the government has done its job right, they've scrubbed you of individuality, retrained you that all the things you've learned at home don't apply anymore. Until you enlisted, society worked hard to tell you to be nice, don't hurt people, stifle your violent impulses, get along with others, and don't fight. These are good things in civilian life, but when you want warriors, you need people who are OK with killing, brutalizing, living without remorse. You need people who can handle death—causing it, watching it happen to people they care about, risking their own. We need Spartans and Vikings—we need meanness from those who carry weapons and go do the dirty work—not sensitive, compassionate men who are taught to have respect for other people. Those are the ones who have the most difficult time. It's the hard truth of war and postwar, and civilians don't get it. They don't want to get it, because it's uncomfortable. They don't really want to think about what they ask these guys to do in their name—to turn civility on and off, compassion on and off, morality on and off, deployment after deployment after deployment, year after year. It's easy to watch the news from your couch and cheer for Team USA to kick some ass. It's not easy or without consequence to actually go do that.

If you're a normal person, after a while you can't load bombs without thinking about what they do, wondering how many people they are about to kill, who they are, and how you are a part of it, wondering how many have already died, and if they were the right people. Your parents and your teachers have told you to be nice. Your country has asked you to facilitate indiscriminate mass killing. And you have to hold both those things in the same brain. You watch the news at home and suddenly you start seeing things from the other side of the bomb.

"You feel like working here? Seeing if it works out?"

He looked stunned.

"I . . . I . . . I guess so. That's it? OK."

"OK, man. Good to have you on board. Come in Monday at nine o'clock."

On his first day, Terry showed up three hours late smelling like a distillery and left two hours early. But he showed up. I gave him that. By the second week, we had talked to his wife, and we were making sure he took his meds when he was supposed to. One Thursday morning he showed up on time. Sometimes he couldn't get out of bed, and his wife would call. And one of the other guys would fill in.

"Been there," said Sherlock. "I'll cover his mornings as long as he needs it."

I did have to explain to him one day that the six polar sleeping bags he sold for fifty dollars apiece were actually marked 50 percent *off* for our summer sale, making them $200 apiece. I could see his eyes widen with fear.

"Oh, shit. I'm so . . . I'm sorry . . . I'll make it up."

"It's OK, Discount," I said. "Shit happens. You're covered. Everyone fucks up some time. Just try to pay attention, OK?"

In a few months Discount was showing up on time and working an eight-hour day. He made bank deposits on his way home. And he didn't give discounts unless he was supposed to.

After six months, he was ready to go on a mission. Being depended on again made him dependable. And it didn't happen from a therapy session or a new med—it was being part of something again, being a soldier again, being of use. And being around a group of guys who got it and who didn't judge. Guys sitting around a fire has been some pretty legit therapy since there were guys and since there were fires. Discount had a reason to get up and get out of his house. And now he'd have a gun back.

As Discount and the others grew and matured into their work and became more professional, Drop Zone did too. Granted, we started with a pretty low bar, but we evolved. Thanks to Sherlock, we grew our list of rules to include "no telling customers they're assholes and don't know shit, even if they are and they don't." I broke that rule sometimes when some jackass refused to keep his ignorant racist mouth shut or take his gay-bashing bullshit some-where else. This invariably was met with utter confusion, and one of the guys saying to the startled customer, "No, he's serious, man. We really don't say that shit here. He'll throw your ass out, we've seen it happen," and with me explaining that I really didn't need his fucking money and that GI Joe's Surplus Store was only a couple miles away.

There was no question that my customer base was strongly right-leaning and libertarian politically. They identified themselves that way, any-way. I tried a few times to explain that you can't actually be a real libertar-ian and a fundamentalist Christian social conservative at the same time. But eventually I just gave up. They had no reason to think I wasn't one of their own, so they felt comfortable sharing their brilliant solutions to world problems and deep level of hatred and fear of the government. I didn't want to disabuse them of the idea that I was one of them for two reasons. First, I liked having customers. They kept me in business. Second, I felt like I was keeping watch. If the crazies confided in me, I could tip off the cops to real dangers and maybe prevent something bad from happening, or maybe I'd hear a good tip about something that already went down.

There was a strong militia presence in the state. The official Alaska state militia, the Alaska State Defense Force, reports directly to the governor, as commander-in-chief, so it held little appeal to anyone distrusting the intentions of the government. So instead, they gravitated toward private militias, which are organized and led in a paramilitary style by command-ers who may or may not have gone through any formal military training or assessment of leadership skills. Some are relatively benign—guys who never quite grew out of playing soldier in the woods, and want to feel like they'd be useful in a disaster. They focus not only on the military aspect, but also on prepping and survivalist skills. I got that, totally, because I was one of those guys. I'm all about being able to brew my own beer and have fresh eggs from the chicken coop and some kickass tomatoes after the end of the world. And many militia groups had gathered vets like I had, who needed a gun and a purpose, which I also understood. But the lon-ger I brushed up against my customers, the more I saw cults of personal-ity that arose when a particularly charismatic leader took the reins and began fear-mongering. The groups mostly engaged in simple preparedness exercises and target practice, but there were those who fantasized about going back to a "simpler time," some hyper-idealized Christian-based eighteenth century life. Those were the good ol' days—if you happened to be a white Christian male. The need for power, belonging to a cause bigger than themselves, the need to feel chosen, to feel independent, led them to stand defiant, wrapped in a flag with an AK-47 in one hand and a Bible in the other. Muslims were the problem—and for others it was also black men, or gays, or women being uppity, or immigrants, or liberals, or socialists, or environmentalists. But for all of them, it was the government—which coincidentally some believed was run by a liberal, black, gay, immigrant, Muslim socialist. Funny how that worked. I kept waiting for Fox News to say he was really a woman and all the bases would have been covered. Self-determination, and freedom itself, was on the line as the government sought to make everyone equal by raising up inferior or undeserving groups of people, and thereby exterminating American culture. American liberties too are destined to wash away in a One World government where everyone is the same—all slaves to a malevolent power structure. A good-versus-evil world is very neat, and you always know where you stand when you are the good and "they" are the evil.

A few of my regular customers asked if I was "a sovereign." When I told them I had no idea what the hell that was, they told me to read up. So, I read up on sovereign citizens. For the most part, they, like many other Alaskans, just wanted to be left alone and not have the government in their business. But they viewed regulations like vehicle registration, driver's licenses, traffic fines, fees, and taxes of all kinds as an unconstitutional intrusion on their freedom. Any government agency—including law enforcement—robbed them of that God-given individual liberty. They found support with each other in meet-ups and online groups. Paranoia was a common trait, and they wanted to believe they were somehow exempt from laws they didn't like, preferring to commiserate about some fantasyland where they were "free men on the land" and didn't have to deal with society or authority of any kind. Some of them had joined private militias so they'd be prepared when the government collapsed under the weight of its own illegitimacy.

The hard-core Sovereign Citizens are the conductors of this crazy train, denying the very existence of the United States government itself and all its agencies. They believe that the government is no longer legitimate and that law enforcement literally has no legal jurisdiction over them. They have "renounced their citizenship" and all connection to any government process—no fishing licenses, no marriage licenses, no dog licenses; they alter driver's licenses and license plates to proclaim their sovereign status. These are the "you're not the boss of me" kids in sixth grade who grew up and decided that the laws no longer applied to them and that nobody was going to tell them what to do. They do everything from clogging up the judicial system with acts of "paper terrorism" like filing false liens against the homes of judges and police officers they don't like, to even kidnapping and murdering law enforcement agents and federal officials. By 2014 this group would officially be named by the FBI as the number-one threat to law enforcement, surpassing Islamic extremists, militias, and a host of other radical organizations—despite being largely unknown to the general populace.

And yes, these were some of my best customers. Crazy as shit.

A guy once bought a bunch of armored plates he wanted to retrofit and mount inside the driver's-side door of his car. I asked him why, and he explained it was to save him from a shootout with the police. He hadn't done anything yet, and wasn't going to, but was preparing in case he ever got pulled over for a speeding ticket or a burned-out headlight and things "escalated."

"They got no damned authority over me, or you, or anybody," he said. "The US Corporation has no lawful authority over Private Sovereign State Citizens acting in the capacity of free men on the land. So no goddamn corporate fed is gonna make me get out of my own goddamn car. I'm nobody's slave, and I'll eat a bullet before I bend my knee to the tyrant."

What. The. Fuck. I wrote down his license number, make, and model as he drove off with his stack of armor plates. The cops got a call.

"Ah, yes. The 'sovereign citizens,' " said Rod Potter of the APD. "I'm surprised you haven't seen them before now. Crazy and dangerous. Appreciate the tip, Bill," he said. "We never know when a routine traffic stop is going to go bad because of one of these guys."

If anyone seemed like a credible threat, I'd tip the cops, but for the most part they were all bluster. It's hard to explain how, but you could just tell the difference.

While these armchair patriots fanned the flames of their own paranoia, Drop Zone fugitive recovery did the harder work, getting violent
criminals off the street. We had neither the time nor desire to obsess over
the hypothetical demise of the government and the dream of converting
the country to a white-male-dominated Christian theocracy. There were
assholes to put in jail.

"Hey! Didn't we just see that guy last week?" Suicide pointed to the face on
the office TV. "Seriously, when we nabbed that meth head on the East side.
Sitting on the couch! Remember? That's that guy!"

A lumpy-faced man with a large, distinctive nose stared out from the
screen. His photo was followed by two more.

"*You* could get a cash reward for up to a thousand dollars for providing
information that brings these most-wanted fugitives to justice. If you have
information that could lead to arrest, call Crime Stoppers now."

Lumpy Face was one of Anchorage's top-three most wanted, apparently, and we not only had information that could lead to his arrest, we
could probably save them the trouble and arrest him ourselves. That would
be way more fun. Guys like him tended to hang out in the same place a lot.

"Who's down?" I asked. Suicide, the Big Mexican, and Hippie Alpha
were all on board for an impromptu mission. Within the hour we
had our gear checked and loaded, and wheels were rolling toward the
always-exciting section of town known as Mountain View. We felt pretty
sure that if the guy had been sitting on that ratty couch banging meth last
Thursday night, he'd probably be doing the exact same thing this Thursday
night. It was worth a shot, anyway.

We knocked on the door. It opened. It was usually as easy as that.

"Hey! Holy shit, you guys. It's the shadow people again!" a thin,
unwashed man said talking to the room behind him where various people
were sprawled on furniture tweaking their asses off. "Are you? Wait. Are
you guys shadow people or people people? I don't remember. I don't . . .
Were you? And how do I know whether to believe you? Oh, shit . . ." The guy
looked like he hadn't blinked in days and was having a hard time thinking.

"We just want to talk to that gentleman right there on the couch," said Suicide, entering the room and walking over to Lumpy Face who was slumped over, mouth hanging open, sitting next to a woman who was picking fluff out of a hole in the couch. Lumpy was cuffed in about four seconds flat, and the Big Mexican guided him out the door.

"Oh, shit, oh, shit, oh, shit . . ." said the thin man, clutching his head.

"It's OK, man," said Suicide. "It's OK. We're just going to visit Shadowland to talk to some people. You go back inside now. It's fine." He closed the door.

"How the fuck did you find me?" Lumpy asked on the way to the police station. "I don't even know you guys . . ." You could tell his whole world was operating in slow motion. Probably heroin. Something. Who knew?

"Your little friend sold you out, man. What's his name . . ." I grabbed the printout from the Crime Stoppers website sitting on the dashboard that listed the names of the three most wanted. They'd all been involved in a series of robberies. "TJ, that's it. Your friend TJ Wilkerson had some not-so-nice things to say about you. Told us where you'd be so we'd go easy on him. See? This is his statement right here," I said holding up the papers and shaking them a little. Suicide suppressed a laugh.

"That little motherfucker," Lumpy said, looking out the window. "What a back-stabbing little fuck."

"Yeah, that really sucks for you how he did that," I said. "Of course, there's still one more of you three musketeers out there. You can still cut a deal . . . do yourself a favor and tell us where we can find him." I held up the picture. "Because I'll tell you what, if we find him, he's gonna talk first and it'll be double bad for you."

Lumpy spilled his guts immediately. Clearly he had no qualms about joining the "back-stabbing little fuck" club, and we got the address where a certain Jason Balas was living with his mother. We dropped Lumpy off at the police station.

Jason Balas's mom took some convincing but called her son on his cellphone and talked him into turning himself in. They would go easy on him, she said, if he'd just turn over the location of his friend TJ Wilkerson and give himself up. TJ was bad news, and she knew it from the beginning, from the first time she saw him. It was all his fault Jason had gotten into this mess in the first place, according to his mom. Jason got home, told us everything we needed to know about TJ, and we slipped the cuffs on. The APD arrived and the flashing red-and-blue lights lit Jason's way to jail.

"Go easy, he turned himself in. He's just been hanging with the wrong crowd," I said. Mrs. Balas gave me a grateful smile.

We set out for our third arrest at a motel by the airport.

"Aww, fuck," said my buddy Derek at the check-in desk when he recognized me. "You guys are killing me! He's in 108. Just don't break the door down this time, please?" He handed me a key.

"This is too easy," said the Big Mexican as he stood towering over a dejected TJ Wilkerson, who sat on the bed in the motel in a pair of brightly colored boxers. He'd been lying low in the same motel where everyone who's worried about being arrested lies low. He was watching an Adam Sandler movie when we opened the door.

"What the fuck is that, dude? Are those moose?" the Big Mexican said, pointing at TJ's shorts.

"Yeah, moose."

"Why they got red noses, man?"

"It's like Rudolph the Red-Nosed Reindeer. It's supposed to be Merry Chrismoose."

"Dude, it's fucking July. That ain't right."

"We're gonna get three grand for less than two hours' work. Not half bad," Suicide calculated as we waited for APD.

"Are you guys done for the night?" Officer Rod Potter asked when he arrived and saw us for the third time. "It's not that we don't appreciate your little entertainment for the evening, but it'd be nice to have a heads-up if we're gonna get called again in the next twenty minutes."

"This is the last one," I said. "Gotta keep you gentlemen on your toes."

Back at the shop we high-fived, sat back down in our chairs, poured some fresh beers, laughed our asses off, and got on the phone. We were pumped.

"Yeah, Crime Stoppers?" I said. "Name's Bill Fulton. I just want to report that I've got some information that will lead you to your three most wanted."

I had to tell the guys to hold down the celebration while I was on the phone.

"Yup, all three of them. My tip? Well, they're all back in custody with the Anchorage Police so they should be easy to find . . . Because I arrested them . . . I did, yes, ma'am. Well, me and three other guys did . . . Yes, ma'am, it was a lawful arrest . . . Yes. Yes, they are there right now. Yes, I personally arrested them. Bill Fulton. Drop Zone over on Spenard. You can talk to Officer Rodney Potter. Yes, ma'am . . . Hold on. What? . . . Your commercial said . . . Are you fucking kidding me?"

All eyes were on me.

"No . . . Your ad said 'bring them to justice.' And we did. We brought them *to justice* directly. All three of them. We handed them right to justice, and justice didn't even have to do shit. And now you're saying that doesn't *count*? I'm sorry, I was under the impression that you actually wanted to stop crime. I mean when you call yourselves 'Crime Stoppers,' it kind of leaves people with that impression."

There was no convincing them. They had a strict policy of not dealing with "bounty hunters."

"We are freelance fugitive recovery agents!" I explained. "It says that right on my damn business card!"

It didn't work. We were all pissed. Yeah, we had a good time, and we got Anchorage's three most wanted off the streets in less than two hours. But it would have been nice to get at least some gas money out of the deal instead of just a story.

"I knew it was too good to be true," said the Big Mexican.

"Fuck Crime Stoppers!" Hippie Alpha said, raising his red plastic cup.

"But it was fun," said Suicide.

Nobody could argue that.

CHAPTER 7

★ ★ ★ ★ ★

THE ROTTING ELEPHANT

"America is looking for answers. She's looking for a new direction; the world is looking for a light. That light can come from America's great North Star; it can come from Alaska."
—Sarah Palin

"The voice of the Republican party is up for grabs. It's a contest right now."
—Former Republican Governor of New Mexico Gary Johnson

Sometimes you don't even notice the days that change your life. The day I met Stacey seemed like a regular day. I had no idea that my world would turn upside down and that one event would change everything that followed. Those days always seem clear in the rearview mirror, though. Like the day I met that weasely little prick, Francis August Schaeffer Cox.

The visor was down and my Oakley sunglasses deflected the morning light of March as the sun crested the mountains. I was a delegate to the State Republican Convention. No matter how many times I said that to myself, it still seemed absurd. Anchorage was gaining about six minutes of sunlight a day this time of year, racing to summer solstice when it would never get completely dark. This was cabin-fever time, when people went a little nutty after months of dark and cold. Soon, a couple of missing-persons cases would get closed when bodies melted out of the snow or showed up when the river ice broke up.

I'd dipped my toe in the world of politics once before, volunteering for former two-term Democratic Gov. Tony Knowles, who decided to try his hand at a Senate run. He was not a typical Democrat, but he was a typical Alaska Democrat—pro-business, pro-gun, pro-development, pro-oil drilling, skeptical of the feds. Alaska Republicans call Democrats leftist, socialist, communist, atheist, anti-family, big gubmint, gay-marryin', tree-huggin' union thugs. In any other state, they'd be running as moderate Republicans.

Knowles went down in flames, and election night found me in a cheap, smoky motel room downtown, crying in my beer with the broken-hearted college Dems who had knocked on doors with me. Politics sucked. The next morning, nursing my political hangover, I swore I'd never touch the stuff again.

I made good on my vow until my path crossed a former state legislator and epic shit disturber named Ray Metcalfe. Ray would chew anyone's ear off about politics, usually about some scandal behind the scenes, and we hit it off immediately. He was a fellow Montanan, born on the Crow Indian Reservation, and had hitchhiked to Alaska in 1969 with fifty-three dollars in his pocket. He was fifteen years old. Man after my own heart.

My mishmash of conservative, liberal, and libertarian beliefs often left me feeling like a man without a political party. But Ray had started a new one—the Republican Moderate Party. It embraced fiscal conservatism while keeping bigotry and religion out of the mix. It sounded good to me, and I became a member.

I had taken my first trip to Fairbanks with Ray years earlier. He needed someone to swap off driving his powder-blue Cadillac on the fourteen-hour round trip through the hundreds of miles of wilderness between Alaska's two biggest cities. Pretty sure it was the only powder-blue Cadillac in the state. We crossed rivers and crested mountain passes, traversed Denali National Park and the sprawling Goldstream Valley—all the while debating political philosophy and commiserating about the sorry state of the Alaska Republican Party.

Alaska's previous Republican governor, Frank Murkowski, had spent most of his one term in office using his influence to grease the palms of Big Oil—tax breaks, closed-door meetings, and reigning supreme over a culture of massive corruption that saw a full 10 percent of the state legislature (all Republicans) convicted of bribery-related charges for selling their votes to oil interests—sometimes for only a few hundred dollars. These legislators proudly called themselves "The Corrupt Bastards Club," and even had baseball caps embroidered with the "CBC" logo. Nothing like subtlety. These dumbasses thought this was hilarious. But after FBI phone taps and a hidden video camera in a hotel suite in Juneau that recorded cash changing hands, they stopped laughing. By the time the massive sting operation concluded, almost a dozen legislators ended up behind bars, and the FBI had plans to build a massive new Anchorage headquarters. You couldn't make this shit up.

Ray's Republican Moderate Party eventually died a slow, lingering death. Alaskans are not moderate people, especially the Republicans. "Moderate" was basically code for "Marxist," they assumed, and he never got his membership past critical mass. But even though Ray became a man without a party, he was always on high alert for a scandal and always to be found where anti-establishment plans were brewing. Anywhere else, Ray might be considered the village conspiracy theorist, but Alaska provided plenty of political conspiracy *fact* to keep him busy. Above all, he was laser-focused on his burning obsession with the snake pit that was the Alaska Republican Party.

Now that the Republican Moderates were defunct, I changed my party affiliation yet again. I became a Republican proper. Republicans were my people in the business community and also my best customers. I needed to network, so my presence at events like these made sense. But it was more than just a calculated business decision that brought me to the convention. Recent changes in the party had piqued my curiosity. A new wing had begun to take shape. These folks didn't like entrenched Republican politicians either, or their corrupt ways, but they veered off from the mainstream not toward the center but in a distinctly libertarian direction.

The standard-bearer of this wing, Gov. Sarah Palin, had vowed to clean up the corruption in her party. Backed by a wave of populist support and a sea of red yard signs proclaiming "Palin for Governor—Take a Stand," the young mom and former Wasilla mayor swept into the governor's mansion with promises of change and reform. She turned out to be ahead of the national curve in a movement that would knock the Republican Party on its ass and turn the party against itself like some kind of cannibalistic Frankenstein elephant. It didn't have a name in 2006 when the Corrupt Bastards were going to jail and Palin took office, but it would eventually be called "The Tea Party," and its national poster boy was Texas Congressman Ron Paul. His combination of libertarianism, conservatism, and populism struck a chord in the Alaskan heart and he enjoyed wide support at the convention I was headed to.

I liked some of Ron Paul's economic ideas—smaller government, local control, and states' rights—but it was his non-interventionist foreign policy that really grabbed me. We'd been at war for seven long years. PTSD wasn't really talked about a lot yet, but I looked it in the face every day. Guys like Discount, they were my friends, my co-workers, my brothers, my team, and they constantly wrestled with the demons of war. It was not an acceptable cost of doing business. "Foreign policy" was anything but foreign to me, and it was sure as shit more than "policy." It was very personal, and I was ready to support anyone who wanted our intervention in foreign conflicts to end. And so here I was—a Ron Paul delegate. I'd cast my one vote, and I'd try to meet some people who might need security services, and I'd hand out business cards to drum up some new customers. That was my mission.

I turned onto Fifth Avenue, and the Captain Cook Hotel came into view—a pair of blocky, mustard-colored concrete towers by the water. Almost the tallest buildings in the Anchorage skyline, they stand at only fifteen and eighteen stories, appearing even smaller against the backdrop of the Chugach Mountains. The tall tower is just four feet shy of the tallest in the city—the Conoco Phillips building.

"Treat my baby right," I said as I handed the keys to my mud-spattered Hummer to the valet-parking guy. Every vehicle in the state looked like a mud bogger in March.

Although the Captain Cook Hotel was named for James Cook, the explorer who first sailed up Cook Inlet a few blocks to the north in 1778, it was a man named Walter J. Hickel who owned its legacy. Wally was Alaska's second and eighth governor, a barrel-chested, badass boxing champion. Born and raised in Kansas, he had big dreams, a tough work ethic, and he was drawn to the possibilities of this open and wild land. He'd wanted to go to Australia but couldn't get a ticket. And so he headed north and found that Alaska fit him like a boxing glove. He started out as a construction worker in 1940, and by the end of World War II, he'd made his fortune and owned his own construction company. "The Cook" was his crowning achievement.

Wally was connected, and he urged politicians in Washington to vote for Alaska statehood in 1959. Republicans needed to be persuaded to let what was then the "liberal" territory of Alaska into the union. After massive oil deposits were discovered on Alaska's North Slope, and the Trans-Alaska Pipeline was built, the influx of oil workers from Southern states brought their conservative ideology and religious dogma, and the politics and religion of the state swung steadily to the right.

As I pushed on the carved wooden door rail, the ugly detention-facility vibe of the building changed. Twinkling chandeliers, dark wood paneling and carved trim, brass rails, expensive boutique shops, marble floors, and large oil paintings of three-masted schooners.

No crappy depressing Democratic motel room for me as I returned to the world of politics. I was a Republican now, in the best hotel in the state, with a sea of people who were used to winning and used to raising boatloads of cash.

I held the door open for the man behind me. I looked back to respond to his "thank you," and realized the tall man in the beige suit and wire-rimmed glasses who flashed me a vapid smile was Pastor Jerry Prevo, Alaska's very own Pat Robertson. He was the monarch of his own media empire, and his Anchorage Baptist Temple was a huge, gleaming megachurch with multiple ministers, a Christian school, TV and radio stations, and a score of tax-exempt properties. The weekly flock had grown to 2,000 true believers under the roof and thousands more in front of the TV. When election time came, the sheep in his flock voted whichever way the pastor's voter guide told them to. Prevo even hosted political debates right in the church, where Republicans tried to out-God each other, pandering to the cabal of religious powerbrokers. Prevo, for decades, had good success handpicking candidates, influencing those already elected, and inserting religion into politics at every opportunity. The government should stay out of your business, he said, except when he wanted it to legislate his own rigid brand of Christian morality.

The Republican Party worshipped two higher powers that guided it to victory—a militant and judgmental God represented by Pastor Prevo and good old-fashioned secular cronyism handled by Party Chair Randy Ruedrich.

And right on cue, there they were, holding court in the lobby—Ruedrich, plump and silver-haired, with a hint of Southern drawl, laughing and shaking hands with a couple delegates who worked for BP, and Prevo with his far-away smile, schmoozing a couple of state senators.

"That's the way it is, and don't you know it!" Ruedrich gave a hearty frat-boy laugh. "We'll talk. You have my promise on that. We'll talk." He winked, clapped the guy on the shoulder, and moved on to the next waiting suit. "Richard! How in the hell are you? How's the wife?" Ruedrich was the power broker, the kingmaker, the glue that kept the administrative end of the Republican Party together; he was the oil money that kept it funded, and a big reason it kept winning elections.

Loud "How are yous," and "I'm so glad you're heres" drifted from all corners of the bustling lobby. A flock of hair-sprayed biddies from some Republican women's club huddled in the corner, cackling like hens. Many had husbands in the oil business who'd been sent to Alaska to work. You could usually tell whether people had chosen Alaska or whether Alaska had chosen them, and they were simply making the best of it. Embroidered on their matching vests was the outline of the map of Alaska tilted on its side to look like the Republican elephant, with the Aleutian Islands chain as its trunk. It ended up looking like it had some kind of congenital birth defect and had accidentally wandered through a minefield.

I took my place in a short line at the front desk to pick up my key.

The man in front of me wore the typical uniform of rural Alaska—brown canvas Carhartt work overalls, a flannel shirt, and a pair of mud-colored XtraTuff rubber boots. A grimy duffel bag was his only luggage.

"Are you here for the convention, sir?" the woman asked him from behind the counter.

"Yes, ma'am. Time to do my civic duty, I guess."

The woman behind the desk took his dog-eared ID and shuffled through some paperwork.

"Where are you here from?" I asked him. He turned around and gave me a crinkly smile. His hair and beard were grizzled and unkempt, and he smelled like a pile of old laundry.

"I come down from the Interior. Got a little cabin up in Fox, near Fairbanks." He looked me over from my "high and tight" military haircut, to my crisp white shirt, charcoal suit, flag pin, and down to my shiny black shoes. "You must be from Anchorage."

"Yes, sir. I'm doing my civic duty too."

"So, you must know that Wally Hickel built this hotel." I could tell I was in for an old-timer's "quiz." How Alaskan was I, really? He wanted to find out.

"Yes, sir. I did know that."

"And did you know that the second time he ran in the nineties, he ran with the AIP, and he won?"

The AIP was the Alaskan Independence Party, founded in the 1970s. It sought exactly what its name implied—Alaskan independence, secession from the United States. Its founder, Joe Vogler, was another Kansan like Wally Hickel, who fell in love with the Last Frontier and stayed. "The fires of Hell are frozen glaciers compared to my hatred of the United States government, and I won't be buried under their damn flag!" was Vogler's money quote. After he was murdered in an explosives deal gone bad, his body was found in a gravel pit near Fairbanks, wrapped in a blue tarp wound up with duct tape. His last wishes were granted. He wasn't buried under America's "damn flag" but laid to rest in Dawson City, Canada, where he waits for Alaska to become a free and independent Republic so his bones can be brought home.

"And Sarah's husband Todd was a member too. Seven years he was, but he left when she started moving up the political ladder."

"Well, they gotta do what they gotta do to get elected. You know how that goes," I said. "Sometimes it's easier to change things from the inside."

"Well, now if that ain't the truth!" he nodded. "I sure do like that gal, though. I had one of her big signs propped up on a sawhorse in the bed of my truck. She gave a speech to the AIP convention this year on the video, did you know that? She's sympathetic, even though she can't say it right out because it ain't politically correct." He rolled his eyes.

"Well, I voted for her," I said. I wasn't lying.

"Did you know that when Wally passed on, they buried that ol' sumbitch standing up, facing Warshington, ready to give 'em hell?" He laughed until he coughed. "Ain't never gonna be another Wally. He was a straight shooter."

I was tempted to remind him that Wally Hickel, who had been tapped by Nixon to become his secretary of the interior, put seven species of whales on the endangered species list, shut down offshore oil drilling after a spill off the coast of Santa Barbara, and got fired from the Cabinet for overtly opposing Nixon's participation in the Vietnam War. But I could tell that this guy, along with today's strain of uber-right Republicans, preferred their selective memories. So I kept my mouth shut.

"Well, if you have some time while you're in town, come by my shop. I have a feeling you'd like it," I said and handed him a card.

"I just might do that," he said.

Key in hand, finally, I headed for my room.

"Mr. Fulton," came a soft voice from the elevator as the massive doors slid open. It was Ray Metcalfe.

"Holy shit! How the hell are you, man? I haven't seen you in forever." The heavy doors shut and I punched the button for the tenth floor.

Ray had a strange intensity. He was fairly short, with eyes that absorbed everything. Balding, with prominent ears and a sharp nose, he seemed almost elvish.

"I'm well," he said. "And yourself?"

"I'm living the dream, man. What the hell are you doing here? I hate to be the one to break it to you, but I think most of the people in this building fucking hate you."

If Ray was here, it wasn't to press the flesh and chitchat with the Republican establishment. He was up to something.

"Ah, but not *all* of them." His eyes twinkled. "If you're not busy, you should come by my room in about twenty minutes. Number 803." The chime of the elevator bell sounded and the doors opened. He stepped out and turned over his shoulder. "It's good to see you, Bill."

He knew I'd show up. Something was happening, and he was dangling the bait. I looked at my watch. I had just enough time to drop my bag in the suite, sample the bottle of "networking scotch" in my bag to make sure it was worth the two hundred dollars I'd dished out for it, and get to room 803 in twenty minutes sharp.

My tenth-floor suite had oriental carpets and lush dark red furnishings, including a sitting area with a little fireplace and several stuffed wing chairs where I could conduct business. A sweeping view of downtown Anchorage with the snow-covered Chugach Mountain range behind it almost looked like a painting.

Ray's room was a little smaller and already held five or six people by the time I got there. I didn't know them by name, but at least two worked closely with Gov. Palin.

"Bill Fulton, I'd like to you meet Frank Bailey, Governor Palin's director of boards and commissions and one of her true trusted insiders," said Ray with a smile. I shook Bailey's hand—a warm, firm shake. He'd been with Sarah from the very beginning of her gubernatorial campaign, and his influence was far wider than his official title would indicate.

"Ray's been telling me about you and your store in Spenard. Good stuff, man. I'm totally going to make it a point to come by there. And you're a Ron Paul guy, huh?"

Bailey was in his thirties, shorter than me, and balding, with an easy manner and a casual, surfer-dude tone. He did not seem like a politician.

"Yes, sir. I'm a Paul delegate. There's a lot of us around here from what I hear."

"Totally! Yeah. It's awesome. It's gonna be a great weekend, man, I can feel it," he said.

"The Paul delegates are the ones we're really counting on, Bill," Ray explained. "There are big things happening. Things are moving forward, and we'd like your support. I think it's time we finally gave Randy Ruedrich his walking papers, don't you agree?" Ray locked on me with his usual penetrating gaze. He looked like a man ready to behead a snake. His desire to topple the Republican Party still burned hot.

"You know how I feel about that asshole. Count me in on whatever," I said.

"If the majority of Republican delegates vote no confidence at this convention, he'll lose his chairmanship," Ray went on. "There are many here who are tired of his rules, and tired of being marginalized if they don't play by them. Power corrupts and he's had too much of it for too long."

Ruedrich's humiliation would be devastating, and Ray Metcalfe and Frank Bailey could taste it like an ice-cold beer on a summer day. Ousting Ruedrich carried hefty symbolic weight—corrupt bastards out, Ron Paul people in. The Republican Party, which had been pulling in two directions for some time, would be torn apart from inside its own ranks, with the blessing of the governor herself.

The establishment had been in Palin's crosshairs for some time. She'd worked on an oil and gas commission with Ruedrich years earlier while he continued to hold the position of Republican Party chair. Palin had ratted him out for doing party business on his government computer, and he received the biggest ethics fine in state history for passing along confidential documents to oil and gas interests. He had Palin to thank for being exposed. She never hesitated to remind voters of this, and called Ruedrich's operation "the machine" and those who ran it "the good ol' boys." She'd slathered on the anti-establishment rhetoric and never pulled punches. Despite Ruedrich's unsurprising lack of support for Palin in the gubernatorial primary, she still managed to annihilate Murkowski, who limped off the political stage with 19 percent in a three-way race. Palin was all about remaking the party and the state, and she was every bit as ruthless as Ruedrich. So it didn't shock me to see Frank Bailey, a member of her inner sanctum, at the hub of this coup attempt. This was going to be the Battle of the Titans. It was time to pass the popcorn—and the scotch.

"This plan to overthrow Ruedrich is coming from the governor?" I asked, looking from Ray to Bailey and back.

"No, no, no," Bailey immediately piped up. "This is something we're doing on our off time. It's not that Sarah . . . Governor Palin wouldn't secretly love it, of course, but this is *not* her telling me directly to do this. This is *not* her being active in this. This is me and some others *on our own* doing this, apart from her. But we do know when it happens she'll be pleased about it. We're sure of that."

Bailey was tap dancing like Fred Astaire on Red Bull. Clearly the governor was all about sledgehammering Ruedrich and knew exactly what was going on—but as governor she couldn't "officially" be part of a partisan coup attempt. Plausible deniability. I got the picture.

"We believe we've got enough votes to oust him, but it's going to be close," Ray said. "We need to convince these folks to dump someone who's won for them, who has created a lot of power for the party. It's a leap for a lot of people—to throw over the establishment. We need allies who can drum up votes and get the delegates fired up for some change. We've been back and forth about who we want to take over. It looks like it'll be Cathy Giessel who's been vice chair of the party. She's running Congressman Young's re-election campaign right now. And Plan B is Joe Miller. You heard of him?"

I hadn't. But I knew Cathy Giessel definitely wasn't Ray's cup of political tea. A rigid, controlling, red-suited Christian conservative, she was severe, looked a bit like a bird, and was wound up tighter than a monkey's nuts. Eminently dislikable, she'd managed to alienate almost everyone she'd ever worked with. Her husband had a habit of sending letters to the editor of the *Anchorage Daily News* about how the earth is 6,000 years old and "evolution" is a trick. I was no fan of the slick, oily, corrupt bastards like Ruedrich who had taken over the party, but I didn't see how Jesus was going to save the day riding sidesaddle on a dinosaur with Cathy Giessel. Ray's priority was clearly to get Ruedrich out, come hell or high water, and deal with the aftermath later. The silver lining was that Giessel's brand of Republican wingnuts sounded an awful lot like my customer base. These were the ones who bought the camo-covered Bibles and the End of Days body armor. Not to be cynical about the whole thing, but I'd make some business connections if I got in with the party revolutionaries. I agreed to a get-to-know-you meet up with Frank Bailey and Joe Miller in my suite later that night.

"You'll totally like Joe," Bailey smiled. "He's one of the good guys. I respect him. He walks the talk, you know what I mean? He's one of the ones you hope will run for office someday."

My head was brimming with thoughts of the coup. I loved being in the thick of something that would rock the political boat. I made calls when I had a minute, urging other delegates I knew to vote against Ruedrich when the time came.

I caught a glimpse of Palin herself, who would be speaking later. A small line of people waited in the lobby to have their picture taken with her, and she was all smiles, and happy to pose and shake hands. She had fired the first shot across the bow of the Republican Party establishment. The fact that she sat behind the governor's desk kept plenty of the bastards up at night, and I was just fine with that. Now her people were poised to split the party and wipe the good ol' boys off the map. It was going to be damn good political theater.

Don Young, Alaska's only congressman, was standing by a table on top of which was a row of coffee urns and Styrofoam cups. It was hard to miss his too-loud laugh, and his sense of bravado. He was wearing his signature bolo tie decorated with the Alaska flag—the eight gold stars of the Big Dipper on a dark-blue sky. Every Alaskan knew that flag and that bolo. I decided to grab a cup of coffee, and if an opportunity presented itself, I'd shake his hand and introduce myself. Young had been in office since 1973, and showed no signs of slowing down.

"That's the damn problem," he said to the small crowd gathered around. "We think that life is all about staying comfortable. We think we're all entitled to this life where nothing happens. The liberals want the world to all stay the same—'Don't let it get warmer! Don't cut the trees! Save the whales, and some damn owl nobody ever heard of!' And while we're busy doing nothing, they want the government to take care of everything. I wrote my college thesis on the benefits of war, and damn near got kicked out for it. But I can show you that the greatest advancements of mankind come under stress and strain, not comfort. But I can't convince you to put the drink down if you're an alcoholic. I can't convince you to stop eating the cookies if you're a diabetic. You have to want to do that. *You* have to do that. And that takes responsibility."

I knew Young had served in the Army in the late 'Fifties, and couldn't quite grasp the fact he was still standing here, half a century later with our troops in the Middle East, boasting about his pitch for the "benefits of war" for the economy. I opted to skip the handshake and just go for the coffee.

"How did Hitler take over Germany?" he said to a bearded man in an NRA baseball cap who had come to shake his hand. "He took the weapons away from the people. How did the Jewish people get put in those ovens? They had no weapons. How did Stalin kill fifteen million people in his own country? Because he took the weapons away. Well, I hear people say that would never happen in the United States. Well. Don't take that for granted." He was on a roll.

"We wonder why we've got the Freemen or the militants. We wonder why we have got unrest in this country. It is because our government has got out of hand and out of line, with the Endangered Species Act. You tell people they can't use land and they get mad . . ."

I walked away drinking my coffee while Don Young drank his own Kool-Aid. This was going to be a long weekend.

By five o'clock, I was exhausted from a day of backslapping and standing around in dress shoes. I got back to my suite and flopped on the bed. A soft rapping on the door popped me awake. I rubbed my face and brushed the front of my suit coat with my hands. On the other side of the door was Frank Bailey. Joe Miller was coming, he said.

I had hoped for some good networking at this convention, but I had no idea that I'd end up with such high-level access in such a short time. As some guy who owns a military surplus store, I felt more than a little over my head. This morning had been a normal day, and now here I sat with one of the most powerful figures in state government, plotting a political coup. He didn't know me from Adam at the beginning of the day, and now we were talking strategy and tactics over a finger of scotch. It was surreal.

"So, how did you end up working for Governor Palin?" I asked.

"It was kind of a funny thing," Bailey said. "I heard Sarah on the radio, on some talk-radio show when she was the mayor of Wasilla, and I just liked what she had to say. I'd been really turned off to politics for a while, and I heard her talking about the corruption, and the political machine in Alaska—how messed up it is—saying all the things I felt. So, I looked up her number and gave her a call. My wife thought I was nuts."

He smiled at the memory.

"So Sarah's really gracious, thanks me, and I told her I'd be happy to support her if she ever decided to run for governor. And when she threw her hat in, I called again and I was like, 'Hey, Sarah! Remember me? I'm serious, I'll totally scrub toilets if that's what you need!' and sure enough I ended up spending Thanksgiving weekend painting her campaign office, washing windows, and scrubbing toilets. It was crazy, man. The rest is history."

"So, who were you working for at the time?"

"Alaska Airlines. I wasn't into politics at all, until Sarah."

The smoky golden liquid slid down my throat with a delicious burn that made me settle into the moment in all its absurdity. I was right. Frank Bailey was not a politician, and apparently I wasn't the only one who got high-level access quickly. This guy with zero political experience, working for an airline, picks up the phone and calls the former mayor of Wasilla, whose number is listed in the book, and goes from scrubbing toilets to sitting at the right hand of the governor a year later—and spearheading the overthrow of the Alaska Republican Party a year after that.

"Here's to Alaska," I said, raising my glass.

Another louder rapping came at the door. Joe Miller was tall and lanky with lots of teeth and a fifteen-day growth, by my estimate. He used some kind of hair product, which put him in the tiny minority of Alaskan men. I detected the remnants of "foo foo juice," known to the rest of the country as "cologne." He lived in Fairbanks, but here he was no Alaska mountain man—charcoal suit, white shirt, gold tie. I was glad it wasn't red, or the three of us would have looked uncomfortably like triplets.

I asked if he wanted some scotch. He paused for a second before saying no. Then he noticed the Oban label.

"Maybe just a drop," he said.

That bottle was paying for itself already.

I settled back into the armchair by the fireplace and looked at Miller. "So, I hear we've got a mission." The clock was ticking. The vote would happen tomorrow afternoon.

"Well, before we get started, I'm gonna ask you to bear with me here for a minute," he flashed a crooked smile. "I've taken the liberty of inviting someone else to sit in with us—Schaeffer Cox. A real up and comer. He's running for the State House in Fairbanks against the establishment candidate." His deep baritone said "establishment candidate" in a way that made it very clear that like Palin, "establishment candidates" were not his bag. "He'll be a help to us in wrangling votes."

As we waited for Cox's arrival, I got Miller's story—Yale, West Point, pretty blonde wife Kathleen, bunch of kids, Christian conservative, small government, family values, Fairbanks lawyer, guns guns guns, and yet another Kansan who came north to seek his fortune. Wally Hickel became governor twice, Joe Vogler got duct-taped in a blue tarp . . . I wondered what lay in store for *this* guy.

I'd begun to think that the energetic, up-and-coming Mr. Cox wasn't going to show, when another knock came—the one you give when you expect an answer. *Da-dada-da-da.*

I popped up and swung the door open.

"Hi! I'm Schaeffer!"

Standing before me was a fifteen-year-old newsboy straight from 1925. Big brown wide-set eyes, freckles, and a wide grin. Sitting on his dark shock of hair was a tweed newsie cap. Beside him stood a woman taller by several inches, with long dishwater-blonde hair in a frumpy dress with a silver cross around her neck.

"I'm Bill Fulton. Come on in," I said, shaking his outstretched hand and that of the woman who peered at me through oval glasses and shook my hand like hers had no bones. Miller introduced her as Marti Cox, Schaeffer's wife.

Cox himself was not wearing a suit coat or a tie. A vest over a black button-up shirt was covered with a brightly colored cluster of political buttons—Alaska Right to Life, the NRA, Second Amendment Task Force, Fairbanks Republicans, Ron Paul for President, a red-white-and-blue elephant, and a bright-red Cox for State House. There were more than a dozen in all. He looked like a wide-eyed kid who'd taken his first trip to a big-city political rally. He walked into this room of power players in suits and ties clueless he'd botched the dress code. Marti was his campaign manager, he said, so she'd be staying for the meeting.

"Nice cap," I offered.

"Thanks! It's kind of my trademark, you could say," he reflexively grabbed the front of the brim and adjusted it. "And thanks for asking me here," he said looking from one of us to another. "It's always good to be with like-minded souls. The good thing is that I think there are more of us all the time, more people waking up and seeing the truth. It's just this ongoing assault on our liberties, and it never ends. They chip away at our right to keep and bear arms, and not just that, but all of our rights that we have naturally as human beings that are supposed to be recognized in the Constitution. I mean, I'm trying to do what I can, rallying the troops in Fairbanks. Joe knows that. I mean, at some point you just have to realize that the Congress, the federal government—they've all flat-out rejected the Constitution. It's like people are blind, or they just don't want to see. They're scared to rock the boat. They're preoccupied with this belief that the laws of men are above the laws of God. But at the end of the day, if you follow the higher law, you can sleep at night. You know?"

He'd been in the room two minutes and I already wanted to bash my head against the wall. Or his. I couldn't put my finger on it, but I knew right then we would never get along.

"OK. So, let's leave the God talk, and crunch some numbers, shall we?" I said, ignoring his stump speech. He showed up almost half an hour late to an important meeting with important people and presumed everyone was here to listen to him talk about political philosophy. The next hour was a constant battle between trying to figure out whose vote we had and whose we needed, and corralling the runaway mouth that was Schaeffer Cox talking about himself.

My phone buzzed. *We need to talk when you have a minute.*

It was Stacey. I'd asked her to grab a stack of business cards from my office and drop them at the hotel.

Did u find the cards?

Yes. On the desk. Call me.

K. In a meeting. Call soon.

"The two-party system is part of the problem. Even though it feels like this new movement we have going is a third party, we don't need a third party—we need a second government. Things are so far gone at this point. I mean, you can't unpickle a pickle. You can't put the crap back in the horse, you know? This corruption has been baked in the cake. It's done. The blueprint, the documents of freedom are all fine, but we need to restart the computer—wipe the hard drive, maybe."

I wasn't sure how many useless, trite metaphors could be jammed into one sentence, or how this self-obsessed, nonstop talker had managed to gather a following. But if we wanted to actually pull off an overthrow of the Republican Party in the next two days, we needed tactics, not philosophy.

"Look, we can worry about horse crap and wiping the hard drive of the federal government later, OK? Let's keep some focus," I said.

Bailey, with the help of others, had been calling and persuading Republican delegates from Anchorage for months now; Miller had been making the calls in Fairbanks. And Cox said he knew many more from the Interior. Running the Ron Paul effort put him in touch with exactly the people we needed, and I was guessing this was why Bailey and Miller put up with his babbling. I was a doer and had little patience for talkers who wasted time when there was shit that needed doing.

Cox was perhaps savvier than he looked. It became clear as the hour passed that he wasn't willing just to volunteer to participate in this coup unless there was a tangible benefit to his own cause. He wanted to know that when the new chair was installed, he'd get something out of it. Cox wanted firm positions on income taxes, abolishing the Federal Reserve, the gold standard, and other economic planks to be inserted into the Republican Party platform. None of these additions would affect policy in the real world, or require any action, but the platform defines on paper the philosophical heart and soul of the party. And if Cox could change the mission statement, he'd be happy, and have another feather in his cap.

"That's eminently doable," Miller said, looking at the bullet points he'd written on a notepad. "There's no reason those things can't be included in the platform, Schaeffer. If you do what you say you can do and get everyone fired up tonight with your speech, if you can push people over the edge and get those last votes against Ruedrich that we need, the new party will be indebted to you—there's no question about that. I think it's only right that when we remake the leadership of the Republican Party, we redefine what it stands for. If you can work your magic, you've got your planks. I guarantee it. Do we have a deal?"

"Absolutely," said Cox grinning from ear to ear. "This is really great." He grabbed Miller's hand in both of his and shook. Then Bailey's. Then mine. He was practically beaming. "I feel optimistic about getting some new leadership. I really do. I'm looking forward to a fresh start."

I was glad when everyone left. I got out of my suit as fast as I could and called Stacey. I could tell immediately something was wrong. She had gone to the shop that morning with Emma to grab the business cards.

"So, guess what I found when I walked in?"

If this involved Clay and a pile of tents I was going to strangle him with my bare hands.

"Who's that guy who opened this morning, 'Discount'?" she asked. "Yeah, he was really professional." She dripped sarcasm.

"What did he say?"

"Nothing. He was too busy sleeping in his own puke on the counter at ten o'clock in the morning. It was really charming. So, I cleaned up and had to sit there until Suicide showed up."

"Oh, shit, babe . . . I'm so sorry."

After I called and chewed Discount's ass and grabbed a quick shower, I was back in the elevator. A woman looked at me nervously. She had no makeup, new white sneakers, and a T-shirt covered in tiny rose-buds. *Fairbanks formal*, I thought.

"Excuse me, I'm so sorry to bother you, but are you a delegate, by chance?" she asked.

"Yes, ma'am."

"Well," her voice was hushed, even though we were the only ones in the elevator, "I'm supposed to let you know that there's going to be an informal meeting tonight in the Tikhatnu Room downstairs. It starts in just a few minutes, and Schaeffer Cox will be speaking about something very import-ant. Do you know Schaeffer?"

"I've heard of him," I said.

CHAPTER 8

★ ★ ★ ★ ★

GOONS

"It does not take a majority to prevail . . . but rather
an irate, tireless minority, keen on setting brushfires of
freedom in the minds of men."
—Samuel Adams

We just love Schaeffer up in Fairbanks," said the woman in the elevator. "He's a young man, but he's done so much up there for the Second Amendment and liberty. He's running for office now. He's the future. I hope you can make it."

"That's where I'm headed," I said, and she smiled. At the other end of the building, in the Tikhatnu Room, Cox had the troops out in force. This was good.

The official convention events had wrapped up for the night, but when I shut the doors of the Tikhatnu Room there were about 150 people inside—many more than I expected. Miller and Bailey didn't want to be seen anywhere near the event, so I was to keep them posted in their rooms via text.

"Bill! Hey! Would you like to take the mic? It's all yours if you want to say a few words, buddy." Cox held out the mic.

"Noooo, no, no . . ." I laughed. "I work from the shadows, man. I'm just the background. Now it's your turn to talk, so get up there and do your thing. My job is to count votes at the door when everyone leaves, after you get them all fired up to oust this prick. Break a leg." I slapped him on the back and found a spot by the door.

I looked at my watch. It was 9:10 p.m. He had half an hour to make it happen.

"Good evening! Are y'all awake?" His smile was genuine, and he looked absolutely in his element. "I know it's been a long day, so I want to thank you for spending a few minutes with me tonight."

The crowd did look a bit bedraggled.

"Well, let's get right to it—I've got some news for you in case you missed it. We are goin' to Hell in a freight train!" The crowd laughed.

"It's OK to laugh about it a little. But let's talk frankly here a minute, about what's going on in the state and the nation. And even though we're in a lot of trouble—you know we are—it's you people right here who give me hope. You do! It's late at night and you're tired. Many of you have driven in and flown in from all over this great state—and this is a pretty big state! But you're here. You are the ones who care. Give yourselves a hand!"

A whoop went up from the crowd.

"And I know why you're all here. Not just to cast a vote tomorrow, or see your friends, or hear some speeches. I know why you're *really* here. It's the same reason I'm here. You all know in your gut that something is horribly wrong. You don't have to be told. Nobody *told* you something was wrong. You know because you have a heart, and a spirit, and a mind that's perceptive to those things. And you have sense, and you know when something bad is going on."

He walked back and forth making eye contact across the room.

"When I look at this current debacle we're in, that's been going on for years and years, I feel like there's just this *huge* power out there that is incomprehensible! It's impossible to imagine influencing it, never mind stopping it. And all I want—and I think all *you* want—is to just be free, to respect other people, and to have them respect me, to be protected by the law, and be able to do what I want, and not hurt anyone else, and have *freedom*. You know? That's it! That's all I want. It's pretty simple. And I have a feeling that's what you want too. Am I right?"

He paused to take a drink from a plastic water bottle, and the audience clapped loudly. He'd been talking only a few minutes, but already the crowd was his. I had no idea where he was going with his speech, but if the level of interest of the crowd was any indication, we might just pull this off in a spectacular fashion.

Hey boss we had an issue today. A text from Hippie Omega.

I heard. Discount. I talked 2 him.

No. Clay.

Oh shit. Who was it this time?

Bananas wife.

I wanted to throttle Clay. And how the hell did these women keep falling for his lines? And how did he even meet her? If he could bottle his secret, he'd retire a billionaire tomorrow.

Fuuuuck. Does he know?

Oh, yeah.

I'll call soon. Hopefully.

k

"...I don't know how to argue for that inherent knowledge I have of what's right by using all these nitty-gritty statutes and laws. And I don't understand all the ins and outs of this giant monster that's coming our way and bulldozing over our freedom, but *I feel in my gut a resentment*—and I think you all identify with this—that you shouldn't *have* to understand all that stuff. You shouldn't have to!"

"How have I never heard of this guy?" a smartly dressed white-haired man in front of me leaned over to the woman next to him.

"He's from Fairbanks. He's running against Mike Kelly for State House in the primary and coming at him from the right. He's doing well, I hear," she whispered back. "You can see why."

I was starting to see why too. I was surprised at how quickly and adeptly Cox had managed to wrap the audience around his finger. It made me uneasy. I thought this kid was kind of a narcissistic douchebag, but apparently the feeling was not widely shared by this crowd. Sheep who wanted to be led, I thought. Confidence was intoxicating. The minutes ticked by and he hit the themes one by one: the government is coming to take our guns, God's will for free men, the right to life, the liberal threat, the evils of government education, the TSA groping us at the airport, the IRS taking our homes, the feds who want to steal our liberty . . . and on, and on. I heard this kind of stuff every day in my store from the people stockpiling ammo and weapons and canned food.

". . . We can't forget that our rights are our *rights*, and we shouldn't have to *buy* our rights with hassle! You know, you hear about these guys who fought the IRS, and they're like, 'Yeah, I beat 'em! It took me thirty years, and seventeen thouuuusand dollars, but I showed 'em!'" He laughed.

"And you're thinking to yourself, 'Well, that sounds like a prison sentence!' It shouldn't have to be that way. They still gotcha . . . they just gotcha the other way."

An audible murmur went up from the crowd. Even the Anchorage people who weren't used to this level of anti-government rhetoric seemed mesmerized.

"It makes me sick, and it makes a lot of people sick. It makes me worry. We're getting to the point where they can just lock you up for anything they want! If they want to, if they don't like you, if they think you're a threat, they can pretty much just make you disappear. And that's not the way it's supposed to be. That's a police state. That's not what our founders intended. So, we show up here. Why? Because we don't know what else to do. We want to try to influence the monster and make it behave.

"It makes you feel like you got kicked in the teeth by a government-issued boot, because we feel like all we can do is beg the tyrant to change, and commit ourselves to a long drudge uphill to try to reform this monster. And your heart sinks, and you wonder, 'Is that really the price of freedom?'"

He spoke more quickly as his rhetoric heated up. What did he even know about the "price of freedom"? He'd never served his country or fought for freedom. A government-issued boot? *I'll show you a government-issued boot, you little shit*, I thought. I wore one of those for years, and I was ready to plant it in his backside if he didn't cut all this crap and just throw Ruedrich under the bus already.

"And there comes a point where you get tired of trying to be a good influence on tyranny. So, you decide to run for office, to become a part of it, so you can change it from the inside. And that's what I'm going to try to do. I'm out there working hard to get to Juneau to represent the ideals of liberty in the State House of Representatives."

A very loud and sustained bout of applause shook the room. I felt like I was watching The Schaeffer Cox Show, and I wasn't allowed to change the channel. This was becoming a stump speech, or a tent revival, and we'd already been stuck in the basement almost an hour without a word about tomorrow's vote. I was worried people would start to leave, but the crowd seemed rooted.

"I'm hopeful. I'm hopeful that I'll find a few like-minded people when I get there, and we'll start pulling the brakes on this runaway train, bit by bit. I hope I can count on your support, because I'll tell you what. It can feel like a lonely ride sometimes."

The white-haired man from Anchorage reached into his jacket and pulled a checkbook out of the inside pocket. He made a check out to "Cox for State House" for $150.

The whole meeting was morphing before my eyes, following another agenda entirely, "like a runaway train," to use Cox's analogy.

My phone buzzed. It was Frank. *Hey where r u? any news?*

Still talking. Send.

Jesus. This was getting ridiculous. I was tired, and needed to be up early in the morning. And so did these other people.

"While we're at this convention, we've got to remember to know our enemy, and be realistic about who our enemy is."

Finally! The enemy. Here we go. Cue the disemboweling of Randy Ruedrich in three, two, one . . .

"Our enemy is anyone who would take away the rights that are intrinsically yours and that God gave us—your free will. When you ask someone what their authority is to tell you what to think and what to do, and the only thing they can say is, 'Because I said so,' then *that's* tyranny and *that's* our enemy, and we have to learn to recognize that. And I know that puts a whole lot of people in our enemy category," he chuckled. "But you know what? That's OK. We can handle it, because we keep our eyes on God's laws and God's rules."

My phone buzzed. It was Stacey. *U never called me when ur meeting was over! Did you forget? ;) xoxo*

STILL HERE LISTENING TO SOME EFFIN DICKBAG FM FBX TALK ABT HIMSELF. SHOOT ME. WILL CALL SOON. LOVE U. Send.

"You know what my dad told me once? He's a Baptist minister up in Fairbanks, and he said, 'If you don't control yourself, then someone else will control you.' Profound, right? That's the thing that'll let us look at those storm clouds on the horizon and be OK with it. How many of you get those emails all the time: 'Oh, no! Something really bad is going to happen!' How many?"

Hands shot up across the room.

"Right? I get those darn things all the time. But I don't think it's all going to be gloom and doom. We just have to have a cause that's higher than self-preservation. We have to have some skin in the game. I really do believe that we are ready to write a bright page in history for our state, and our country, I really do. Are you ready?"

Wild cheers. "Hell, yeah!"

My watch said 10:15 p.m. My feet hurt. And I wondered what I was going to have to clean up at the shop. I'd rather clean up puke than another one of Clay's messes.

"I want you to know that I've been talking to people here—people who say they want a change in this party. They say they want to root out corruption."

Finally, he got to the whole purpose of this meeting. At least the crowd was in his pocket; I'd give him that.

"And those people—they want to tell you how to vote tomorrow. Heck, there are people who want *me* to stand up here and tell you how to vote tomorrow. And I'm not going to do that."

I did a double take.

"I tell you this, I can't look into the future. I can't tell you how this will turn out, or what some new leadership will do, or how they will guide our party. Will the new boss be any better than the old boss? I don't know. What I do know is that the establishment always talks down to us, and tells how to do things and exactly what to do 'for our own good.' Have you noticed that?"

He made air quotes around "for our own good." I stood stunned. What the fuck just happened? We were in the same room, three hours ago. He shook hands. He made a deal. Votes for planks. Suddenly, we, the insurgency trying to oust the establishment, *became* the "establishment" that no one was supposed to listen to?

"At the end of the day, you have to answer to yourself, and to a higher power than yourself. Ron Paul believes in individual choice, and so do I. God gives you the power to choose. He gives you free will. That's what personal liberty means. That's what individual freedom means. Don't listen to me, because I'm not going to tell you what to do. Don't listen to anyone who *does* tell you what to do. Tomorrow, you do what your heart tells you to do."

I could feel my face get hot. That little bastard had totally screwed us. I grabbed my phone and texted Frank.

WE JUST GOT ROYALLY FUCKED.

Buzz. *????!*

BE THERE IN A MINUTE TO EXPLAIN.

The crowd was on its feet cheering. He waved a humble good night, and almost instantly had a line of people wanting to talk, wanting to donate, pulling out checkbooks. And we looked like jackasses—meet the new boss, same as the old boss. In the end he acted on self-interest only. He wanted votes all right, but he wanted them on Election Day for himself.

As people filtered out of the room, I tried to get a feel for where they stood.

"I don't really know much about these new people they want in there."

"They're all the same, anyway. It doesn't really matter."

"Well, I'm going to have to think about it. I'll decide tomorrow."

It was a disaster.

I marched to the front of Cox's receiving line.

"Got a minute?" I asked in the form of a command.

Cox suddenly looked uncomfortable. Without the crowd as a buffer, he didn't seem quite as confident facing one of the people he had just hung out to dry. I put my hand on his back and physically led him away from the line, as he indicated to those waiting that he'd be right back and gave an awkward smile.

"What the fuck was that?"

"Hey, look. I've always been about personal freedom and people making their own choices. I never . . ."

"I'm going to tell you something, Schaeffer. I just met you, but you need to hear this from somebody, so it may as well be me. Any of these people who donate to your campaign right now should have their fucking heads examined. You're going to lose, and do you know why? You don't *do* what you just did. You don't stab people in the back when they reach out to you. You don't tell them one thing to their faces, and then turn around and make it all about you. I don't give a shit what your politics are. If you want my advice, you'll get yourself a campaign manager who knows what the fuck they're doing and get your head out of your ass. You need to stop right now thinking you're the most important guy in the room. This is not about you and your campaign. The people trying to get rid of Ruedrich have worked their asses off for months, and now I can't even get a fucking vote count from this room because of what you said. I'm done."

I headed to my room, fast-walking and pissed off. I needed more information about Cox. I decided to call Brian Beazley, my best friend in Fairbanks. I'd helped him set up a shop there, similar to mine, called Dark North Tactical. Brian was a full-on, dyed-in-the-wool anarchist who ran his own militia but didn't call it a militia because anarchists don't have militias. He was smart, and rebellious, and a little crazy. We were tight.

"Yo."

"Hey man. What can you tell me about Schaeffer Cox?"

"He's a fucknut."

"I think I figured that out. Anything else?"

"He's done a bunch of stuff up here with the Interior Alaska Conservatives, and the Second Amendment Task Force, and a bunch of shit. He loves to hear himself talk. He just loves himself in general. Dude moans his own name in bed I bet. And he's fucking crazy. Why? Where are you?"

"I just listened to the guy talk for over an hour, and then he flipped out and fucked over a bunch of Republicans."

"Sounds like him," he said. "I'd stay far, far away, man. I don't get it. People up here worship the dude. I go along to get along, but . . . And hey, when are you coming up? Why do I always have to come to Los Anchorage to see you?"

"Soon, man. Miss you, bro. I gotta run, though."

I dialed Hippie Omega next.

"What the fuck happened? How did he even meet her?"

"Banana came in last week to pick up his paycheck, and she was out in the parking lot having a smoke waiting for him. I guess he took too long, because Clay was out there and they started talking . . . You know how that goes."

"Goddamn it. I can't leave for one fucking day?"

"Apparently not."

"This is why we have the goddamn 'No wives and girlfriends' rule! And he found out?"

"Well, technically she wasn't *in* the shop, so no rule violation. But yeah, Banana came tearing in here and fucking flattened him right on the porch and then took off. He's all swollen up and purple. I gave him a couple small stitches over his eye. Nothing too medically serious, but he looks like he got hit by a beer truck."

"All right. Make sure they're not working the same shift until I get back."

"Roger that, Boss."

The next morning I sat over bacon and eggs in the café downstairs, wondering why the hell I thought it was a good idea to get back into politics and why everything at the shop seemed to fall apart the second I left.

Joe Miller looked like someone had died after I debriefed him and Frank Bailey about the shit show the previous night. Bailey had been agitated and red-faced but kept saying, "It'll be OK." I wanted to smack that stupid cap off Cox's head for fucking everything up. I'd seen Ray, too, who somehow managed to take it all in stride. He'd gone up against so much bullshit in his political life, failure didn't ruffle him. He just figured that he was one failure closer to success the next time. I just wanted to get out of this shark-infested cesspool and go back to doing something normal and uncomplicated, like selling body armor to crazy people.

Miller slid into the seat next to me as I ate. Every muscle in his body looked tense, and he glanced around the room, scanning, like a rabbit looking for the foxes.

"I've ruffled a lot of feathers around here," he said. "And I'd like to enlist your services if you'd consider it. There are people . . . people with enough money and power to make things happen. People who don't want change. It's not in their interest. I'd like to hire Drop Zone as my personal security."

"You feel there's a threat?"

"Yes, I do. But you're a delegate, and I don't think you can do both things, so I understand if . . ."

"Done," I said. I was looking for a reason to walk away from the insanity, and I took it. I'd noticed Miller getting overt glares from passersby. Hair-sprayed ladies in elephant vests mumbled to each other. Oily executives in suits threw eye daggers.

"I'm yours."

I pulled a threat-assessment form from my briefcase. Although Miller was pretty sure "people" were out to get him, he couldn't tell me who. The nuts on his tires had been loosened, he was almost positive. Shots were fired at his house last month, he thought, but he hadn't called the police. For someone else, I might have walked away and filed it under paranoia, but I'd be crazy to turn down this job. No harm would be done, I'd stay close to the governor's inner circle, Miller would be happy, my guys would get paid, and I'd get out of this political shit heap. Win-win-win-win.

Miller wanted the full executive treatment and that's what he got. Two phone calls later, my team was on the way with thermal-imaging cameras, sound extenders with headphones, and handcuffs, ready to track Miller's every move. It would be good practice.

In a matter of a couple of hours, four guys in black suits, black ties, white shirts, earbuds, and Oakley sunglasses flanked Miller. We were like Mormons, only scarier. As team leader, I wore a red tie—a visual cue in a crisis situation so everyone knew the go-to guy.

Everywhere Miller went, we "walked the diamond" with one guy to the left, one to the right, one in front, and one in rear—far enough away to be inconspicuous, but close enough to "collapse the diamond" if needed to protect the client in a threat situation.

Miller said he wanted out of the convention room the second the vote was called. Suicide and Sherlock trailed him into the ballroom and took positions in the corners of the room, scanning to make sure no one in the crowd drew a weapon. The Big Mexican and I staked out the hallway to maintain positive control over the evacuation route. A car and a follow vehicle waited.

My earpiece crackled, and Suicide told me the vote had failed. Randy Ruedrich had won the day, and there would be no Tea Party/Ron Paul coup. The ballroom doors flew open and out came Miller with my two guys behind him. We formed the diamond and headed for his car while angry shouts were hurled at Miller.

"I hope you're happy!"

"Nice try, idiot. You need to back off!"

"You got goons now, Joe? Are you kidding me?"

I held the door open on Miller's white SUV, which was running, and we followed in Gunny's black one. This was all in a day's work for us. But it was anything but normal for a political convention in Alaska. Here, it was all about Miller having "goons."

"Hey, dude. Did you hear that?" I said to Sherlock. "You're a goon."

"Goons!" he said, with a fist in the air. "Yaaahhh!"

"Goons," said Gunny and let out a syllable that might have almost been a laugh. "Huhh."

We escorted Miller out of the area and safely to his vehicle, and swung back around to the Captain Cook. It was going to be business as usual with the Republican Party. If Cox had gotten the votes, the shiny new party would have backed him all the way. Instead, he decided to make it The Schaeffer Cox Show, where his first act was shooting himself in the foot. But I wasn't here to save him from himself. He had managed to betray the powers that be in the governor's office, and the leaders of this new movement of insurrection, before he'd hardly gotten to know them. He would reap what he sowed. Don't give support, don't get support.

For our part, Joe Miller didn't die, so he liked us, and I'd gained a couple hundred new customers from hand-shaking, shooting the shit over scotch, and passing out business cards for a couple days.

While I was reveling in the belief that Cox was going to flame out after he lost the election, I could not have fathomed that in a matter of a few years he would take me down with him. Or how hard we would fall. I just knew that life was simpler when you knew who the enemy was, and you had a clearly defined mission. "Get the meth dealer out of the hotel room alive. Take him or her to the police station." Easy. Good guys versus bad guys.

In politics, it was all about strategy of a different kind. The mission was the same—win, succeed. But the methods involved selling out your principles, shifting your allegiances, and deciding who to screw over and when. It wasn't a place where people with integrity survived, especially in the Republican Party. It wasn't like I had any love for Democrats either, but the worst corruption tends to reside in the party with the power. I might have to kiss the Republicans' asses for business, but I wasn't buying into their bullshit. I'd stick with my world, where I knew who the enemy was.

CHAPTER 9

★ ★ ★ ★ ★

SCOUNDRELS, MOLES, AND SLUGS

"I say this to you who may be weak-hearted. If you love wealth
more than liberty, and you love tranquility more than the
animating contest of freedom, then go home in peace. We ask
neither your counsel nor your arms. Crouch down and lick the
hand that feeds you, and may your chains rest lightly upon
your shoulders, and may posterity forget that you were ever
our countrymen. This is our finest hour, ladies and gentlemen.
Don't be hidden. Walk out from under the shadows. When fear
turns into righteous indignation then we can use you. But we
can't use you if you're sniveling and afraid to take back liberty.
You've got to want it so badly that you're willing to die for it."
—**Norm Olson, commander of the Northern Michigan Militia, 1994**

Y ou could look at Clay's face and tell Banana Hammock was a lefty.
Our company whore would be out of commission for a while until
he could open his right eye again. The bruising was bad, and his
lip was split and swollen. Somehow, Banana had turned him into Rocky

in the last round with only one punch, which we all respected in a way, including Clay. There had also been a kick to the ribs once Clay hit the floor, but nothing broken. Just bruised. Clay was one lucky motherfucker and he knew it.

"He took her shoe-shopping," Hippie Omega offered, and rolled his eyes. "Shoe-shopping! Nice m.o."

"Shoe-shopping *and* ice cream," Clay corrected. "I told her she was too skinny . . . needed some meat on her bones. It works."

"Oh, for fuck's sake," I said.

"Well, I did prove one thing," he said. "If I could bang Banana's old lady, then size isn't everything . . . apparently." He grabbed his crotch. "It's quality, not quantity."

"Not fucking funny, man. Did you hit him back?"

"Nah . . . I had it coming," he said. "But it was totally worth it."

"Are we gonna lose him over this?" I asked.

"Already gone," said Hippie Omega.

"Fuck."

He'd been a decent worker. And he'd make the fourth one I'd lost because Clay couldn't keep his dick in his pants.

"Hey! Banana split!" said the Big Mexican, laughing. "Get it?"

"Too soon, man," said Hippie Omega.

Clay still had a black eye a week later when a tall man with grey hair and a mustache came into the store in full camo. That by itself happened pretty frequently, but this was different. I felt like I'd seen him before but couldn't place him. He looked at me, scanning as if trying to figure out if I was me. He had flat, milky-blue eyes and his ears stuck out a bit. He carried himself like he'd been in the military. I was still trying to place him when he introduced himself.

"Norm Olson, nice to finally meet you," he said, holding out a hand.

Norm Olson, co-founder of the Northern Michigan Militia and founding father of the modern militia movement, was legend in the militia world. He'd organized hundreds of people into dozens of militia groups in Michigan. Under his supervision, sixty-eight out of eighty-three of Michigan's counties and forty-six states had armed citizen militia groups by the mid-1990s. He vowed there would never be another Waco under his watch, and if there were, he'd be there to intervene. A retired Air Force veteran, Norm was also a Baptist preacher and spoke like it. Put more than three people in a room and Norm would actually utter words like, "I say unto you . . ." He had been preparing for "The End" for almost twenty years as far as I knew, and "The End" always seemed to be two years away.

But after a couple of his fanboys had blown up the Oklahoma City Federal Building and the day-care center inside, Norm lost his luster. He even got some time in the hot seat, testifying before Congress' Terrorism Subcommittee trying to explain to them how it was that Timothy McVeigh and Terry Nichols considered bombing the Murrah Federal Building "an act of retribution," and defending the role his own rhetoric may have played in ginning up that sentiment.

Eventually that rhetoric became too extreme, even for his own group, and Olson was ousted and moved west to start over, which is how he happened to be standing in my shop. He had landed in Nikiski, a small rural community about three hours south of Anchorage in the religious and conservative land of the Kenai Peninsula. He'd appointed himself commander of the "Alaska Citizens Militia."

He gave a warm handshake, looking at my face for recognition when he said his name.

"I know who you are, sir," I said.

He seemed pleased. He browsed the store, but it became apparent that he really wasn't there to buy anything. He had just come by to talk, and the conversation soon turned to militias. We were on a steady march to a police state, and it was only a matter of time before they came for everyone's guns, he said. I'd heard this a million times. Fear is a motivator, and people like Olson use the fear of gun confiscation, the fear of government threat, to increase membership in militia groups.

"I think we're on a slippery slope to civil war," he said. "But I'm not telling you what you don't already know. As a pastor, I can tell when I'm preaching to the choir."

I nodded.

"You know, when I started the Northern Michigan Militia, it was twenty-nine men in the woods in camo. We were deep in the woods with our cars, on private land. We were afraid to be out in the open, but we realized you can't do that. You have to be out in the open and unafraid . . . How is business for you?" he asked.

"It's great. Brisk. I have no complaints. Lots of people prepping," I said.

"Good. That's very good," he said. "You know, we realized back in '94 that doing what we were doing was probably the last option before armed and open warfare, unless the attitude of this country changes. Otherwise it's inevitable. And I don't want that. I want to protect my children from that. But you know, when you look at your children . . . do you have children?"

"Yes, a little girl."

"Well, when you go home, you look at the face of your little daughter and you hug her close. I try to remind people to remember that one day you're going to be in a graveyard someplace, and your people are going to come out and they're going to look for you and that gravestone, and God help you if they have to push the weeds away. God help you if they come out there to curse your name and your memory because you didn't stand in the valiant hour. But how wonderful it would be if they came out and said, Let's talk about grandpa. Let's gather around this gravestone and talk about how he stood and gave the last full measure of his loyalty and devotion and honor to the principles of freedom, and dignity."

"Amen," I said. It was kind of surreal, getting "the pitch" from Norm Olson.

"The militia is legal, the militia is constitutional. If you're interested in forming one up here, I can tell you how to do it. I'm sure you know many like-minded souls. Are you a veteran?"

"Yes, I am. Army. They retired me. Involuntary medical."

He shook his head in sympathy.

"Thank you for your service," he said. And let me say this to you—you served honorably, and you've raised your hand and you signed on the dotted line. You raised your hand and you vowed to protect this country from all enemies, foreign and domestic. You have never disannulled that vow. And if you were willing to die for your country then, you are willing to die for your country now. Am I right?"

"Yes, sir."

I wondered what Drill Sergeant Mitchell would have to say to Norm Olson. I guessed that they had different definitions of a "domestic enemy," but the sentiment was the same; the call to duty was the same. And it reminded me that in a war, both sides believe equally that they are right.

"The thing that's so frustrating is that we've pretty much fallen asleep at the controls in our country. It's time that we speak up, it's time that we stand up, but by God it's time that we wake up. And if we're going to be the men and women of honor, and if we're going to have the dignity and we're going to have the principles that God intended that free men and women ought to have, then we're going to have to do the job. We've fallen asleep and it's time to wake up. The militia is the answer."

I felt like I was looking into a time machine at Schaeffer Cox in forty years.

"There seems to be a lot of militia activity up here," I said, hoping to encourage him to say more.

"Well, we've had enough of the tyranny. Enough is enough. You want to think about taking this nation back? Then think about eating an ele- phant. You don't eat it all at once, you just grab hold and start gnawing where you are. And that's why we have so much local militia activity in this nation. And I've tried to do my part to make that happen."

"You've certainly had influence," I said.

"But ultimately it's not me. I'm only one man. But I pass my advice. I say, Get a group, meet, elect an officer who will be your commander. Give him the rank of major. Your staff officers hold the rank of captain. You orga- nize, you speak, you hold rallies, and we network across the state so if something happens you can get in touch with other brigades. It is critical to network across the state. If you have trouble down here, we'll be here to help you. There is strength in numbers," he said, and looked at me with grave seriousness. "Are you interested in joining up? You are the kind of man we need."

I'd been thinking of how I'd answer this question.

"I support you one-hundred percent, you know that, I hope. But I have a role here. This is where I belong. I get things that are needed, and I get them into the hands of people who need them. This is my place, and how I've chosen to fit in to it all. I hope you understand that this is my service, but if the shit ever goes down, I'm with you. You know where to find me."

"I respect that," he said. "We need a good supply sergeant." He put his hand on my shoulder and smiled, but I could tell he was a little disappointed.

"I tell you what," I said. "I've got some extra BDUs and I'd like to make a donation to the cause if you'll take them. You have men who could use them, right?"

The Army was in the process of phasing out the old Battle Dress Uniforms in favor of a new digital pattern. Nobody needed the old ones anymore and I had two big duffel bags full. I took him back to the office and pulled the bags down from the top shelf of a large metal storage rack. He looked around the room, eyeing the racks of rifles, helmets, and gear we used for fugitive recovery.

"Impressive," he said.

Then he noticed the list of "Fulton's Rules" on the wall and began to read.

"We need a lot of rules around this place," I laughed.

"You want to know what things *I* tell people to look out for?" he asked and started counting on his fingers. "Nothing illegal, no drugs, no illegal weapons. If they connect illegal activity to any of us, it will taint the militia. We will lose our purity, and we cannot afford to lose that. Be politically pure also," he went on. "This is not about politics, or what party you are in. Don't make it about race. No racism. We welcome anyone and everyone. That's what America is all about. And favor no denomination. I'm a Baptist preacher, but that doesn't mean anyone else has to be. America defends your right to a religion or no religion. Are you a political person?"

"Well, funny you should ask. I just went to the Republican convention as a Ron Paul delegate but ended up leaving early. I made some good business contacts, but politics is too frustrating for me, and I think I'll be putting it aside," I said.

"While you were there, did you happen to come across a young man named Schaeffer Cox?"

"As a matter of fact, I did," I said, bracing myself for what was coming. They already knew each other.

"I think he's worth watching. He's different. We need more zealous young patriots who aren't afraid to tell the emperor he has no clothes. I think we'll be seeing a lot more from him. The older I get, the more pleased I get when I see our future leaders in action."

God help us, I thought. I knew that Olson liked to fan the flames of discontent with rhetoric, and then step back and watch the crazies "follow their own conscience." It was all about plausible deniability. Even if he wasn't wishing directly for an Oklahoma City, it was hard to imagine how Commander Olson could hope to get his troops pumped for battle and then be shocked when the battle came.

Olson was a hero to many. But his power was waning, and he'd need to pass the torch. Cox was perfect. He was passionate, charismatic, and, I had to admit, one hell of a persuasive orator.

"Did you hear the boy speak?" he asked.

"I sure did. He can really work a room," I said.

The thought of Olson and Cox—the figurehead and the future—steering the ship made me seasick. Nobody wanted a repeat of Oklahoma City. Maybe I'd spent too much time in the company of paranoid people. Maybe my mind was running away with me. Maybe not. If I were trusted, though, I'd be privy to information. There was no better way to know what the wolves were up to than to pretend to be one of them, I reasoned. So I'd be a sheepdog in wolf's clothing. It would help me sleep better.

"The last thing?" he said, "is watch out for three kinds of people—the moles who are working for someone else to report on your activities, the provocateurs who try to sow the seeds of discord and division, and the dissipaters who seek positions of power and then steer you the wrong way. There are many whose purpose is to discredit us. Trust me. I have learned from experience."

"I bet there are," I said. I threw a box with a half-dozen pairs of black combat boots and a garbage bag full of white cotton T-shirts onto Olson's pile. Outreach and good will to the granddaddy of the militia movement would only mean more business, and more contacts. I said my goodbyes and shook his hand.

"It was a pleasure to meet you, Commander Olson."

"Likewise," he said. "God help the scoundrels, and the moles, and the slugs. God help any that touch those children, but there are those trying to put the chains of tyranny on those children's shoulders. I'm glad you're in the fight. God bless you."

CHAPTER 10

★ ★ ★ ★ ★

CHARLIE AND OSCAR

"The better I get to know men, the more I find myself
loving dogs."
—Charles de Gaulle

We've heard this nine times in the last six months," Suicide said into
the phone. "I know because I've been keeping count . . . You are
totally sure? Right now. She's there . . . OK, man. You keep eyes
locked, because we're gonna move on this and I don't want another dry
run. Call my cell or the Boss's cell if there's any movement. OK?"

It was the Princess. That's what we called our most elusive fugitive.
Her name was Prinsesa, a repeat felon who lived in a dilapidated green
trailer with her enormous Samoan boyfriend and a litter of kids. She was
wanted for armed robbery and assault for knocking over a convenience
store and pistol-whipping a customer on her way out. She never surfaced
at trial, and she never surfaced during *nine* attempts to arrest her. She and
her boyfriend probably weighed 700 pounds combined, and yet somehow
she managed to become invisible when we showed up. It was maddening.
But our source (the kid in the trailer across the street who we'd promised
$100 at arrest) just swore he saw her go in. Again.

This time, it was going to be different. We had a new strategy. Charlie and Oscar stood on call. They were a highly trained team, in search and rescue and in police work. They could literally smell a fugitive from 200 feet away. Because they were dogs. Charlie was a border collie and Oscar a German shepherd. They'd be the new recruits today on their first Drop Zone mission, along with their handler, a former MP named Tony.

"Remember, we don't get paid if they're dead," I told Tony.

"Roger that," he said.

It was late afternoon when our four SUVs rolled up in front of the trailer. Hippie Alpha was in full tracking mode and had binoculars on the residence from the lead vehicle—my red Hummer. "I've got a visual on the target," he said. "Big window on the right. Yup, it's definitely her. She's in there."

"Well, this is kind of fucked up," said Sunshine looking at the half-dozen kids running around in the neighboring yards playing "keep away" with a wiffle ball.

"OK, we've got a bunch of kids here near the premises today, so extra caution, please," I said into the radio. "We've got confirmation on the target inside, so let's do this. Fast and careful, please. Nobody gets hurt. Let's go."

We exited the vehicles and walked past the kids who seemed completely unfazed that sixteen armed guys in camo were marching up the walk. We had been here nine times before, so they were used to this.

We were preparing to breach the door when it flew open, and the boyfriend stood there like a wall. He had to be six-foot-eight and so wide we couldn't see past him. His legs were like tree trunks. A Samoan version of Gunny.

"We're here to talk to Prinsesa," I said.

"She's not here," he said.

"Yes, she is," I said.

"No, she's not," he said.

"This is not a game of yes she is, no she's not," I said.

"You got a search warrant?"

"We don't need a warrant. She's technically already in state custody, but she has violated the terms of her release. We know she's present. We can breach the door without a warrant."

"I got a gun," he said, squinting, and there were several seconds of awkward silence.

"Well, that's a really fucking stupid thing to say in front of the sixteen guys pointing guns at you right now," I said. A wiffle ball bounced off my helmet.

He froze for a second, his hand held at an awkward angle, as though reaching behind him. I knew he was going for a weapon. So did my guys. Time got very slow, and I could see him moving his eyes from one weapon to another. I did not want to have to shoot this stupid fucker. And I really didn't want to have to shoot him in front of a bunch of kids. And I felt incredibly uncomfortable being between him and the row of muzzles behind me.

"You got kids here, man. They don't need to see this." And by "this" it was either going to be gunfire or several of us being broken in half and the other dozen sitting on this guy.

"No, sweetheart, the doggies are not here to play. They are working right now. You need to go back over there with your friends, OK? Be good, and maybe you can see them later. Go on, now. Good girl." I could hear Tony behind me.

The Samoan looked at the dogs and his face changed. He didn't like dogs.

"Are the dogs ready?" I called out, gaze still locked on the Samoan.

"Roger! On your command, sir."

"NO DOGS," he said, still frozen, his voice tight.

"All right, if you don't like dogs, then what I need you to do is put your hands up where I can see them. Nice and slow. Do it now."

He inched his hands up and followed my orders. "Palms out. Let me see them. Walk forward slowly, down the steps, walk ten feet . . . Now down on your knees, cross your ankles. Thread your fingers behind your head."

Oscar barked.

I zipped the cuffs on, and four guys stood around him, weapons still pointed. I was so damn glad we didn't have to sumo wrestle this guy. Charlie and Oscar were already the heroes of the day as far as I was concerned. They were like doggie kryptonite.

"Jesus!" Sunshine scooped up a toddler who was climbing on the prostrate Samoan trying to play horsey. "This is seriously fucked up!" he said. "Oh, shit . . . sorry! Language! Fuck! One of you take this kid!" he called out to the group.

Suicide patted the Samoan down, looking for the gun.

"He's clean. No gun," he said, and everyone looked even more relieved that we didn't shoot the guy.

"Yeah, there is," I said. "Keep looking." I could tell a bluff, and when that guy reached for a gun, he was not bluffing.

"Awww, fuck, I found it," said Suicide a moment later. "Hey, Tony! You're the new guy, here's your initiation. Get this fucking gun out of this guy's ass."

It took a minute to rearrange the ample butt cheeks of the Samoan and get down his pants so Tony could get the .38 revolver out of his crack. Tony muttered something about bonus pay and hazing, while Suicide called APD.

Now it was up to Charlie and Oscar. They took off in tandem, bypassing the open door and ducking under the trailer, letting out a series of sharp, rapid barks. We'd looked under the trailer nine times before, but maybe we'd missed something. Hippie Alpha was on their heels, weapon drawn. He got down on his belly and shined a mag light into the darkness.

"Oh, shit, I see it now!" he called. "Son of a bitch! There's a box! Rear right side!"

Six of us headed inside the trailer, following Hippie Alpha. He did a mental calculation of the floor plan and homed in on the kitchen table. Underneath a sheet of peeling yellow linoleum, a hole had been cut. He pulled up a grimy slab of plywood flooring and underneath was our Princess, crouched in a makeshift box only slightly bigger than she was. That's why we'd missed her. They'd even painted the outside black so we didn't see it when we looked underneath.

"You had us running, Princess," I said.

"Yeah, I did," she smiled, her eyes crinkling up on the sides. "You guys were dumb."

"Well, you know what they say—tenth time is a charm."

Tony patted Charlie and Oscar and gave them a couple Yummy Chummies salmon treats from his pocket. Even Alaskan dogs love salmon. The canine team worked cheap and had as much fun as we did. We worked cheap too. We made $5,000 for the arrest, but multiplied by ten trips out there, and divided by sixteen guys, nobody got rich. But it was never about the money. Other people went mud bogging, or fishing, or snowboarding. We arrested people.

Outside, we handed over the Princess and found out that the boyfriend was on probation, so APD had a double arrest.

Tony let the little neighbor girl pet Charlie while the cops contacted relatives of the kids whose guardians were both headed to jail. She said he was like the doggie in the movie *Babe*.

"Do you have a piggy too? I like piggies," she said.

"No, no piggies. But I'm glad you like Charlie. He likes you too. He says when you grow up, you should stay out of trouble because you're a very nice little girl."

"He said that? How do you know?" Her eyes went wide.

"It's my job to know," he said. "I can understand him."

"My name is Mary," she said. "Tell Charlie I'll be good!"

"I will," he said and gave Charlie the sign to put his paw out for a shake. Mary let out a giggle and shook his paw.

After six months of tracking the Princess, this victory was sweet and called for a celebration. Instead of our usual campfire and home brew, we opted for a local watering hole instead. The Carousel Lounge was just down the road and the perfect place for after a mission—pool tables, jukebox, barely enough light to see the regular power drinkers and scumbags at the bar, and a fight was always a possibility. Plus the booze was cheap and the drinks were stiff. A perfect Alaska dive bar.

Tony joined us after he got Charlie and Oscar home and fed.

"Hey, it's K9!" Sunshine announced to the bar when he walked in.

"K9!" came an unknown voice from the corner in the dark.

"That was so much fucking fun," he said as he slid into an empty chair. "I'm all jacked up, man. I haven't had a rush like that in a while . . . But that gun smelled like ass."

We all laughed, and I ordered him a shot of whiskey and a beer.

"Speaking of smelling like ass . . ." said Sunshine looking pointedly into the dark corner where a guy sat, leaning against the wall. His bottom half was in filthy sweat pants and his top half was an equally filthy Army uniform.

"What's up, man?" Suicide called over into the dark.

"Nobody gives a fuck," he called back. "Nobody fucking gives a fucking flying fuck . . . and they don't. Give. A. Fuck."

"That guy is messed up," Suicide said, and he didn't just mean drunk.

By the end of the night, we were all shitfaced, stumbling back to Drop Zone holding up our new buddy, "Soap," and making sure he didn't stagger into traffic, because contrary to what he thought, we actually did give a fuck. He had nobody and nowhere to go. He'd been in Iraq, Fallujah. I asked him if he needed a shower. He said no. I asked him again. He said no. I told him he could crash on the cot in the office so he wouldn't have to sleep on the street. And was he really, really sure he didn't want a shower? He was very sure. We'd talk tomorrow about getting cleaned up and getting him set straight.

The whole system was so broken, and so many men were so broken. You either had to throw up your hands and be hopeless, or you had to take the situation presented to you and do what you could do. Like that story about the starfish. The kid is throwing stranded starfish back into the water and his grandfather says don't bother—you'll never get all those starfish back into the water and it doesn't matter. And the kid says it matters to the ones I throw back. In life, you're either the grandfather or the kid, and you have to commit or you'll go crazy.

It was clear that Soap had some major problems, aversion to water being one of them. Maybe it was a trigger for something, a reminder of something that had happened. We never did find out. And for a year and a half he lived in the shop and never took a shower. Not one.

He sat on the cot and looked at the green wool blanket and the pillow.

"This is good," he said and fell on his side. He was asleep in seconds.

CHAPTER 11

★ ★ ★ ★ ★

THE RIGHT THING

"The truth of the matter is that you always know the right
thing to do. The hard part is doing it."
—Norman Schwarzkopf

The 2008 election was epic. Alaska held its breath, wondering if
somehow, maybe, we'd feel relevant on the national stage. By
November, we felt a mix of pride and embarrassment. Our home-
town hockey mom had wowed the country, but the wow wasn't always
particularly flattering. For a few weeks, we thought that our Sarah would
be the magic bullet for John McCain's foundering campaign. But soon it
was obvious that the magic bullet was about to shoot him in the foot with
her "maverickyness" and her lack of knowledge about anything beyond
Alaska's borders. Her record of bipartisanship as governor went right out
the window, and playing to the camera with divisive rhetoric became her
primary focus.

Palin and McCain went down in flames, and Barack Hussein Obama
moved in to the White House. Many in my core customer base had been
huge Palin supporters. Many believed the new president was a foreigner
and a liberal gay Muslim socialist come to promote the New World Order,

cede the power of the United States to the United Nations, take their guns, and round them up into FEMA death camps. I nodded, took their money, bagged up their supplies for the end of the world, and face-palmed when they left.

There was no limit to the conspiracy theories. And the "black man in the White House" part didn't help. The escalation of paranoia was palpable. The militias went on high alert for the collapse, and recruitment soared in Alaska and nationwide, far more than it had even in the Clinton days when standoffs between citizens and the government at Waco and Ruby Ridge were fresh in everyone's mind. Even those not involved in organized groups, the lone wolves, were nervous and they all wanted to talk about it. This, they said, is why they lived off the grid. This is why you could never have enough ammo, enough guns, enough precious metals, enough Spam. This is why they needed a secure perimeter. Nobody in or out. They were ready to hunker down, and spend the rest of their days eating moose and dehydrated military MREs, and staying vigilant for raiders come to ravage their zucchini garden.

A customer offered me a poster for my window with a picture of Obama's face in makeup like the Joker from Batman. It had the words "Fascism. Socialism." That was it. Like this idiot had any idea what either one of those things actually was, or that they were different and couldn't exist simultaneously. I hesitated for a second.

"What, you don't want it? You like that sonofabitch, huh?"

It was a bit extreme, especially for my little neighborhood, which had voted for him by a healthy margin, but I took it and put it up right in the front window. A local community blogger marched into the store one day to read me the riot act and tell me we were divisive and a "malignant presence in the community." We ended up having a beer and talking about the merits of social libertarianism. She left thinking we weren't actually evil assholes, but the poster stayed up. A photo of it showed up on her blog with commentary:

> *The "Drop Zone" (corner of Spenard and McCain) has been open way too long. The last thing Spenard needs is more guns. You can't see the posters they have in their windows when you're speeding by*

in a car. You read about this crap on line. You see the images. But when you see it for yourself, on the street, it affects you differently. Racism. Racism. Racism.

We weren't a gun shop, which she apparently hadn't noticed. We weren't racists. If I couldn't convince her of that after a half hour of shooting the shit over a beer, I wasn't going to be able to do it now. And if the left thought I was a crazy, right-wing gun nut, then so be it. I didn't have the time or desire to correct every idiot with a blog and too much time on their hands.

I'd been helpful to the cops and to CID only because the bad guys trusted me. And I was trusted only because I let people think what they wanted to think about me. The truth was that putting up the poster, even though personally I found it repugnant, was like pouring honey on a bag of dog food and waiting for the bears to come along and take the bait—just like our new TV ads. I'd hired a local right-wing in-your-face radio talk-show host named Eddie Burke to do the voice work. Eddie was former Navy and as conservative a blowhard as you could find. I don't think he believed half the shit he said, but he was a good showman. It was never about logic with Eddie, it was all about ratings. He was an entertaining professional bully. Eddie was nuts, but for some reason I loved the guy. He was quick with a laugh and a good story. His unmistakable booming voice on our commercials, and a backdrop of fiery explosions with a death-metal soundtrack, was perfect. It was self-parody, but it totally worked. "If you need to defend a small country, or bring back a big one," he snarled, "head to the *Drop Zone*." KABOOM!

Everything was working like a charm. It was raining and I was the guy selling umbrellas. Stacey and I were even able to buy our "dream house." Most people would have thought our dreams to be modest, but it had everything we wanted. Three bedrooms for a growing family, nice garage, nice dog yard, beautiful kitchen. I'd have paid double just to see the look on Stacey's face when they accepted our offer and we knew it was ours. I felt like maybe it made up for all I'd put her through lately.

I loved my shop and my life. And then one of those days happened. The ones where you look back and say, "If I'd only known then what I know

now." A small-framed man in a denim jacket, dirty jeans, and work boots walked into the store, saying he'd heard our ads and wanted to check us out.

"I listen to Eddie Burke every day," he said. "He's the only one worth listening to. He ain't afraid to tell the truth," he said. "All them others are full of shit."

"We love Eddie," I said.

"Now, him . . . He's on thin ice," he said pointing to the backside of the Obama poster. "I seen your sign from outside. I seen it come from Infowars."

"Damn straight," I said, because the customer's always right.

After some FEMA-death-camp-fuck-the-feds chitchat, he said, "I been in here a couple times now, and I got a feeling about you, and my feelings, well . . . I'm pretty good with feelings about people. Can I show you something?"

"Sure thing, man. Whatcha got?"

He pulled a piece of folded graph paper out of the pocket of his denim jacket and spread it out on the counter, smoothing it flat with his hands. It looked like a floor plan of a building with doors and windows noted and arrows. Another nut who's booby-trapping his house so the feds don't get him in the night, I assumed.

"If we want to stop a thing, and not just complain about that thing, we gotta do something real, right? I'm sick of talk all the time. Talk, talk, talk," he said, tapping the paper with the tip of a grimy finger. "You want to wipe out the pests, you gotta get to the hive."

I pulled the sheet over into the light so I could see what the hell he was talking about. The building didn't look like a house. It looked like a store or an office building in a strip mall. There were indications of doors and which way they opened, areas where someone could take cover, drawings of stick figures where people were located.

I tried to be casual.

"What is this? This isn't your house . . ."

"No, it's not," he said. "It might could be a recruiting station." He looked at me to gauge my response. "I'm not saying it is, but I'm not saying it ain't. I'm just saying if someone were to want to get at the source of the problem, then that might be one way to make that statement."

I looked back at the paper again. It was all worked out—access points, times of occupancy written in the margins, escape routes, points of cover, parking, and strategic locations in the building marked with penciled red Xs. The roads next to the building were marked, too, with direction lanes.

"Y'ain't gonna stop 'em altogether, of course," he said, "but you sure's hell gonna make the little bastards think about it before they sign on the dotted line to lick the jackboots of the tyrant." He looked to me for an approving nod.

Time felt slow. My brain had to catch up with what was happening. This guy standing here in front of me was planning on killing people, recruits and recruiters. Not just talking shit. This guy had fucking graph paper and red arrows and times. He was going to do this and I knew about it. I looked at the paper and each stick figure; if all went according to plan, someone or more than one would be dead. It was all I could do not to flatten this guy with a throat punch. I needed time to think, though. I learned a long time ago that just like you don't go shopping when you're hungry, you don't pound the shit out of a guy when you're angry. Nothing good comes of it. Suppressing my urge to arrest this fucker took everything I had.

"I feel you, brother. But it's probably best for you we never had this conversation, right?" I said with a wink as I took a last look at the paper, trying to memorize every detail. "Is that gonna do it for you today? Just the armor plates?" I rang him up. "You take care, man. Don't take no shit."

I got his license plate as his truck rumbled out of the lot. Anger welled up inside me like lava, uncontrollable. I grabbed a piece of paper and began recreating the image so I wouldn't forget. Suicide came in from a smoke break and knew something was wrong the second he saw me. I could tell my face was red.

"What happened, man? What's going on? What are you writing?"

"I'm gonna call CID on that fucking bastard," I said.

"Whoa, whoa, whoa. Dude. Take a breath."

I told him what had happened so he'd understand. He was a Marine. He'd been a young recruit. He would get it.

"OK. Let's just take a second. Let's have a smoke."

I finished the drawing. It wasn't perfect, but it was damn close. The screen door closed behind us. The day was perfect—blue sky, bright sun, a hot seventy-degree summer day. A couple of kids were biking down the street. Suicide lit a Marlboro and handed it to me. It wasn't my brand, but I didn't give a shit.

"First of all, you can't call CID. This guy's not military; he's a civilian, so it's out of their jurisdiction. It would have to be the FBI," he said. He was right. "So, just calm down, man. Think for a minute what that means . . . because you can't do that."

Calming down and thinking for a minute was uncharacteristic of Suicide, to say the least. But when my moral compass, such as he was, said to calm down and think for a minute, I had to stop and think. I took a deep drag, looked up at the sky, and blew a long stream of smoke.

"You don't want me to call this in? You don't think that's the right thing to do? What the fuck?" I couldn't understand why he was reeling me back.

"Dude, we get crazy idiots in here all the time. But you're talking about tipping off the *FBI*. CID is one thing. You've done that; you're military. You have history there. They still might think you're a narc, but people get it with CID. But if you have any FBI connection at all, and it comes out . . . it's the end of this place, everything we have, everything we've been working for. Nobody trusts you. Nobody supports you. I don't care how crazy this guy is . . . We're done. We're toast. End of story."

We smoked in silence for a minute.

"The guy just sounds like a nut. He's not going to do anything. Nobody ever does anything. They're all bark. Don't mess all this up over one crazy delusional moron. He'll go back to his cabin and jack off to some YouTube video about how to make your own explosives, and we'll never see him again."

"You didn't hear him. You weren't here," I said. "This was an actual plan."

"Bill, if we get in bed with the feds, no one will trust us, no one will shop here. You will be a pariah, and Drop Zone will dry up and blow away. Including all of us. Where are these guys gonna go? This is all they have. And think of all the dirtbags we put away. It's not worth the risk. You're not thinking right. You need to just chill out and sleep on it. Seriously."

I took another drag, down to the filter, and flicked it into the bucket.

"Do you promise me you'll sleep on it?"

"Yeah. I will."

I drove home without remembering the details of how I got there. My brain was like a combustion engine. This was so fucked up. These people who talked all the time about liberty and freedom . . . what the fuck did they mean? You're going to send a message to Obama the "tyrant" by blowing up a bunch of kids? And you call yourself the patriot. Well, then what were they? What was I? What was my grandfather? Those were the people who said, "Take my life in service to my country and do with it what is best." They are the ones who risked everything. Who was this asshole? Some dentally challenged lunatic who was mad he had to live by rules and pay some taxes and not get to do whatever the hell he wanted. Some fucking "patriot."

I remembered exactly what it felt like when I wrapped my hand around the heavy cotton handles of my duffel bag on my seventeenth birthday. I remembered walking out the door into the early morning Montana sun, breathing the cool air into my lungs, feeling it on my face, and finally having purpose. Finally being able to leave that shit heap behind me and serve something, do something good with my life. It was the day my life became mine and my choices became mine. And when those kids, wherever they were, went to the recruiting station, they were filled with those same feelings—the exciting, glorious fear of a new beginning that maybe meant a hell of a lot more to them than what they were leaving. And that's what that guy in my shop today wanted to take away. He had it on fucking graph paper—how he was going to wipe those kids off the face of the Earth.

How could Suicide be balking? He was always my voice of reason. He was right, though, that the FBI was toxic. He was right that I was responsible for my crew. What about their lives? Half of them had nothing when we took them in. Where would Soap, or Discount, or half a dozen others go? Back on the street, back in despair, no meaning, broken. What would happen to their families if they lost everything again? How many future Crime Stoppers' most wanted would stay on the streets without my cleanup crew?

During dinner I wondered if I should ask Stacey what she thought. I wanted to know. She was my rock and often she saw things in a way I just couldn't. And she was usually right. But I tried hard not to wind her up in my life at work. The line between my family and the shop had become pretty solid. It felt, sometimes, like I had two lives in separate boxes. It had been hard on Stacey when I started fugitive-recovery work. On nights I got home late, she was usually sleeping in the chair in the living room, where she'd been waiting up. I knew it took a toll, and my guilt sometimes got the better of me. And I resolved to downplay whatever happened. No matter how dangerous or fucked up the night had been, to Stacey it was just dragging some incoherent, stoned-out meth head to the police. Easy breezy. The less she knew, the less she worried. I could give her that, at least. It would be selfish to worry her just so I could vent and get her opinion. I could do this on my own. I would have to.

The following morning, at seven, the Old Man rang. When his number popped up on my phone it made me chuckle. Of course he'd call now, right when I needed him.

"How's my favorite bounty hunter?" he asked.

"You're asking me this at oh-seven-hundred on a Saturday?"

"Well, you're up, aren't you?"

The floodgates opened, and I told him the whole thing. He was quiet for a long time and let out a big sigh. He understood what was going on in my head.

"Let me ask you this," he said. "If you go to the FBI, what is the worst thing that could happen?"

"Well, I could end up losing my business, putting my guys out of work, being an outcast to everyone I know, and unable to provide for my family," I said. "But other than that, nothing."

"And what is the worst thing that could happen if you don't go to the FBI?"

"That lunatic could kill a bunch of kids . . ."

"You need to make your own decision," he said. "But I know it will be the right one."

"But which one is the right one?"

"You already know the answer to that," he said.

"Yeah . . . but why isn't the right one the easy one?" I asked.

"It usually isn't," he said.

CHAPTER 12

★ ★ ★ ★ ★

NO EXPIRATION DATE

"Our integrity is never worth so much as when we have
parted with our all to keep it."
—Ovid

The building looked like a box made out of red cement Legos. Grey concrete barriers on the sidewalk made a ring around the structure to prevent vehicles packed with explosives from ramming into it. There was a tall wrought-iron fence, security cameras staring at the surroundings, and plain black lettering: *Federal Bureau of Investigation*. The architecture was post-Oklahoma City, and it was obvious the occupants knew they weren't liked.

On one side was an Office Depot, and a block or two down was the Anchorage 5th Avenue Mall, with Nordstrom on one side and JC Penney on the other. Glass-sided "sky bridges" led over the street to a covered parking garage so shoppers could stay out of the snow in the winter.

I looked around on the chance I'd see someone I knew, which was always a possibility in Anchorage. It was all clear and I darted into the lobby, my heart beating faster than I wanted it to. Two geriatric security guards stood by a large body-scanning metal detector and X-ray machine.

Their uniforms said "Securitas," a private security company based in Switzerland. Way to go, FBI.

Plain walls, beige paint, cheap plastic floor tiles—the building had about as much personality on the inside as it did on the outside. The floors reminded me of the ones I had to buff every time I "pushed the limits" in the Army.

"How can I help you?" asked a guard.

I told him I was there to talk to an agent about a domestic terrorism threat. He raised an eyebrow and pushed some buttons on a black wall phone with a curled cord that looked like it had been resurrected from the 'Sixties.

"Says he wants to speak to someone about a domestic terror threat. Yes. Yes. Right. OK."

They irradiated my stuff, took my cell phone and my ID, and sent me to the second floor. The only thing I brought with me was a piece of paper with my copy of the drawing of the recruiting station. I had tried to burn into my head where the Xs were, where the arrows were, the times, the shape of the building, and re-create what I'd seen. I'd also written the make, model, and license-plate number of his rig.

After my conversation with the Old Man, I'd called my handler with CID. Just in case. I had been working with him since we opened the store. "We can't help with civilian threats. Call the FBI," he said. There was no other way to handle this.

The elevator smelled like a recently cleaned hospital bathroom. I stepped off into another beige lobby. The FBI seal hung on the wall along with a picture of the president and the FBI director. A series of wooden doors lined the grey-carpeted hall.

I found room 222, which contained a large bulletproof-glass window, a table, and two blue plastic chairs. On my side of the glass was another chair, a wall clock, and a camera bolted to a corner of the ceiling. It looked like every prison's visitors room in every bad movie I had ever seen. The window even had one of those metal slide-out trays like they use to take your money at the gas station on the bad side of town. I took a seat and waited. I looked up at the ceiling camera. I waved. And I waited. And waited. I tried to imagine who was going to pop through the door on the other side of the glass. It had to be a typical Hollywood G-man to fit the rest of this place. Buzz cut, white shirt, black tie, and shiny shoes. He'd be "Special Agent Anderson," I guessed. The minutes ticked by on the black-and-white wall clock. I could hear each second. What the fuck was I doing here? I told Suicide I needed to run an errand. He didn't think anything of it. At least I didn't think he did. But what if he had suspected? And what if he'd been right and this was all for nothing—all risk, no benefit? I was coming out of my skin, drumming my fingers on the table, watching the clock. And someone was probably watching me watch the clock from that camera on the ceiling. Fuck. Tick, tick, tick, tick . . .

The door opened on the other side of the glass revealing not the soulless robotic G-man in my mind but my mom. Not *my* mom, literally, but every soccer mom or Girl Scout leader you've ever met. She was attractive (in a second-grade-teacher kind of way) and thin, with short wavy blond hair. She was wearing khaki pants and a blue-and-white-striped button-up shirt. The only clue that she wasn't from the PTA was the Glock pistol on her right hip and the FBI shield on her left.

"Special Agent Sandra Klein," she said through the microphone on the window. "Nice to meet you, Mr. Fulton." My ID had made it here before I did, apparently. I was sure they'd done all sorts of checking up on me while I sat waiting.

"You don't look . . . I would never have thought . . ." I stumbled.

"That's kind of the point, right?" she said, smiling. She had dimples. Of course.

"True," I said. "Well . . . well done."

The conversation started the way every conversation in Alaska starts.

"So, what brought you to Alaska?"

"Military."

"How do you like it?"

"Love it. I always had a dream that I wanted to live in Colorado, but this is like Colorado on steroids. Best place on earth."

The more we talked, the more comfortable I felt. I had a half-thought that she probably had the job she did because she was good at putting people at ease, but it didn't change the fact that she actually *did* put me at ease. I explained about the shop. I told her about the guy and the graph paper.

"Oh, that's not good," she said. I felt like I was tattling to the teacher and also having a session with my therapist, but she made me feel that coming here was the right choice. I slid my copy of the drawing through the tray and she looked at it with her eyebrows crunched together.

"Wow . . . I can sure understand how this concerned you," she said. She stopped and looked up at me. "And I want to tell you that I know it took some courage to come here, and I just want to say that you've done the right thing. Thank you."

It may as well have been my mom telling me she was proud of me for acing a test.

"Would it be all right with you if I asked a colleague of mine to join us?" she asked.

A minute later, the guy I expected earlier made his appearance. Special Agent Dirk Ellison was tall with a chiseled jaw and dark hair short enough that I knew he'd been in the military. He was a former Marine and looked the part. He was in khakis, too, and a white dress shirt. There was no way he blended into the background of daily life like she did, and I was pretty sure he had never made anyone milk and cookies in his life. But I liked him right off the bat. I understood the team—good cop and badass cop, and I liked both of them right away. It was not supposed to go like this.

Special Agent Ellison looked at the drawing. It was obvious he'd been listening in and watching because he was already up to speed. He didn't say much, but his eyes scanned the paper, and occasionally he'd say, "Hm," or clear his throat.

"Are you going to be able to do anything?" I asked.

"Well, not us directly," Ellison said. "This is going to go up the chain to the JTTF . . . the Joint Terrorism Task Force. We won't be able to share any further information with you, but I'll just echo Special Agent Klein and say you've done the right thing."

"I don't get to know what happens?"

Klein smiled in sympathy. "I know. It's frustrating, but the FBI works on a 'need to know' basis. There are times it even frustrates us, believe me. But it has to be that way so things are done cleanly. Information needs to be contained. Less chance for screwups. And screwups can have serious consequences in this line of work."

"I like your shop," said Ellison. "Been in there a few times. What made you decide to get into that business?"

And so the conversation went. I told them my story.

I told them about the military, my shop, and about my customers. They told me about the unique challenges the FBI faced in the wilds of Alaska, how the Anchorage office covered the entire state, and about their previous encounters with domestic terrorism. We talked about the "patriot movement," and a lot of what they said sounded familiar.

"You're pretty much describing some of my best customers," I said. My store was a magnet for crazy. I knew this, and now so did they.

"Let me ask you a question," said Klein in an offhanded way. "Would it be all right with you if Agent Ellison and I just sort of bounced some names off you, and you could tell us if you have had any contact or know them at all?"

"Sure. OK."

"OK, well let's start with Frank McClintock?"

"Yup, he's from the Kenai. Kind of a nut case. Buys a lot of survivalist stuff."

"Bud Lauffer?"

"Yup. Douchebag from Wasilla."

"How about Cindy and Gene Majors?"

"Him I know. Religious type. End of Days. Never met her, though."

"Clint Felling? Sometimes goes by Clint Gregory?"

"No . . . oh, wait. Yeah, I think he's the guy we call Wheezer. Sovereign citizen, big time."

"Schaeffer Cox? He's from Fairbanks."

It shouldn't have surprised me. That name just kept coming up . . . like scum rising to the surface of a pond.

He'd lost the State House race (as I'd predicted), but he'd made an excellent showing for a first-time twenty-four-year-old candidate, losing the primary to an incumbent by less than 600 votes. He took the loss hard, though, and had abandoned politics for local activism and organizing. He had recently formed yet another group, which he called "The Alaska Peacemakers Militia" (I could only assume with guidance from Norm Olson) and appointed himself its commander.

"Funny you should ask," I said. "Yes, I do know that little prick. And I wish I didn't."

Cox had been busy since his loss and had had two recent run-ins with the law. He and Marti were driving south from Fairbanks to Anchorage to visit her mother with their two-year-old son Seth in the back seat. They began to fight, and Cox punched her in the arm. She then told him if he ever did that again, she'd leave him and take Seth with her, whereupon he immediately grabbed her by the throat and pinned her up against the window. Nobody was going to leave him, and nobody was going to take his kid. She fought him off, the anger dissipated, and she and her mom called the police the next day. Marti gave a tearful report, met with the cops, and the officer noted bruising and finger nail scratches on her neck when he wrote up his report. Cox was arrested, and Marti posted his $3,500 bail the same day. After that, magically, Marti's story changed. Suddenly it was all a big mistake, and the cops just had it out for poor, poor Schaeffer. She begged leniency from the court, saying she wanted to save her marriage, and his felony got reduced to a misdemeanor disorderly conduct charge with two years' probation and a class on "alternatives to violence."

I pitied Marti and that kid, but I admit I felt a certain level of satisfaction. When your bells go off, and you just know in your gut somebody is a total piece of shit, and then he proves you right, it's a vindication. My spidey senses were on the mark.

Two weeks after the choking incident, Cox got a Liberty Bell Network distress call from a supporter in Fairbanks whose home was being searched. He had established this network so citizens could call for witnesses when they felt they were being harassed by the police or that their liberties were being violated. A hang-up call to 911 from inside the house had triggered a safety protocol by police. The homeowner denied making the call, wigged out when the cops showed up, and called Fairbanks's Number One Son of Liberty to report the violation of her constitutional rights. Cox, newly on probation, arrived at the scene in body armor, carrying a knife and packing a concealed Ruger .380-caliber semi-automatic pistol. He opened his big mouth, confronted an officer at the scene, and ended up getting searched. His failure to disclose to the officer that he was carrying the weapons was another misdemeanor and a giant violation of his probation.

One thing was crystal clear by this point. Schaeffer Cox made really shitty decisions, and not just political ones. This asshole seemed bound and determined to go to jail. And yet, somehow he was released on bail yet again, after explaining to the court that he *always* wore body armor and carried a loaded weapon because he had to protect himself from "all the death threats." Ever know someone who thinks he's way more important than he is? Schaeffer Cox is that guy. He *wished* he were important enough to get death threats. He was starting to sound like Joe Miller, for fuck's sake.

"Everybody's going to think, 'He's not armed, so let's go get him,'" he told the judge. And for whatever reason, the judge bought his line of bull-shit enough that he was allowed once again to have weapons, but only in his home. He still bitched about it, saying his restriction from carrying in pub-lic was "a danger to his family." *He* was the danger to his family. His assault on Marti should by all rights have been a felony and he shouldn't have been allowed to arm himself at all after that, but he weaseled out of it. And now, he'd done it again. But the legal noose was tightening around his neck. The Office of Children's Services told him they needed to come to his home and interview Seth—normal protocol since the kid was present during the assault on his mother. Cox resisted at every turn. It was all a ruse, he said. His mother-in-law was plotting against him. His political enemies were in on it. So was the police department. Now, OCS was coming to take his kid, and nothing anyone could say was going to convince him otherwise. They were out to get him because they were afraid of his political speech. The men in black perceived him as a threat, a leader who would save the people from the government boot on their necks and bring them to free-dom. At this point, I was just sitting back with a bucket of popcorn waiting to see what stupid thing he'd do next. The fact that the FBI had him on its radar actually made me feel better. Someone was watching—someone who wouldn't let him talk his way out.

Klein and Ellison rattled off more names, and there was only one I didn't know. They tried to keep cool, but I sensed that they were extremely inter-ested in the fact that their "people to keep an eye on" list meshed almost entirely with my customer list. Klein asked if it would be all right if they called in the future some time, if they had any questions or concerns. They also said to call them Sandy and Dirk.

"I respect that you're still serving your country," said Dirk.

I said yes, they could call, because at that point I'd already made the hard decision. How could I turn in one asshole and not help with others?

They slid two business cards through the slot and I stuffed them into my pocket.

I stepped out of the cement box, past the concrete barriers and back into real life. I entered the contact info of my new "handlers" into my phone under "SK" and "DE" and chucked the business cards into a trashcan on the way to my truck.

There was no point second-guessing what I'd done. I wasn't even going to be able to find out if they arrested the guy I'd just reported on. I'd provided a lot more information than I'd gotten. That was OK, because now I was just walking away from all of it, clean, with no harm done and nobody the wiser. And at least I'd be able to tell the Old Man that I'd done the right thing. I was a good Jedi. That was something.

CHAPTER 13

★ ★ ★ ★ ★

COME TO JESUS

"Liberty built civilization. It can rebuild civilization."
—Ron Paul

The literal next day my phone buzzed as I was having my morning coffee and smoke on the porch behind the shop—*DE*. I stared.

"You gonna get that?" Suicide asked, looking at my face.

"Nah. I'm good." I dismissed the call, and put the phone back in my pocket.

A ratty maroon Buick pulled up to the curb on the other side of the lot, and Kevin got out. Kevin was our intern. We didn't really need an intern, but Kevin needed us. He was a hulking high school kid who was feeling kind of directionless. He lived near the store and decided he liked it. He liked us. He wanted to join. I told him he could be an intern, paid, part-time, if he kept his grades up. You'd have thought I was his fairy godfather. "I won't let you down, Boss!"

"Hey, it's the birthday boy!" Suicide called out as Kevin navigated his considerable frame out of the passenger side of the car. He smiled and looked at the ground. His dad pulled away.

"What do you want for your birthday, man? You're fuckin' eighteen!" I said.

"Not 'til tomorrow," he grinned. "I told you guys what I want. All I want is to go on a mission. Come on, Boss, please?" Kevin said, looking at me and sounding more like the kid he was growing out of than the man he wanted to grow into. He'd been bugging the shit out of me for months.

"We'll see what we got tomorrow," I said. "But right now there's an inventory printed out on my desk that needs to be checked."

With a sigh, Kevin lumbered inside.

"You gonna take him?" asked Suicide.

"Yeah, I'll take him. We've got a couple nonviolent ones we need to pick up."

"So, you're just torturing him, basically," Suicide laughed.

I smiled. "I gotta go return a call."

I decided to walk the block rather than call the FBI in earshot of anyone at the shop.

"You free for lunch?" asked Dirk Ellison.

"Do I need to be?"

"It would be helpful. Don Pepe's in midtown at 11:30?"

"OK, fine. I'll be there."

"There's a room in the back. Later."

Of course there was a room in the back of Don Pepe's where I had to go meet with the fucking FBI on my lunch break. Because that is how surreal my life became in a matter of two days. Again I wanted to throat-punch that stupid fucker with his drawing. If he had kept his goddamn mouth shut, my biggest worry would have been finding some heroin addict for Kevin to arrest as a birthday present. Now I was some kind of ridiculous secret agent man who had to walk around the block to make a phone call.

I got back to the store and gave Kevin his wish. We'd go pick up someone named Kiki VanDerWeeg who was likely an addict and a prostitute. His face lit up as if I'd told him we were going to Disneyland.

"You sure this is how you want to spend your birthday? No booze? No strippers?"

"I am so sure," he said. "You're the best boss ever!" He was easy to please.

Lunchtime rolled around, and sure enough, there was a back room at Don Pepe's Mexican Cantina. The table inside could hold ten or twelve people, but only two chairs were full. A waitress stood ready to take an order.

"Long time, no see," I said as I walked in and slid into a chair. "It's been like twenty-six hours, I was starting to miss you guys." I much preferred this setting to the bulletproof-glass window.

"I recommend the taco special," said Dirk. "Trust me, you won't be sorry."

My stomach felt like I'd swallowed cement, and the last thing I wanted was a taco special. "I'll just have a Corona," I told the waitress.

"Two taco specials, two Cokes, and a Corona. I'll be right back," she said, closing the door behind her.

"It's about Schaeffer Cox," said Sandy, not wasting a second.

"How did I know it would be about Schaeffer Cox?" I said. "What did he do now?"

"Here's the thing," said Dirk. "We've gotten information that he's been saying things in public. Confessing to crimes, basically. And these things concern us. We don't know if they're true, partially true, or if it's just bluster. But we have a window of time, thirty days, that we can conduct an investigation. If we find something, we can act on it. If we find nothing, then we have to close it and move on."

"Why do you have to close it?" I asked.

"Contrary to what some people think," Sandy explained, "we actually need a valid reason to investigate someone. We can't just keep monitoring people forever or for no valid reason. They give us thirty days to find out whatever we can, and then we either proceed with the intent to prosecute, or we're done. That's what makes it frustrating sometimes. When somebody does something terrible, they always say, 'Where was the FBI?' but we don't have license to just arrest people because we don't like them, or because we're pretty sure that sometime in the future they'll do something bad."

"So, we're in our thirty-day window with Mr. Cox," Dirk said. "I'll just put it like that."

"Well, I really don't talk to the dude," I said. "We didn't exactly leave things on good terms. So, I don't know what you want from me."

"You're going to Fairbanks next weekend, yes?" Sandy asked as though this were common knowledge.

"Well . . . yeah. But . . . how do you even know that?" Did these people talk to my employees? Were they listening in on my phone? What the fuck?

"Drop Zone is mentioned on the flyer," Dirk said and shoved a piece of paper across the table. It was a printout from Brian Beazley's website. He was having a fundraiser at his shop, Dark North Tactical, to benefit Cox's Interior Alaska Conservative Coalition, and I'd told him I could come up and sell some stuff to help out. It was networking, and it was a good excuse to go hang with Brian Beazley for the day. I'd also promised Stacey for a while that we'd take a little family vacation, and the Fairbanks road trip was perfect. After I did my thing at the fundraiser, we'd hit the local fairgrounds, eat a fried Snickers, and take a quick trip to the nearby town of North Pole to visit the famous Santa Claus House. Santa himself lived and worked there for the other 364 days a year and was always available for photo ops. Santa had a team in North Pole who answered his mail from all over the world in the winter and sold shot glasses, snow globes, tiny mosquito leg-hold traps, and gold-plated moose-nugget jewelry during the summer (and by "nugget," Alaskans mean "shit"—tourists will buy anything). So, even though it would be summer solstice in the Land of the Midnight Sun, Santa was on the job.

"All we're asking is if you could give Schaeffer a call while you're there. Maybe say you want to mend fences or something. Just sit with him. Talk. See if anything comes up. Find out what he's up to. Nothing hard-core, just . . ."

She stopped mid-sentence when the waitress came back with a tray of food. As soon as the door closed again, she resumed.

"Just have a conversation and let us know if anything concerns you," Sandy said before taking a mouthful of chicken taco.

"So, just have a beer with my ol' buddy Schaeffer is what you're asking me."

"That's it," said Dirk. "Just tip one back and shoot the shit." Sandy nodded.

"He probably won't even meet with me," I said. "But I'll give it a shot."

"You really should have gotten the tacos," said Dirk. "Outstanding. Maybe next time."

Next time? This was going way too fast. There was not enough Corona in the world right now. I ended up having another, and as lunch went on I began to feel better about the FBI. They were really just doing what I was doing, hunting bad guys. I knew enough to know they weren't always right, but at least in my world I had a good feeling about Sandy and Dirk. They were sheepdogs too. And now we were on the same team.

I drove back to the store with the windows down. It was seventy-five degrees, hot for Anchorage. Houses had giant flower baskets hanging from porches, kids were out on bikes, people were jogging with dogs, gardening . . . summer was in full swing and Alaskans were sucking the life out of it, enjoying every minute. It didn't feel like the right backdrop for a clandestine meeting with the FBI about thwarting domestic terrorists. It felt like I should be having another Corona in a lawn chair watching my kid play in the sprinkler.

Schaeffer Cox's contact information was still in my phone from the Republican convention. I punched his name. I might as well get it over with.

"Schaeffer? Bill Fulton. We met at the Republican convention. You came to my room . . . Joe Miller, right. Listen, I'm going to be up in Fairbanks for that benefit for the IACC at Beazley's shop. I know you started that organization, right? . . . Cool. So, I didn't know if you had any free time that day, but if you want to get together and just shoot the shit for a little . . . Yeah. I'm staying at Pike's Lodge . . . Awesome. Yeah, I'll text you the info . . . Great. Thanks, man. Later."

That had gone much easier than I'd thought it would. Cox seemed relaxed, almost in a good mood. And our less-than-friendly parting of ways didn't even come up. Maybe it wouldn't be that uncomfortable. Of course, at the time I was blissfully in the dark about the things of "concern" the FBI had been hearing, and "uncomfortable" was about to become an understatement.

Since the election, Cox had started attending militia conventions in the Lower 48, and quickly became a rising star, drawing large and enthusiastic crowds. As much as his life in Alaska seemed to be falling apart, his influence and status in the patriot community were on the rise. He talked about not trying to change the current government from within anymore but creating a "second government" and boasted about the readiness of his Alaska Peacekeepers Militia to take on the existing one.

"We've got a 3,500-man force, militia force, in Fairbanks," he said to a large group in Montana. "It is not a rag-tag deal. I mean, we're *set*; we've got a medical unit that's got surgeons, and doctors, and medical trucks, and mobile surgery units, and stuff like that. We've got engineers that make GPS jammers, cellphone jammers, bombs, and all sorts of nifty stuff. We've got guys with airplanes with laser-acquisition stuff, and we've got rocket launchers, and grenade launchers, and claymores, and machine guns, and cavalry, and we've got boats. It's all set."

Somewhere in the audience an undercover FBI agent wearing a "Don't Tread on Me" T-shirt was probably crapping his pants.

The FBI didn't tell me any of this at the time, of course. That whole "need to know" rule. But the sovereign-citizen movement was giving them more than a few sleepless nights by that point. They knew and understood that in any situation if speech or action fell under the protection of the First or Second Amendment, there wasn't much they could do. But when threatening language and a plan to harm comes from someone with weapons, who actually believes he is above the law and tries to convince others that they are too—things get dangerous. The FBI walks a constitutional minefield, but even with the little information I had at the time, I was pretty sure Schaeffer Cox was going to detonate it, one way or another.

I called Kevin. "OK, you asked for it. You gonna be ready tomorrow? Be at the shop at 20:00 . . . Roger. See you there."

"Come in!" a woman's slurred voice called out when we knocked on the door. It was unlocked. The room was trashed. Fast-food wrappers, empty bottles, cigarette packs, blankets, clothing. It smelled like BO, ashtray, and cat piss. A woman lay sprawled out on the couch looking at the sky through the window. I signaled to Kevin and we did a quick sweep of the apartment, which didn't take long. Nobody else there.

"What's your name, sweetheart?" I said.

"I don't like you. I feel happy, and you should go now . . ."

"Well, you're gonna have to come with us now, OK? We're gonna go for a little ride."

"I don't have to go with you. I don't like you. I feel warm." She smiled. It was obvious from the lighter and the residue on the small square of aluminum foil on the table that she'd just gotten high.

"I hate to interrupt your appointment with Dr. Feelgood." I rummaged through a handbag on the floor and verified the picture on the license with the woman on the couch. I showed Kevin, and he nodded.

I motioned to Kevin that we'd get ready to move her. I took her upper arm and tried to get her to sit up. She struggled and tried to claw my eyes.

"I don't like you! You're the devil!"

"I've been called worse," I said, holding her wrist.

Then her eyes fell on Kevin.

"Him! Oh my god! Are you Jesus?"

Kevin looked at me.

"It's Jesus! You came to me, my Lord and savior! I will go with you!" She stretched her arms up and Kevin, wide-eyed, went to her and pulled her up off the couch. They stood in an awkward embrace, like they were slow dancing, and she started trying to undo the buttons on his shirt.

"Ma'am! Please don't do that," he said, trying to act professional. I tried to keep from laughing because this was funny as shit. While he was holding her up, she ran her hands down his back and grabbed his ass.

"Boss! A little help here!"

"You don't got no boss, you're Jesus Christ, and I want to thank you for coming to save me . . ." she laughed through an opioid haze. She had dark circles under her eyes and a mop of tangled curly brown hair. "Let me thank you," her hand moved around to his crotch. He let her fall back on the couch, looking completely horrified. Junior ROTC had not prepared Kevin for this.

After keeping her from taking off her own clothes by putting the cuffs on, we got Miss Kiki to the police station. The whole while she was begging Jesus to save her soul and offering sexual favors in exchange. I hadn't read the Bible in a while, but I was pretty sure that's not how it was supposed to work.

The cops hauled her out of the rig and took her off our hands.

"Come to me, Jeeeeeesus!" her pleading faded away as they dragged her down the hall, and we filled out the arrest paperwork. I donated my half of the $500 she brought in to Kevin as a birthday present.

"So, what did you think?" I asked, laughing, as we pulled out and headed back to the shop.

"Well . . . it wasn't really what I was expecting," he said. "I thought it would be more . . . different."

Back at the Drop Zone campfire, the guys were waiting to congratulate Kevin on his first mission and welcome him into the fold. They wanted to hear about how the arrest went down. The telling fell to me.

"Oh, Jesus!" I said, in a high squeaky voice as I recounted the events. "Save me, Jesus! But first let me take your clothes off!"

The guys were several beers into the evening and roared with laughter. Kevin, who was blushing like a tomato, was given his handle, whether he liked it or not. He was Jesus from that day on.

But as awesome as Jesus's rite of manhood was, it wasn't the campfire story of the night. The story that left everyone speechless came when Sunshine said that Gunny had a girlfriend. Gunny. Had a girlfriend.

"Wait. Our Gunny?" said Clay. "Like, *Gunny* Gunny?"

"Gunny Gunny," said Sunshine.

"Holy balls!" said Sherlock. "That's some sick shit! Who the fuck is she?"

Nobody was surprised to find out that Gunny and his lady hadn't met at a church social or in the produce section of the grocery store squeezing melons. The match made in heaven had happened at the Great Alaska Bush Company, an infamous local strip club.

Gunny and Sunshine were sitting at a table enjoying the show when a drunken patron who didn't think the "no touching" rule applied to him tried to rush the stage while "Dusti Snow" was dancing. Dusti Snow was Gunny's favorite, so harassing her right in front of him was a really bad fucking idea. The drunk dude lunged to grab a handful of Snow, she screamed, and Gunny took off like a horse out of the gate. He jumped from the floor on to the stage with a guttural growl, grabbed the back of the guy's head like a basketball, and slammed it down into nose-shattering contact with the floor. Gunny's giant boot on his neck probably wasn't necessary at that point because the guy lay motionless, bleeding out his nose and mouth, but Gunny had a certain MO that nobody wanted to critique. The cops showed up in minutes, and the harasser was revived and carted out moaning to a waiting ambulance. A stagehand with rubber gloves mopped the pool of blood off the stage with some old towels he threw into a bucket. Gunny asked Dusti Snow if she was OK in a voice gentler than Sunshine imagined Gunny's voice was capable of being, and she threw her arms around his neck, sniffling into his chest. When Gunny sat her down in a booth and slid in next to her, he was covered with body glitter. Sunshine kept that observation to himself and ordered a Maker's and Coke from a different table. Soon Gunny and Dusti were smiling. And so Cupid's arrow pierced Gunny's leather trench coat at the Great Alaska Bush Company.

As Sunshine finished telling Gunny's love story, the only sound was the crackling of the fire and the deafening silence as all the guys tried to picture in their minds what this relationship would even look like. Stripper and Deathbot.

"That's so crazy, it just might work!" said Sherlock, and laughter filled the parking lot.

"Can we suspend the 'No wives or girlfriends' rule just this once?" Clay pleaded. "I gotta see this!"

"You've got to be fucking kidding me," I said. "*Nobody* gets within a fucking mile of Gunny's girlfriend. *Nobody!*" They all nodded. "Seriously, did I have to actually say that to you motherfuckers?" And they all shook their heads.

I headed home to a nice bottle of wine and some high-end cheese in front of the TV—my nightly post-arrest ritual. I liked knowing that at the end of my insane, testosterone-fueled day my girls awaited me—Stacey, Emma, and now a new baby girl on the way. I was going to be drowning in estrogen, but that's when life felt comfortable and safe. They gave a little balance to my life. I sank into my recliner and Emma, in her fuzzy pink nightgown, climbed into my lap. She showed me her half-eaten cracker and smiled. "You look like a little pink cupcake," I said and munched her belly. She squealed, and Stacey smiled at us from across the room. She was puttering around, getting things rounded up for our road trip to Fairbanks.

Stacey couldn't know about the other reason for our trip. I would have to lie. I didn't like lying to her. I hated it, actually, but I told myself she would understand if she knew. And she worried enough about me anyway, doing fugitive recovery. I couldn't imagine what she'd think if I told her I was an undercover FBI informant. It would stress her out, especially with the baby on the way. I could hardly comprehend it myself. The best and kindest thing—the only thing—I could do for her was to make sure she would never know. I would compartmentalize my life, and I would do it well.

On TV, my other girl, Rachel Maddow, interviewed Kentucky's new Republican Senate nominee, Ron Paul's son Rand Paul. I watched with Emma nestled up under my arm and a glass of Montepulciano with silky plum notes and a pleasing acidity that made me happy. The Tea Party had embraced Rand from the grassroots up, just like they had embraced his father. I liked Ron, but Rand was no Ron. They just wanted someone to believe in and figured they'd stick with the same gene pool. Candidates like Rand Paul, Scott Brown, Nikki Haley, Mike Lee, Christine O'Donnell, and Sharron Angle were throwing red meat to the base ahead of the primary: The government is broken, the Second Amendment is under threat, death panels, too many taxes and regulations, federal overreach, constitutional crisis. Angle, the governor of Nevada, even went as far as to say that the "cure" for tyranny and a Congress out of control was "Second Amendment remedies."

The Tea Party had started with a grassroots movement sprung up from the ashes of Ron Paul's 2008 presidential campaign. I remembered Tax Day 2009, when I'd shown up at the big Tea Party protest in downtown Anchorage. There had been several hundred people with signs like "**TEA**—**T**axed **E**nough **A**lready"; "Time to Clean the House! And the Senate!"; "The Bigger the Government, the Smaller the Citizen!"; and "Don't Spread My Wealth, Spread My Work Ethic—Revolution Is Brewing!" There were people with Lipton tea bags dangling off straw beach hats like pompons on a sombrero, and the bright yellow Gadsden flag with the coiled snake—"Don't Tread on Me"—flapped against the blue of the late winter sky. We sold a shitload of Gadsden flags after that event.

Once the politicians figured out people were pissed off, and this populist discontent might be the key to their own primary victories, and once groups like Americans for Prosperity (funded by billionaire brothers Charles and David Koch) got their hooks in the movement, it got pulled up by its grass roots and went to shit. The candidates, fueled by populist rhetoric and roaring crowds, started ramping up the accusations and the fear. The blogs and publications noticed they got more clicks when people had the shit scared out of them and when they were pissed off. Whether they knew it or not, they'd all adopted the Norm Olson strategy: If you throw enough shit out there, something somewhere will eventually stick. Then, just fan the flames and see where that "brushfire of Liberty" crackles to life. Palin did it with her now-infamous accusation that the president was "pallin' around with terrorists!" Suddenly Saul Alinsky became a right-wing household name. Nobody cared that Todd Palin had been a member of the secessionist Alaskan Independence Party for seven years. He was never called un-American.

The term "federal overreach" sounded catchy—so did calling things "unconstitutional." So did using the term "We the People." A new vocabulary was taking over right-wing politics. The first time I'd really heard it was from Schaeffer Cox in the Tikhatnu Room at the Hotel Captain Cook.

The divisions being sown were deep. And what crafty, opportunistic politicians saw as a way to shore up the base, some of the base saw as a genuine call to arms against a government that they saw as tyrannical and supporters of it who were liberal communist socialist fascist Marxist traitors. Politics had become a clusterfuck.

"OK, cupcake . . . Kiss Daddy goodnight. Time for bed!" I got a sticky cracker kiss on the cheek.

"Kiss baby night night," Stacey said, and Emma kissed her belly.

"Night night, baby doll!" I said.

"So, do you think that a private business has the right to say, 'We don't serve black people'?" Rachel Maddow asked. Rand Paul looked like a bug on a pin.

"I'm not in favor of any discrimination of any form. I would never belong to any club that excluded anybody for race. We still do have private clubs in America that can discriminate based on race. But I think what's important about this debate is not written into any specific 'gotcha' on this, but asking the question: What about freedom of speech?"

CHAPTER 14

★ ★ ★ ★ ★

THE FRIENDLIEST HOTEL IN FAIRBANKS

"A lot of people in this country think we're actually headed toward a Revolution, like 1776. What's in their food?"
—**Chris Matthews**

In Fairbanks on the summer solstice, the sun would rise at 3 a.m. and wouldn't set for twenty-two hours. It was an odd city, not just because of its extremes of light and dark or heat and cold. It seemed somehow to be lost somewhere in the 'Fifties, both in its architecture and its attitude. Many of the bars in the center of downtown had their original neon signs, and there was a little clock tower next to the flag-covered bridge that spanned the Chena River, which divided the city in half. If Norman Rockwell, Daniel Boone, and Billy Graham had gotten drunk and dreamed up a city, it would be Fairbanks.

We'd be staying at Pike's Waterfront Lodge on the outskirts of town. The rustic lodge of a building filled the narrow space between the road and the river. Huge baskets of flowers were everywhere, and gardens with freakishly huge flowers were in full bloom soaking up the almost endless sunshine. Dandelions pushed two feet tall and two and a half inches across. A life-sized sculpture of a moose made of twigs stood near a sign: "Welcome to the Friendliest Hotel in Fairbanks."

Jesus, who hauled up our merchandise for the fundraiser, would be staying in the main hotel, but I had rented one of about a dozen tiny one-room log cabins scattered next to the building for me and the girls. They got settled in and set off to grab dinner on the riverside deck and then go for a flower walk.

At the designated hour, I went to Jesus's room to meet up with Cox. I wanted my lives absolutely separate—a border fence a mile high. Stacey and Emma had to be as far away as possible from the world of Drop Zone, and militias, and sovereign citizens, and Cox. There was no way he was setting foot in my room.

I opened the door when the knock came, and Schaeffer Cox (once again in his tweed cap) stood there with a doughy, red-faced companion—a white-haired gentleman introduced to me as Les Zerbe.

"Hey, Schaeffer! Thanks for coming to see me, man. I know we got off to a bad start . . . Emotions were running high and all that." We shook hands. "I don't get up to Fairbanks that often, so I wanted to make sure just to touch base, see how you're doing."

Zerbe was a missionary pilot and also second-in-command of Cox's Alaska Peacemakers Militia. He and Cox settled into a pair of chairs at a wood-laminate table by the window.

Despite our confrontation and hostile goodbye at the Republican convention, Cox seemed not to hold a grudge. There was no awkward silence. He started right in talking, just as he had in Joe Miller's room all those months ago. He boasted about the rapid growth of his Second Amendment Task Force and how he now had direct (and very public) support from Congressman Don Young.

He pulled a document out of a small leather satchel. It was a declaration, with dozens of signatures—including Rep. Young's. He handed it to me:

Let it be known that should our government seek to further tax, restrict, or register firearms . . . thus impairing our ability to exercise

the God-given right to self-defense that precedes all human legisla-
tion and is superior to it, that the duty of us good and faithful people
will not be to obey them but to alter or abolish them.

"Dude, you got the most senior Republican in Congress to threaten to abolish the government if they tax guns?"

Cox's face softened into a broad grin, and he looked even younger than his twenty-six years.

Don Young had always been a patriot, Cox said, but this new movement now officially known as the Tea Party had emboldened many politicians to express opinions that used to be considered too radical—like acknowledging that the government may need to be "abolished" and that there were laws that superseded the ones made by men. The more liberty-minded patriots there are in DC, the easier it will be to topple the whole house of cards, he said.

"We've got Don Young in DC, and Joe Miller ready to go after Lisa Murkowski for Senate. There are people waking up," he said.

Despite this trend in the right direction, as he saw it, Cox said he had given up on running for office, and was no longer interested in changing the system from within.

"I give them credit for trying, and it'll help, but the ultimate solution is to create another government." The more he rambled, the more it became clear that he had become radicalized, fully believing the sovereign-citizen ideology that the laws enforced by this "tyrannical government" did not apply to him. I didn't know what the FBI was looking for, but Cox's radical ideology and unpredictability made him dangerous in my book. Brian Beazley's opinion when we talked after the Republican convention confirmed it. Norm Olson's association with him confirmed it. The FBI's report of Cox seeking a national stage confirmed it. And what I heard right then confirmed it.

The transition to Cox's new government would not be smooth sailing, he said. "They're after me. They are looking for excuses. They don't like when people speak truth to power. They feel threatened, and I tell you, Bill, they will stop at nothing. Any action against them by a free individual will escalate, until death is the outcome. Or life in prison. They do not tolerate dissent. Think that through, and you'll come to the same . . ."

"Beer?" I grabbed a Heineken out of the little refrigerator next to the desk.

"Sure," he said. Zerbe waved me off and shook his head.

". . . same realization. But it's not me I'm worried about. It's my family," he said as I popped the bottles open. "The Office of Children's Services wants to interview Seth—my three-year-old! They want to come to my house and do it there so they can find something, create some story that we're not fit parents, and take him." He took a long drink. "That's how they'll get to me."

The OCS wanted to talk to Seth because the boy had been in the car when Cox assaulted his wife. I had my doubts whether interviewing a toddler would amount to much, but that was the policy. Cox was totally convinced that it was the beginning of the end and being done only to persecute him.

"What kind of man would just stand by and let the government take his child?" he asked.

The feds saw that he had huge support from militia forces that would come to his aid against law enforcement, he explained. He envisioned another Ruby Ridge incident in which federal officers shot and killed the wife and young son of an anti-government activist named Randy Weaver in a 1992 standoff in Idaho. I remember Brian Beazley telling me he'd actually been there at the time. He lived in Idaho and was there at Ruby Ridge when the whole thing went down. It left an impression. That fiasco had outraged many, and had a big part in sparking the modern militia movement with my new customer Norm Olson at its forefront. Twenty years later, now that the infrastructure of the militia was in place, the network of militias across the state would be there for Cox in case of a standoff, and the feds would pay a heavy price, he said.

It may have been the Heineken, but he looked like he was seeing something play out in front of his eyes—like he was watching the movie of how this was going to go, which was showing on a screen somewhere in the middle distance. After several seconds he snapped himself back.

It wasn't just he who was being persecuted, Cox said. It was everyone.

"This supposed government makes a crime out of freedom. You can't drive without a license, hunt or fish without a license, marry without a license, you can't exercise your constitutional right to bear arms without registration and paperwork. Heck, you can't even die without a license," he said. "And if you refuse to support the tyranny, the IRS will repossess your home, or the feds will lock you up for illegal weapons, or you get fined even more money. This is our basic right to liberty, and at some point we're going to have to take it back.

"The Tea Party and the Libertarians are great, and God bless 'em," Cox went on, "but what we need is not a third political party, it's a second government. And if we can't take down this one outright, then it needs to be replaced one branch at a time, beginning with the judicial."

He had already begun to create and utilize a "Common Law Court," a pseudo-legal system in which jurors are paid in silver, and there are no attorneys—only a legal consultant to answer basic questions. Each person states his or her case before a "judge," and if you're found guilty, you are ostracized from the community. I thought of some of the dirtbags I'd arrested, and somehow I didn't think that being ostracized by the community was going to be an effective deterrent for them or just about anyone else. No one in this system uses last names, because sovereigns believe they are an artificial construct the government uses to own you. First and middle names only—the mark of sovereign citizens.

The Common Law Court that Cox had put together presided over by "Judge Leo" in the back room of the Denny's restaurant in Fairbanks had already found him innocent of all charges in the domestic violence case and the charge of failure to disclose a concealed weapon to police. You couldn't make this shit up.

"That is the true court, a jury of your peers," he said. The Denny's jury was so composed of his own peers that he knew many of them personally. Cox argued his own case, but the law enforcement officers who were "subpoenaed" to testify did not show up. Go figure. And, of course, the jury found him not guilty.

"So, you kind of got the 'Grand Slam' acquittal then," I said, making reference to the famous Denny's breakfast, because this shit was so insane that's what came out of my mouth.

"I get it," he said with a forced smile. "But seriously, Bill . . . I need to ask you something. I know that your line of work includes making arrests of criminals and bringing them to justice, right?"

The "courtroom" at the Fairbanks Denny's.

"Yeah, I do that all the time."

"Well, I was wondering," he paused, "if you could do that for me."

"Do what, arrest people? For you? Who do you want me to arrest?"

"Traitors. Tyrants," he said. "Bad guys. The ones who are part of the problem and have proven by their actions that they are enemies of freedom." He started listing names—a judge who ruled against him, Fairbanks cops who had harassed friends of his for driving without a license, state troopers, a TSA agent, and of course employees of the Office of Children's Services.

This could not be real. This had to be the FBI fucking with me. Somehow.

"So, I arrest them, and deliver them to who? You? Then what happens to them?"

"They will be tried for their crimes—crimes against natural law, against God's law, and against this country. They will be tried in a Common Law Court, and depending on the severity of their crimes, they'll be fined or hung."

Hung. *Hanged.* The word lingered. Time slowed down the way it does in moments when you're trying to figure out a situation that defies figuring out. My brain defaulted back to my orders. Sandy said just let him talk. Find out what he's up to.

"I mean, yeah, I can arrest these guys for you, but I think once that happens, the feds are going to come for you, and beat down your door. You're gonna keep these people in your house?"

"No, we have places."

"Isn't there a way to do this where people don't *die*? I mean, have you seen an attorney about all this stuff with your kid? Can you sue the state?"

"I have seen an attorney, but their laws don't mean anything, Bill. It's past that point. The court system is a joke. The judges fear me, and they respect me because they know I'm right. They know I have the power of truth on my side. There's no winning a game if one side isn't playing by the rules, and *they don't play by the rules.* They choose to do this. Do you understand what I'm saying? They started it."

He sounded increasingly desperate for validation.

"Yeah, man. Yeah. No, I totally understand."

"We have the opportunity to be an example," he said. "Alaska can be an example. Our actions can inspire patriots across the country. Sometimes all men need is a good example—to know that someone else is rising up. And that will make them bold, and they will rise up too, wherever they are. Then you have two, then five, then ten, then a thousand. The Revolution is coming like a freight train, and when it happens I am willing to be the one in front. And that thought terrifies me, because the one out front usually doesn't come back."

Zerbe sat silently, nodding his head now and then in agreement, his fingers interlaced across his belly. He'd probably heard this speech a dozen times before and seemed utterly unfazed by what Cox was saying.

"I don't see how it's you against the troopers and the feds, though. Seriously. That showdown takes like five minutes."

"We're more prepared than anyone thinks," he said. "We've got hidden caches of weapons, armories, stockpiles of ammunition all around the Fairbanks area. We have capabilities of jamming communications. We've got men ready. Thousands. There is more militia than law enforcement here. You should know that."

My brain was vibrating, and I hoped my efforts to keep an outward calm were working. The idea of the nation rising up in armed revolution because Schaeffer Cox didn't want his kid interviewed by the state seemed absurd to me, but Alaska militias alone could do a huge amount of damage if they truly were behind Cox. I couldn't believe many of the people that I dealt with day-to-day in the shop were this radical or this volatile, but I was not in my element here. Fairbanks could be totally different. I found myself wanting to talk to Brian Beazley again.

"You won't be able to do this alone," Cox said.

"Yeah, I can get assets up here to assist," I reassured him, shifting in my seat a little. "For something like this, sixteen . . . twenty guys. All it takes is a phone call. Anchorage is a seven-hour drive away; that's all it takes."

"There's one more thing I have to tell you," he said. "This is full disclosure, so you understand what the situation is." He paused and looked at Les Zerbe. "The FBI's got a hit squad. From Colorado. They're going to kill me—kill my wife and my kid. You have a wife and a kid. You understand what the stakes are here. And when that happens, when they come for us, we're not going down without a fight. But *before* that can happen, the people responsible need to stand trial. They need to answer for what they've done."

Saying the wrong thing at this point, like, "Are you fucking crazy?" would have assured I was instantly cut out of Cox's world. I was not about to tip my hand.

"A hit squad?"

"From Aurora, Colorado. Six men. It's like a shadow unit. According to the government they don't exist. If something happened to them, they would never be missed. But they are very real."

"For me to start arresting people for you is a big step," I said, draining the beer and getting another from the fridge. Cox declined a second. "But I want you to know that I will stand with you. I'm with you. We're all with you. If this goes down, we'll do whatever you need. This is fucking history, man. And I want to be on the right side of it, you know?"

Cox always gave a little wince, almost imperceptible, every time I dropped an F-bomb, and I'll confess to doing it on purpose. But other than that, it seemed to be what he wanted to hear. I told him to write down exactly what he wanted me to do and the names of those to be arrested, their full names, vehicle information, their home addresses, their work addresses, anything he could get me. Cox said he had an IT guy, Michael Anderson, doing research. Anderson had also done some surveillance and was keeping a database. He could tell me what vehicles the targets drove, if they owned property, and where they lived and worked. I told him that details were important and he needed to get me as much specific information as possible. I needed him to write down the plan. Just like that guy in the Drop Zone. On paper.

"When is all this shit going to hit the fan?" I asked.

"Very soon now," Cox said. "It's coming, Bill. That's certain. There's nothing I or you or any of us can do to stop it, but if we want to make it come at the time and place of our choosing, we need to move first and move fast. Otherwise, we give away our advantage, and the outcome becomes more uncertain. I'll have you your list tomorrow at the fundraiser."

"Thanks, brother," I said and held out my hand to him and Zerbe. Both handshakes were damp.

As soon as they left, the adrenaline hit me like a jolt of electricity. Most of the initial shock of the situation had passed since we'd been talking for quite some time, but my fingers shook anyway as I punched the speed dial on my cell to call Sandra Klein. She was on business in DC. It was 3 a.m. on the East Coast. I didn't give a shit.

"Bill? Is everything OK? What's going on?" a sleepy voice asked.

"Good morning, Sandra Klein, this is your wake-up call. What in the FUCK did you get me into?"

"Wait. Hang on . . . where are you, what happened?"

"I just met with Schaeffer Cox is what happened."

"OK, just . . . just breathe for a second. Just focus, and tell me step by step what just happened. Start at the beginning."

At the end, all she could say was, "Wow. All right, well . . . it's going to be OK."

"You don't understand. It's not even close to OK. This asshole is ready to arrest judges and hang people. He wants *me* to arrest them so he can put them on trial! Are you getting what I'm saying here?"

"Listen to me. It will be OK. You've done amazing work. Really, you did very, very well. Just fill out the paperwork we gave you while it's all fresh in your mind, write as much detail about what happened as possible, and go to the fundraiser tomorrow. Get all the information you can. Be our eyes and ears," she said.

I hung up and felt no better than when I'd first called. Just hanging back and "being eyes and ears" in moments of impending crisis was not how I rolled. Fuck that. I needed a plan.

CHAPTER 15

★ ★ ★ ★ ★

THE PLAN

"The supreme art of war is to subdue the enemy
without fighting."
—**Sun Tzu**

The slow, rhythmic breathing of Stacey and Emma would normally have lulled me to sleep, but that night I lay there, staring at the knots in the spruce ceiling while my mind spun itself in circles. I was utterly without strategy, and I hated that.

I had to talk to Brian Beazley before the fundraiser. He was the only person I really knew in Fairbanks, and I could trust him. This was his territory; he knew all the players, and he knew Cox. Brian was an anarchist to the core, and he'd talk himself blue in the face about it to anyone who'd listen. Brian hated the feds, he hated the state, he hated the borough . . . Brian basically hated the entire concept of governance and anyone who presumed to tell him what to do. Brian was his own man. And I knew even Brian thought Cox was bat-shit crazy. He and I didn't see eye to eye about everything, but I loved him like a brother, and I knew he wasn't about to risk his life, or the lives of his men, to follow some idiot in a tweed cap into a war with the federal government because Child Protective Services wanted to talk to his kid. Brian was an ideologue, but he wasn't stupid—far from it. He needed to understand what was going on. I obviously couldn't tell him about the FBI, but I could tell him everything else.

A little chubby hand flailed out and landed on my face. I tucked Emma's arm under the cover. It was cold. Why did I do this? Why were my girls here? My two worlds had become unacceptably close. I didn't know Cox was dangerous when I came here. But I had a feeling that the FBI did know and didn't bother to tell me, which pissed me off. The night went on forever. I couldn't tell what time it was because darkness never came. I may have nodded off for a few minutes, but I couldn't be sure. I put my arm over Emma and rested my hand on Stacey's belly. Olivia was moving in there, restless like her daddy. Finally, I gave up and got into the shower to clear my head. I dressed as quietly as I could and left a note on the table: *Went to Brian's to help him set up. See you tonight. Have a great day. Love you.*

The air was cool and damp, and everything smelled like green. Moisture had condensed in little round water droplets on every leaf and flower and blade of grass and the only sound was a low swoosh of the river. The sun would have heat in it soon, but not yet.

I stopped at the 7-Eleven for a couple of giant foam cups of dark roast and arrived at Brian's shop at about 6 a.m. The light was on. Dark North Tactical made its home in one of the oldest buildings around. It was literally an old trapper's cabin built in God-knows-when, when downtown Fairbanks was the woods. There was moss growing between the logs and on the roof, and the building had settled over the decades with one corner of it noticeably lower than its opposite. Strange windows about a foot tall and six feet long circled the building up by the roofline and some had sheets of yellowed plastic over them.

"Hey, any of this shit for sale?" I called out as I put the coffees on the counter.

"Heyyyy!" Brian came out of the back room and gave me a hug, slapping my back hard. "It's about goddamn time you made it up here."

His store carried scopes, tactical gear, body armor—all the accessories the well-heeled militiaman needed for a tough day preparing to take over the country. He didn't do security or fugitive recovery, but he did head his own private militia—one of many in Interior Alaska. He would argue that it wasn't technically a "militia" because that would be a "statist" organization. But it was a bunch of guys with guns who took orders from him, so . . . he could quibble about the name, but it didn't change what it was.

Brian was a true badass. He was never happier than when he was pulling a trigger or blowing stuff up. Arms and chest covered with tribal tattoos, tall muscular frame, eyes that could bore holes in wood, and an encyclopedic memory for sound bites from the founding fathers to Ayn Rand to obscure Austrian economists, he intimidated the crap out of people on several levels, and I loved him for it. We'd been friends for years. Underneath some fairly significant delusions, and a hard rough edge, he was a good guy. He was the one you wanted to have your back, and he was no fan of Schaeffer Cox.

"If the Revolution happens, you know we're all going to die, right?" he'd said to me once, both matter-of-fact and with a deep intensity. "I'd be surprised if any of us survived, but I'm ready." I had no doubt he was. I knew he was ready to die for the Constitution, for a vision of his country, for the principles on which he stood, but I had a pretty good feeling he wasn't ready to die for Schaeffer Cox's legal troubles with the Office of Children's Services or to save his family from an imaginary black-ops hit squad. I was counting on that.

"I brought coffee. Let's walk," I said.

He scanned my face, trying to read it. "All right, man. Let's walk." He had on a pair of well-worn Carhartt pants and work boots and a black Dark North Tactical T-shirt. I wore my black Drop Zone T-shirt. We were counterparts and dressed like it. He lit a Marlboro as we stepped out into the thin yellow sunlight and crossed the parking lot toward the road.

"You ready for the big day?" I asked. Even though Brian had a visceral dislike of Schaeffer, he was a businessman like me. Schaeffer's people were his best customers, and he'd give 5 or 10 percent of his sales for the day to his Interior Alaska Conservative Coalition just to make friends. He'd learned what I had—you use what you've got to reach your target demographic, and in both our cases the target demographic was the right-wing crazies. The only difference between him and me was that Brian was a true believer, and I was a pragmatist.

"Yeah, I guess," he said. "So, what's up, man?"

"Schaeffer Cox is fucking nuts, is what's up. Gimme a light."

"Well, no shit," he said with a half-smile as he handed me a lighter. "We've been over that. What the fuck . . . you still smoke those things?"

"Yes, I do." I lit an American Spirit. "You don't like the name?"

"It's not the name, man. Who smokes a fucking organic cigarette?"

"I was raised on organic shit," I said. "I'm doing this for my mother."

He laughed.

"Whatever, man."

As our boots crunched the gravel on the side of the road, I recounted some of the conversation with Cox from the night before.

"That asshole's either going to be governor, or he's going to end up in prison. I haven't decided which," he said.

"Schaeffer's going to get us into a friggin' war up here, you know that, right?" I said.

"To be honest, it doesn't surprise me," he said. "Problem is he's got a lot of people behind him. Personally, I can't stand the guy, but he's got some sheep." Brian took a long drag off his cigarette.

"He told me thousands."

"Are you shitting me?" he said, choking on his coffee. "Thousands? I don't think so. He's got like twenty, thirty, tops, who are armed and ready to party. He seriously says thousands? What, is he counting every group in Alaska?"

"You tell me. And this shit isn't about the Constitution, it's not about the government, it's not about the country. The thing he wants to go to war over isn't any of that. This is just about Schaeffer and his own fucking personal problems. This is about child custody and getting arrested for beating the shit out of his wife. This is just The Schaeffer Cox Show. I'm telling you, it's seriously fucked up."

"That's bullshit. That's total fucking bullshit. But I don't know what you want me to tell you. People up here say they're going to help the guy! They'll do what he says. I'd rather have it be for something real and not just his personal problems. It pisses me off. But they're so fucking stupid they might do it anyway. People want something to happen. They're waiting for it. They'll find an excuse."

I handed Brian my coffee while I re-lit my cigarette. We needed to do something. We needed to cut this guy's balls off, and now.

"Here's my problem," I said. "If he's going to drag everybody into this and get people killed, then he needs to let everyone know exactly what the fuck is going on, and what the plan is, and tell them why. He needs to own his shit. Because right now, he's acting like a guy commanding an army of thousands, with all kinds of weapons, and comms and fortifications. He's not acting like a guy with twenty jackasses with guns. And there's a big difference there."

"Well, everyone's here today." Brian paused and thought. "We've got most of the militia leaders in the area and a lot of their guys coming. We've got the people right here. We could just get everyone together and call a meeting after the sale. Tell that little fucker to explain himself. They'll see him for what he is. These guys aren't outright insane," Brian said. "They don't have a death wish."

Things were starting to jell. There was a window of time, an opportunity to erode the militias' confidence in Cox. We agreed that Brian would call a meeting in the store that evening. We would pass the word around that afternoon at the event to the people who needed to know.

"I'm gonna tell you something." Brian stopped walking and stood for a moment, looking at the ground. He flicked his cigarette butt and as it sputtered across the dirt road, he met my gaze. "I'm just letting you know because you're my friend, if he does do this . . . If the balloon goes up, and the party happens, Schaeffer's going to be the one right out in front, waving the flag. He's going to start this war. But on Day One, or Day Two, after everyone's in but before he gets too big and fucks it all up, he's gonna get taken down. This isn't just me talking, either. Mark my words. Somebody's going to put a bullet in his head, and make it look like the feds did it."

"No shit?"

"Someone's gonna martyr his ass, because nobody wants to deal with Schaeffer's bullshit. He can start it if he wants, but he's not going to own it. He talks a good game, and he sucks people in, but nobody wants a little dictator. Nobody wants a little Hitler, you know what I'm saying?"

I knew *exactly* what he was saying.

"Hey, you've got my blessing, dude. Go for it." I couldn't help but laugh to myself at the irony. Here was Schaeffer Cox the night before, wide-eyed like a scared rabbit, telling me that the FBI had some invisible black-ops hit squad "out to get him" and his family, but in the real world the only people who really had plans to put a cap in him were the militias he considered his adoring followers.

"I hear you, man. Nobody wants a little Hitler." I raised my Styrofoam cup.

Brian started walking again. We'd taken a lap of a few blocks, and the store was in sight.

"But if he starts it, we can't stop it, you know. We're in." I knew he was including me.

As we approached Dark North Tactical from the other side, I tried to imagine the meeting that would take place there that night. I knew that the Fairbanks militia scene was more extreme than what I was used to dealing with in Anchorage, but it was largely an unknown. These were hard-core people who thought Anchorage was too civilized—too "big city." As far as they were concerned, anyone within an hour's drive of Anchorage didn't live in "the real Alaska." They had a point. These were the outlaws of the Last Frontier who thought nothing of sixty degrees below zero in the winter, and ninety degrees above in the summer. They filled their freezers with moose, their garages with enough provisions to withstand a siege, and their basements and tool sheds with firearms and ammo—the bigger and badder the better. They could survive anything, and lived every day preparing for some disaster that would cut them off from the rest of the world, and for the collapse of the government, waiting for the sign. The government was the enemy, and they were the true patriots, ready to die fighting it. Many would just as soon have Alaska secede from the Union while they were at it—a Revolution and a Civil War—two for the price of one. They truly believed that Fairbanks and North Pole could be the new Lexington and Concord. I was just hoping that the shot heard round the world wasn't going to be into the forehead of a federal judge. Not on my watch, anyway.

It was clear to me that Schaeffer Cox, despite having only twenty men in his "Peacemakers Militia," held the power to begin that Fairbanks Revolution. Even if it never went anywhere past Interior Alaska, it could be a complete shit show. I ran the scenario in my mind: Cox and his goons expect Drop Zone to arrest tyrant judges and police officers, we turn them over, they stand trial and are killed or kidnapped—regrettable, but hey, that's war. That would precipitate some ugly shootout with Cox holed up in a bunker with a bunch of his guys, and law enforcement and FBI would swarm, and militias from all over would come to back him up. Then we'd get a nasty, bloody street battle in a city where the available militia likely outnumbers law enforcement 100 to one. After that, who knows? Militia hiding in the woods, picking off federal officers with sniper rifles, in some kind of protracted siege ending in the takeover of Fairbanks? It sounded like a Hollywood movie, but it was not totally out of the realm of possibility. My brain hurt.

Whatever happened in Fairbanks, Cox expected that not only the local militias, but militia groups across the country, emboldened by news of the Alaska uprising, would finally spring into action and take up arms against the tyrannical federal government. And then somehow, at the end of the story, they'd all "get their country back." That was the really delusional part. He reminded me of someone who goes on a shooting rampage, knowing they're committing "suicide by cop," but at least they die knowing their name will be in the paper the next day.

Although they fall within the same political boundaries on a map, Cox's country and my country have little in common. He and his type are ready to die for some mythological Christian theocracy that has never existed and never will exist. I am prepared to die defending my real country from all enemies, foreign and domestic. I swore an oath to do that. And at that moment I had a twenty-something domestic enemy in a tweed cap looking more like a paperboy than a terrorist who needed dealing with. How much damage he could do depended on how many people were willing to follow him and that depended on his influence and credibility at the meeting tonight. And that's what I needed to control. I needed to out him for what he was.

The day passed like a slow-ticking clock. I tried to distract myself by talking to customers, but my thoughts kept snapping back to the mission that night. Make Schaeffer Cox inert. Take away his credibility with his army. If he had no respect, and if he knew he had no backup, he'd be powerless.

Large folding tables filled the parking lot. I'd had the foresight to make sure ours had a white awning that kept everything dry during the intermittent periods of rain throughout the afternoon. There was a Federal Firearms Licensee who had several tables selling firearms, giving the event the air of a gun show. Drop Zone sold MultiCam plate carriers (camo vests that held body-armor plates), soft-sided cases for sniper rifles that allowed you to drag them on the ground behind you to keep your profile low, MultiCam uniforms, utility pouches, and a lot of gear that Brian didn't carry. I made sure we didn't duplicate. You don't steal a friend's sales.

There was a decent turnout with several hundred serious buyers perusing the wares, all wearing the standard Alaskan uniforms—Carhartts, camo, baseball caps with the logos of hunting outfitters or aviation outfits, boots, and a wide assortment of facial hair. And one by one they'd stop by the tables. Some I recognized because they'd stopped in my store in Anchorage, and although there were many I'd be meeting for the first time, they all seemed to know me. "You made my brother-in-law a field medical kit when he came to your place last month," or "I've seen your commercials and keep meaning to stop in when I'm in town." I'd already secured a bit of a reputation in Anchorage, and as far as they were concerned, any friend of Brian's was a friend of theirs.

"So, you know Schaeffer Cox?" I asked a militia commander examining a plate carrier vest.

"Yeah, I know him." He squinted a little, and his rough, sunbaked hands kept fiddling with the straps. "You know him?"

"I've met him." I decided I'd better start planting the seeds of doubt now. "He talks a good game. But honestly, I'm not crazy about the guy."

His crinkly blue eyes looked up from under the rim of his baseball cap. "Now, why's that?"

"I gotta be honest, I'm not happy he's playing fast and loose with people's lives over his own personal issues. He seems like a reactionary. I don't trust his judgment, and I think he's got a lot of people convinced to follow him who don't know the whole story."

I'd laid it out there like I saw it. No mincing words. There wasn't time.

"Hm," he said. "Well, he's always been a damn loudmouth—preaching at people all the time—acting like a big shot. I'll give you that."

I'd found an ally. And so it went for the rest of the day, with militia members, IACC members, and anyone I suspected would end up at our meeting. Many agreed with me but some didn't. I got some nods, and some half-nods, but one of the organizers of the event, Maria Rensel, was not having any of it.

"Well, I know Schaeffer personally through the IACC," she said, over-pronouncing every syllable she spoke with certainty. "And I have nothing but good things to report. Schaeffer is an outspoken young patriot. We need more like him, if you ask my opinion. I think he's just wonderful. Maybe you and your opinion and your little sidekick 'Jesus' should stay in Anchorage."

She flipped her shoulder-length blonde hair and walked away. She reminded me of Sarah Palin but not as smart. I could tell there would be no turning her. She was one of those "I've made up my mind, so don't confuse me with the facts" people. There were too goddamn many of those people.

Rensel aside, everyone had no doubt I was there to support the militias because I believed in the cause, which is what I needed.

The day wore on, with zero feedback from the FBI. The situation certainly wasn't conducive for a phone call to my handlers—too many eyes and ears. Hell, the FBI could have been moving an army up to Fairbanks right then, for all I knew, suited up in body armor and ready for a showdown. I was on a need-to-know basis, and I had no idea what else the FBI had on Cox, if anything. I was flying blind.

By evening, the sale had wound down and I left Jesus to load up the last of the gear into the U-Haul, while I went to get supplies for the meeting. Well, only one supply—a twelve-pack of beer. I find that beer helps to settle the nerves when working undercover with crazy people, and this definitely seemed like a twelve-pack kind of night.

In attendance were supposed to be militia commanders, their seconds-in-command, and one guy for security. When the conversation involves the violent overthrow of the government of the United States, and the room is full of people who are more than a little paranoid, it seemed like a good idea to have security standing by outside to keep watch and guard the pile of cellphones that would be prohibited in the building.

"OK, dude. You're my security guy, so wait outside," I said to Jesus, who had just locked up the U-Haul and hurried over to my car. I thought he'd come to ask for a beer.

"Hey, Boss," his eyes twinkled a little. "Can I carry a shotgun? Please?"

"No, you can't carry a fucking shotgun."

"Well, can I carry a rifle, then?"

"I know you're eighteen, but you're not carrying a shotgun, and you're not carrying a rifle." I felt like a dad.

"But some of the other guys have shotguns . . ."

"Oh, for fuck's sake." Sure enough, five or six guys in camo with assault rifles and shotguns were standing around the parking lot, looking not quite sure what to do with themselves.

"Um. Guys?" I walked over to the group. "This is downtown Fairbanks, right? If a cop drives by here and there's a bunch of guys in camouflage with body armor and assault rifles and shotguns just standing in front of this building, do you think maybe that might look just a bit suspicious?" Looks of "shit, I hadn't thought about that" flashed across their faces. "So, why don't you put those in the truck and just keep your side arms."

They may as well have been carrying signs that said, "Something illegal and nefarious is happening behind this door!" And after what Cox had said last night, it was pretty clear he had no moral issues with killing cops. The last thing I or some unsuspecting cop needed was for him to knock on the door in the middle of this meeting.

Brian was striding past. He'd overheard my suggestion to the troops. He flicked his half-smoked Marlboro into the gravel and stepped on it. "Don't be fucking idiots. Do it." He walked into the shop, not stopping to converse.

"And stop standing right by the door," I added. "Christ! You see that little swing under the spruce tree over there? Go swing."

Firearms were stashed, and Jesus and another guy fully outfitted in body armor sat awkwardly together on the swing as ordered.

I left the happy couple and walked through the darkened doorway. Dark North Tactical smelled like the old log cabin it was—that unmistakable half fire-baked, half rotting-wood smell. Musty and pungent with an overtone of spruce pitch. The thing had been built probably eighty years before, in the middle of nothing, but now it sits squarely in the heart of downtown Fairbanks. It looked like a worse mess from the outside than Drop Zone did, which was saying a lot. Its footprint was maybe a thousand square feet.

I'd left my cellphone with Jesus on the swing. Brian wanded the militia leaders as they entered. Not for weapons. Guns were fine. He checked for wires to catch anyone secretly working for the feds. I was grateful I was clean but glad nobody was monitoring my pulse. Jesus and the rest of the armed security detail waited outside.

I'd sold Brian the bug-detector wand a while back. It didn't work. None of the bug detectors I sold actually worked. We made sure of it. I didn't need that on my conscience. Anyone who needed a bug detector was up to no good. The little lights came on, and every once in a while a fluorescent bulb would set it off, so people just assumed they were operational. The only working bug detectors in Drop Zone were the ones we used ourselves for security jobs. I passed the sweep with flying colors.

I set my twelve-pack of IPA on the counter as more guys filtered in. Eventually the trickle stopped, and the outright waiting began. Where was Cox? I was on beer three by the time Les Zerbe walked in. He'd been in the room the night before when Cox detailed the plan. He hadn't said much but nodded in agreement a lot and grumbled words of approval now and then.

"Where the hell is Schaeffer?" I walked up to Zerbe, who instantly got flushed.

"He's talking with his lawyer," he mumbled, eyes darting around the room, taking in the scene.

"His lawyer? Why the fuck is he talking to his lawyer?" I didn't wait for an answer. "You were in the same room I was last night, and that was supposedly all over, remember?" I started counting on my fingers, "The Revolution's coming, I need you to serve warrants, we're going to arrest people, can you bring guys up here . . . So, what the hell is he back meeting with his lawyer for? That doesn't sound like the conversation we had last night."

There was a plan now, goddamn it. And Cox was going to pull one of his famous 180-degree turnarounds? Not again. Not this time.

Zerbe was looking physically uncomfortable. "I don't know, Bill. We'll just have to wait and see what he says. He'll be here as soon as he can."

By this time, there were about fifteen guys in the room, many of whom I'd talked to during the day. As far as any of them knew, I was committed to the cause. But I'd already started to plant doubts about Cox and his motivations in their hearts and minds. These guys were all committed and took the movement seriously and their responsibility for their men seriously. They would rally to someone's aid if it was a real constitutional issue, but they wouldn't want to risk their own lives, or their men's lives, in a manufactured standoff with the government because Schaeffer Cox didn't feel like taking responsibility for the consequences of his actions.

The conversations covered the usual subjects—what guns you had, the quality of whatever beer you were drinking, which night-vision goggles you wore to kill whom, Ron Paul, and the upcoming election. Typical militia small talk.

In militia world it's all about strength and leadership and how many men will follow you when called. If Cox appeared weak and unstable and reckless with the physical safety of his followers, his support from the other militias would evaporate. His violent plans hinged on the belief he had their support, but if he believed no one would be there to follow him into battle, he wouldn't act alone. At the very least we could buy time, but I wanted to utterly destroy him as a player. I'd had enough of this guy. I guess I did have something personal at stake.

It was impossible to predict exactly how it would go, but whatever happened we could not afford to squander this opportunity. Unless the militias jumped ship, Cox would march forward into his bloody confrontation. He must be dethroned or we'd risk an all-out war in the streets.

Everyone was there but Cox. We waited. And drank beer. And waited. And drank beer. An hour and a half after our designated meeting time, Schaeffer Cox finally showed up in a tweed jacket and the ever-present matching cap. It was showtime. Sandy Klein might be fine in her DC hotel room telling me to fill out paperwork and observe, but this was real-life shit. People's lives were at stake. I didn't have to be doing this. I was under no obligation to take orders from the FBI like some criminal informant working to reduce his sentence. I couldn't live with myself if someone got killed while I was sitting there in the back of the class taking notes.

By the time Cox finally showed up, I was a little drunker than I should have been. First things first.

"Hey, man. Before we get started here, do you have something for me?"

He stared at me. "I . . . I'm not sure . . ."

I lowered my voice and leaned in. "You have names, places, right? Who am I supposed to bring in? The plan."

"Plan? I'm not sure what you mean, Bill. Plan for what?"

I remembered the Cox from the previous night. He was serious. Deadly so. This was the Republican convention all over again. Just like the plan to overthrow Ruedrich, when he was all in, and hours later, bailed.

I stood there, an undercover FBI operative, with potential egg on my face in a room full of annoyed badasses with guns, who'd been waiting for "something," and at the mercy of an unpredictable militia leader with homicidal tendencies. In a fucking tweed cap. I knew it wasn't *if* Schaeffer Cox was going to snap, it was *when*. And I was caught off guard for the second time with this asshole. But this wasn't some backroom political vote tally, it was life-or-death stuff, and I couldn't let it pass. If he wasn't going to talk about the plan, I sure as hell was. This was going to end. Now.

"You don't have a plan? What do you mean you don't have a plan? You sure as fuck had a plan last night!" I have a loud voice anyway, but I jacked up the volume to make sure it filled the rest of the room, which wasn't hard. Silence fell immediately.

"You told me to get my men up here and start arresting people! I was on the phone last night setting this up. You can't just tell me it was all bullshit, Schaeffer! Zerbe was sitting right there and heard the whole fucking thing."

Cox looked around the room unable to fix on anyone, and it became clear immediately that nobody there knew about his plan to start a war with the feds. He was counting on them to back him up, and yet they were completely in the dark.

"I think you're overreacting a little bit, Bill. I never said that there was actually a 'plan.'"

"You don't think that arresting judges and *hanging them* is a 'plan'? You are ready to start a fucking war with the feds, and you're expecting the physical support of every asset in this room. You are expecting these guys to put it all on the line for you, and you're hiring me to start it—and they don't even fucking *know*? *Are you kidding me*?"

Cox looked terrified, and Zerbe rose to his defense.

"I don't know who in the hell you think you are, son . . . coming up here and acting like you own the place, with your little assistant out there you call 'Jesus.' You say you're on our side, and you try to act like one of us, but know what? I think you're a damn phony. I don't know you. None of us know you. Why don't you just get out of here and go on home to Anchorage."

That was it. The moment of truth. The alpha-male challenge, and it came from Zerbe, not Cox. I wasn't about to lose a round to that asshole, either. I scanned the room. Situational awareness. Brian at my right. Four-foot-deep counter in front of me. Zerbe behind it. Knife in my pocket.

"Are you calling me a liar, old man?" My face was hot, and I locked eyes like a bull.

"*Yes, I am.*" Zerbe just stood there, his pudgy face absurdly red against his shock of white hair. His fists clenched. My fists clenched. It was Tombstone.

"If . . . you *ever* . . . question my integrity again, I will slit your goddamn throat and bleed you out at my feet, *you fucking son of a bitch*!"

I lunged at Zerbe across Brian's path. Brian grabbed me, his arms around me tight like I knew he would. I struggled. Zerbe's eyes were saucers. Every muscle in my body was taut and straining to get at him.

"Get back here, you fucking piece of shit!" I growled, as he stumbled backwards through the door into the back room. His eyes were glued to me, arms fumbling as he tried to find the door behind him. I was raw emotion, out of control, raging. That's what people saw. That's what I wanted them to see. I wanted to erase Zerbe's accusations from their minds. I wanted to scare them. I wanted them to know that my integrity was never to be questioned. Ever. My life depended on it.

Zerbe, engulfed by the darkness, backed out the side entrance. A motorcycle engine rumbled, and the tires spun through the gravel as he sped out of the lot. Cox had literally backed himself into the corner and was white as ash. His backup was gone. Brian had relaxed his grip, and I wheeled to face Cox, calmer now but still bristling.

"And you listen to me, you little shitbag. I've seen you pull this crap too many times. Your word, and your promises, and your plans mean jack-fucking-shit! Don't ever fucking call me again. Ever. If shit goes down, and someone in this room needs me, I'm there. But I'm taking my orders from Brian, and Brian only. Not from you, you little punk-ass motherfucker."

I was about eight inches from his face, finger in his chest, when he side-stepped and moved silently, trying not to run to the door, and backed out with an awkward nod, adjusting his cap in a last attempt at dignity.

There was absolute silence in the room.

"What the fuck, dude! I never saw you go off like that, man! Holy fuck-ing shit!" Brian's laugh broke the tension. "Remind me never to question your loyalty, bro." He slapped me on the back, still laughing.

The rest of the room visibly relaxed, and I had gained a new respect. In the testosterone power play, I can give as good as the next guy. And right now I was alpha dog, and Schaeffer Cox and Les Zerbe were off somewhere like whimpering Chihuahuas with their tails between their legs.

"I fucking hate that guy," I said, in case anyone missed it, and drained the last of my sixth Heineken. "What a weak-ass, self-serving little prick. You know he was ready to drag you guys into a fucking war because he hit his wife and didn't want to man up to it. That's *his* fucking problem, not yours," I said to the room in general. I began to calm down, now that I realized it had worked, and the balance of power had now shifted from Cox to Brian.

The room was still filled with the energy and smell of a fight. No sooner had the door shut than the smack-talk began. Several guys came over to me, and I felt suddenly like a respected member of the group in my own right. "Right on, brother. I've been thinking that shit for a while." "I don't know who he thinks he is. He's got some kind of delusion of grandeur." "I ain't at his beck and call. He's full of shit." "I finally met someone who can make Schaeffer Cox shut the fuck up!"

There was laughing and backslapping and posturing, and after a few min-utes, the room began to empty. It was then I saw a dark-haired, frail-looking man sitting in the corner, silent. His eyes were fixed on me with a squint.

I'd bought a hot dog from him earlier in the afternoon. He was twitchy and looked like he was trying to be invisible, hiding in rumpled clothes that were strangely big on him. I walked over.

"Bill Fulton," I said, holding my hand out.

"Yeah, I know who you are," he said, arms remaining tightly folded across his narrow chest, eyes staring straight ahead.

"What's your name?"

He looked around like he wanted someone to save him, but seeing no one, said, "Michael Anderson." My brain searched the files. I'd just heard that name . . . Ah. Cox's database manager who had been collecting the information on the people I was supposed to arrest. I had a feeling I wasn't going to win him over, so I memorized his face and turned away with a "Good to meet you."

There was bound to be some kind of repercussion from all this, but I was focused on the present moment. Mission accomplished. That's all that mattered. I'd gotten rid of Zerbe, told Cox to go piss up a rope, and broken the back of his support. Nobody was going to blindly take orders from Schaeffer Cox anymore. It was a good day.

After the group had dispersed, Brian looked at me and shook his head.

"That was nuts, man. I thought you were going to fucking kill him," he laughed.

"Good thing he got out when he did."

"I'm actually proud of you, man. I've never seen you that mad before, and I've known you for like six years. Shit. Way to go."

"Thanks, Bri. Thanks for having my back."

"Any time, brother."

I walked out into the late-evening twilight, which at that time of year in Alaska lasts for hours. It could have been 9 p.m., or it could have been 11, or 1 a.m. I had no idea.

Jesus was standing outside the door.

"I thought I was going to have to come in there. I thought people were going to start shooting people."

"You heard that?"

"Yeah, I heard that. I actually made a call to Anchorage and told the guys to get ready to get their asses up here, because I didn't know what was going on. I told Suicide back at the shop to get ready to come to Fairbanks. I said there's something going on with the boss and it's not good. I didn't know what to do."

Clearly I'd made an impression, even through the log walls of the cabin.

"Well, call the guys back and tell them to stand down. It's all good." Jesus was heading back to Anchorage, and I was going back to the motel to stay another day with my wife and daughter. I'd promised them a trip to Frontierland and Santa Claus House the next day.

"I think I need a ride back to the room," I said. I was still pretty pumped up but I knew I'd blow a DUI badly if it came down to it.

"Hey, Boss?" Jesus said, as we pulled out. "This was cool and everything, and I really appreciate the opportunity, and your confidence in me, but can someone else do the next one?"

"Sure, Jesus, that's fine. I really appreciated your help up here, but you don't have to come on the next one."

"Thanks, Boss. Because I really don't want to die." He was completely serious and utterly relieved. Here he was, hulking and six-foot-three, looking like the guy in the bar who wanted to crush your skull. But in reality, he was still a teenager, longing for action and adventure and adulthood but not quite ready to handle the reality. It never occurred to him that he could just say no or tell me to piss off. He was asking permission first, not to have to die. I loved that kid.

He drove me back to the little cabin, I gave him $200 for the week, another couple of twenties to fill the tank, and sent him on his way back to Anchorage.

"Pull over and sleep if you get tired," I said. "Don't make me worry."

Back at our little one-room cabin, Stacey and Emma were fast asleep. I stepped outside for a smoke and called Sandra Klein.

She said, "Oh, my God" a lot.

"You were supposed to *observe*. Ob-serve, Bill. That means *watch*, and pay attention, and report back. Not threaten to cut someone's throat. Oh, my God . . . Did you really actually say that? In those words?"

"Yes, I did. And, I like to think that a good 'observer' will cut the balls off a fucking psychopath who wants to kill people when given the opportunity, Sandy. So maybe we have different definitions. I don't like to 'observe' people getting killed."

"Well, what's done is done. You're going to have some major paperwork to fill out, you know. I'm not even sure what happens now. I can't believe you actually . . . oh, my God."

I was still so amped on adrenaline that I did the paperwork that night. I didn't care. As long as Schaeffer Cox was no longer an immediate threat, I was happy. He was no longer my problem. And this time, he was out of my life for sure. Bridge burned.

CHAPTER 16

★ ★ ★ ★ ★

THE NAKED BITER

"For if you forgive men when they sin against you, your
heavenly Father will also forgive you."
—**Matthew 6:14**

The weekend in Fairbanks was under my belt, and Stacey was never the wiser. She commented that I shouldn't have had so much to drink but was glad I was responsible and got a ride. I powered through my hangover at Santa Claus House like a champ, and let Stacey take the wheel on the way home.

Now I was back with my band of brothers in the world of Drop Zone, and things felt comfortable again. Normal. I was finished squaring off with insane people I didn't know and content simply to sell camo-covered Bibles and snow boots to the ones I did.

The beer was brewing in the back room next to a big pink Victorian dollhouse I was building Emma for next Christmas. I had no idea how long it was going to take so I had started early. The guys were bullshitting and laughing and working on various little projects, and it was as close to a scene of domestic bliss as you could hope to find at a military surplus store full of bounty hunters with dysfunctional personal lives.

"What's with all the Domino's uniforms?" asked Discount, holding up a red-and-blue polyester polo shirt.

"We got 'em at Salvation Army," I said. "We're going on a mission tonight. Special delivery."

I had learned over the years that the best, most infallible way to get someone to open a door was by standing on the other side of it with a pizza box. It doesn't matter if they ordered pizza or not. People see pizza, they open the door. And since our lucky fugitive for the night was staying in a motel, we were hoping not to have to break the door down and deal with the wrath of management.

"There's pizza too. Eat up, we need the empty boxes."

When we got back later that evening, the fire was blazing in the back parking lot. We racked our guns, inventoried, and stowed the body armor in the office. The store had been closed for at least an hour, but Discount, the Big Mexican, Grease, and Clay sat in a semicircle, faces flickering in the orange glow; they were drinking beer out of red plastic Solo cups in that half-mesmerized way you do anything when you're staring at a fire.

"You get the bad guy?" Clay asked when we caught his eye.

Suicide, Hippie Alpha, Sunshine, and Gunny had rounded out the mission team and we were all glad for the fire and the beer.

"Yup, Mr. Mendoza is now in the loving care of Anchorage's finest."

"No hitches?" asked the Big Mexican.

"Another naked one. Good times." I answered.

They all groaned. Nobody liked the naked ones.

"A biter, too—a naked biter! It was like double good times," said Sunshine. The naked biters were the worst. There was a hierarchy of fugitives, and biters were on the bottom rung of the ladder. Naked biters were below the bottom rung, and the price they paid for making us deal with their shit was that they were not afforded the opportunity to get dressed before we took them to the station. It was a simple matter of principle.

They waited for the rest of the story and as Sunshine gave a deliberate sideways look at Gunny, they realized that it was his story to tell.

"A naked biter . . . No shit?" said Clay, and he and the others fixed their gazes on Gunny, who had pulled up a collapsible camp chair and now sat with his giant fingers interlaced behind his head and his black boots stretched toward the flames. They weren't sure why it was Gunny's story and couldn't possibly imagine that the naked guy was stupid enough to have bitten Gunny, but naked guys had done pretty stupid things before. They leaned forward and waited. Gunny took a whetstone from his front pocket and a knife out of the sleeve of his coat and began sharpening it, like the scary badass version of an old guy on a porch whittling a piece of wood. He took a deep breath and exhaled.

"Motherfucker bit me," he said.

"And?" said Clay after a few seconds.

"I put his head through the wall," he said.

"And?!"

"And it went through the wall," Gunny said with finality.

Gunny had a way of distilling a story down to its essence.

My cell rang. *SK* flashed on the screen—Sandra Klein.

I moved inside where I could talk.

"S'up, lady?"

"Well, I'm reaching out because I need to know we can still count on your help with something. This is kind of a big one."

"You know you can count on me. Just no more Schaeffer Cox. What's going on?"

"We need you to call Schaeffer Cox and apologize."

". . . You're fucking kidding me, right?"

"I know this is difficult for you . . ."

"No, Sandra. That was an actual question. I'll repeat it. You are fucking kidding me, *right*?"

"Bill, you have to."

"You seem to forget, I don't owe you anything. I'm not one of your criminal informants. I'm a volunteer. I don't *have* to do shit."

"I remember when a guy walked into my office and said he wanted to serve his country. He wanted to protect people. He wanted to save lives. I need to know I'm still talking to that guy."

She knew what buttons to push to override my good sense, and even my hatred of that little pissant, Schaeffer Cox. All I had to do, she said, was call and mend fences. That was it.

"You're killing me. You know you're killing me, right?"

"We are so grateful, Bill. Really. Thank you. I know this is a lot to ask."

It took me three tries before I could actually dial Cox's number all the way through.

"Hello?"

"Hey, Schaeffer. Bill Fulton."

"Oh . . ."

"Hey, hear me out for a second, don't hang up . . . Look, I know we've had our rough spots. I get passionate sometimes . . . and I know I kind of . . . went a little too far. Zerbe kinda pushed my buttons, you know? I just want to bury the hatchet and tell you I respect you, and this state is too small to hold grudges, so I hope we can start over."

There was a long pause.

"I'll be honest with you, Bill. I wasn't expecting this call from you, after Fairbanks. Your behavior to me and to Les up there was really . . ."

"Yeah, the way we left things has really been bothering me. And I just felt like I needed to call. We're really on the same side, in the big picture. And that's what we should be focusing on. I can get a little carried away. I lost sight of things. I'd had a few beers . . ."

I went out of my way not to actually apologize. Just for my own self-respect.

"Well . . . it takes a big man to admit he was wrong, and apologize like this, Bill . . ." This phone call was going to kill me. Physically kill me. "If there's one lesson we get from Jesus Christ, it's to forgive, right?"

"You said it, buddy. Amen." I wanted to throw the phone. Throw it, and stomp it with my boot, and hurl its mangled remains into the fire. "I just hope you can see it in your heart to give me another chance."

"Well, I really do appreciate the apology, Bill. Let's let bygones be bygones, then. We can let all that go."

"That sounds awesome, man."

"You know, it's actually funny you should call right now, because I've got some guys coming down for the big militia conference in Anchorage next month. I'll be there if I can, but Marti is expecting around that time, so I might send them in to see if you can help us acquire some equipment."

"Congratulations on the baby! We're expecting one any day now too, a little girl. What do you need? I can see if I've got it in stock."

"Well, that's great! And thanks, we're pretty excited. But I think that this is probably a transaction better handled in person rather than over the phone lines."

Suddenly it clicked in my head. Cox was looking for illegal weapons, and *that* was why the FBI wanted me to make contact. Because, of course, the FBI never told me anything. It was all "need to know," as I was constantly reminded. They told me what to do; I did it. They asked me what was said; I met with them and told them. My relationship with Sandy and Dirk was like gossiping with a friend who never gave you anything back. One-way information. No context. Minimal disclosure.

And now they needed another favor. Unless I mended fences with Cox, he'd go to someone who wasn't me, and the FBI would be in the dark. I was ready to bet money they wanted me to be the "illegal weapons dealer" for this transaction.

"I hope you're fucking happy, Sandy." I called her back as instructed after the call to Cox.

"You did it?"

"Yes."

"You're awesome, Bill! I know that sucked. I'm sorry."

"Yeah, but you don't know how *much* it sucked. I hate that guy."

"I think I've heard you say that before," she said.

I told Sandy that Cox was sending down two of his militia members. She was pleased and told me the FBI would be wiring my hotel room for the militia conference with audio and video, and that I was to invite them into my room when the time came, and be sure to clearly establish that they were acting on Schaeffer Cox's behalf. That they were working for him. Get them talking. Whatever they asked for, say yes. Buy them dinner, promise weapons they want, give them enough rope to hang themselves, and send the receipts to the FBI.

As I made my way back out to the fire, I thought to myself that I was perfectly happy to have them hang themselves instead of someone else.

CHAPTER 17

★ ★ ★ ★ ★

AIN'T NOBODY GONNA KEEP ME DOWN

"What is good for Alaska is good for the country.
Transferring power from the federal government to the
states provides opportunity to all states, not just Alaska."
—Joe Miller

I don't know how I got talked into being Eddie Burke's campaign manager. And I don't know how he thought he was going to become the lieutenant governor of the state of Alaska. All that right-wing talk radio had warped his brain and also given him a taste for politics, so there he was on the Republican ticket. It was more about building his personal brand than the idea that he could actually win. And I understood that. It was the reason I went to most of the events I did. The brand makes the business. Besides, Eddie was fun to be around, and when he asked me to run his campaign, after he'd recorded our latest radio ad, I said yes. Running the campaign was a challenge, particularly when my candidate became known in the news media for brandishing a gun (for emphasis) while making a joke about Barack Obama at a holiday Toys for Tots fundraising banquet. Nothing says Merry Christmas like making the $250-a-plate crowd gasp and cower in their chairs. It was all great, if you subscribe to the belief that any attention is good attention. Despite his bull-in-a-china-shop cluelessness, and his Yosemite Sam campaign tactics, I managed to raise $10,000 for him, which may not sound like much but it wasn't easy. I also made a lot of Republican political contacts for myself.

On the August primary night of the 2010 midterm election, Eddie and I were at Election Central, a large venue in the downtown Anchorage Convention Center where all the candidates and their supporters go when the polls close. Supporters rally, the media sets up interview locations around the perimeter of the room, and four large screens display the vote tallies of the races as they come in. Volunteers for the campaigns stake out a local watering hole, and at the appropriate time they abandon their celebration, march half-loaded from the bar to the convention center, and usher their candidate into the room with balloons and campaign signs. There's even a full bar in the corner so they can start drinking again. Alaska knows how to do elections.

Eddie was holding steady at about 15 percent of the vote.

"That ain't half fucking bad," he said, with his arms folded across his chest, looking pleased. And considering what I had to work with, he was right.

Campaigning for Eddie Burke in 2010.

After the unsuccessful coup attempt at the Republican Convention, Joe Miller had retreated back to Fairbanks to regroup. He decided to ratchet up his political aspirations with a run for the US Senate against moderate incumbent Republican Lisa Murkowski. He'd attacked Murkowski hard from the right. Miller supporters from the Second Amendment Task Force marched in a July parade wearing "Miller for Senate" T-shirts and waving signs with semiautomatic rifles slung over their backs. News of a candidate marching with "assault rifles" touched off a media firestorm in the Lower 48, and Miller told ABC News, "You know, guns are a pretty big thing up here in Alaska. It's not unusual at political rallies and parades to see that kind of thing. Probably, though, in the Lower 48, it does raise some eyebrows."

It raised some eyebrows in Alaska, too.

Sarah Palin had put her full weight behind Miller again. By this time, she'd quit the governorship to go on a lucrative book tour, but she still had some influence. She had caused a huge rift in the Republican Party in Alaska, and after her national tour with John McCain, she'd been even more successful driving a wedge into the party on a national level. She was the Queen of the Tea Party.

That night as we watched the screens update with new vote tallies, it became clear that the far-right base had turned out in force to vote, and apathetic moderates stayed home believing Murkowski was a shoo-in. The room was buzzing. This could be a huge upset. TV stations were seeking out Miller for interviews. Murkowski never retook her slim lead, and when the race was called for Miller, people in the room looked utterly shocked. In the end, Miller won by a mere 2,006 votes, but it was a win. Nobody was more stunned at the victory than Miller himself.

Eddie Burke was not so lucky. He came in third, with 13.91 percent—just over 14,000 votes—losing to a much more moderate Republican, Meade Treadwell. But he'd gotten his moment in the sun.

I felt someone grab my arm from behind.

"Hey, Bill. I'm trying to regroup here, and I'm just wondering if you happen to have any body armor I could use for the night."

I'd been looking for nominee Miller, but he found me first.

It was time for episode two of being Joe Miller's Secret Service, guarding him from shadowy establishment Republicans who might want to kill

Primary night 2010—Eddie Burke (L) shakes hands with Joe Miller (R), while I look on. Photo by Zach D. Roberts.

Joe Miller's 2010 campaign T-shirt. Photo by Zach D. Roberts.

him for some unspecified reason. I knew the drill. I ran out to the Hummer and met him in the men's room to fit him with a spare set of body armor under his designer-suit.

"We mobilized the base," Miller said as I slipped the vest around his shoulders. I could feel the heat and adrenaline coming off his body in waves. "Everybody thought Lisa was just going to walk away with it, because she's the incumbent with the power of the office. Nobody thought we could do it, but I'm telling you—Alaska is ready for a change. It's in the air."

"My hat's off to you, man. You pulled it off. Unfuckingbelievable. Murkowski HQ has got to be drinking heavily about now."

"They want someone who is actually concerned with the liberty of the people. They want someone who believes in sovereignty, freedom, the culture of life . . . They want someone who will defend them against Obama's gun policies—not a Democrat in Republican clothing. The ones paying attention show up. The ones content with the status quo stay home."

"You realize nobody knows who the fuck the Democrat is in this race, and you just toppled the Murkowski dynasty. You're the next senator, man."

"Change is coming," he said, adjusting his new body armor and straightening his tie in the mirror. "And the people are ready for it."

Miller mingled and did interviews and nobody knew about his extra layer. As the evening wore down, I escorted him to his hotel room a few blocks away, but I still had work to do that night. I would much rather have gone home and seen my new little Olivia before my girls went to bed. But duty called.

Salty Pete's Seafood Buffet was many things, but an upscale fresh Alaska seafood restaurant was not one of them. I never understood how Alaska could support a crappy frozen, imported seafood chain when amazing fresh fish was everywhere to be found. It must have been either the ridiculously stocked bar, the fishbowl-sized tropical drinks, or the all-you-can-eat fried clam bowl known as "The Barge," but Salty Pete's always drew a crowd.

Summer crowds were often rowdy, and during the tourist season they hired Drop Zone to work security at the doors—checking IDs, brawl prevention, calling cabs for drunks. Tuesday was "All Night Happy Hour" and the Big Mexican and Suicide were on the job. But the Big Mexican wasn't feeling well and I told him I'd come relieve him when I was done with Miller.

The drink special that night was the "Blue Parrot," a goblet the size of my head filled with eight kinds of rum and what looked like pool water and fruit salad. And, of course, an umbrella.

The Big Mexican took off, and Suicide said we might have a problem at the end of the bar. He pointed to a group of three women who were laughing loudly and calling out to other patrons at the tables. Not surprisingly the worst offender was sitting before an almost empty goldfish bowl and digging out chunks of blue, alcohol-soaked pineapple with her fingers.

"What are you lookin' at?" she called to a group of college kids at a table. "You got a problem?"

They turned away, quickly, and Ed the bartender looked at me with a raised eyebrow.

"I need another one! I loooove me some blue parrot! Another drink, bartender!"

Ed leaned in to her and said something I couldn't hear.

"You said what? You are cutting me OFF? I don't think so, honey." She held up a finger. "I am a proud black woman, and nobody gonna cut me off."

"Oh, shit, here we go," said Suicide.

We walked down to the end of the bar where I dutifully explained the finer points of alcohol service law to the woman and her friends and offered to call them a cab.

"A cab? A CAB? We ain't takin' no cab. This night hasn't even started!"

"Ma'am, I really think you should consider just going home at this point."

"You do, do you? Well, I think you ought to consider leaving me the fuck alone," she slurped the dregs of the blue parrot with a straw, "at this point."

Ed made a motion across his throat with his finger and eyeballed the woman.

"Ma'am, I need to inform you that this is private property and if you do not cooperate I will have to arrest you for trespassing."

"You a cop?" she said, jabbing me in the chest with a long purple fingernail. "You don't look like no cop. If you a cop, let me see your cop papers. Let me see a badge."

That was never a good sign. She tried to get off the bar stool and almost fell. Suicide and I both grabbed an arm so she wouldn't hit the deck. And her fate was sealed. Fingernail in chest, arms held—we had no choice but to arrest. She screamed bloody murder. Suicide slipped the cuffs on, and I brought her back to our customary holding area—an old unused coatroom. She was more compliant than I thought she'd be and I was relieved because I guessed she was about six feet without the heels and probably outweighed me by 150 pounds at least. She didn't look that big on the barstool.

Two chairs were set up in the coatroom, which was about four-by-six feet. I shut the door.

There are rules about putting people in cuffs. The first one is you can't leave them alone in case they injure themselves. I'd sat in this coat closet many times before, and it wouldn't be my last time. It was uncomfortably small, but the police were usually quick to the scene. My charge glared at me from the chair.

"You can't arrest me," she said.

"And yet I just did," I said.

"You got a smart mouth."

"That's what I've been told."

She went to stand again and swayed dangerously.

"You need to sit down, ma'am," I said and grabbed her arm to guide her back down on to the chair.

"Did you just touch me? Did you TOUCH me? You do not touch me! Do you know why?"

"Because you're a proud black woman?"

"You damn RIGHT!" she said and on the word "right" I felt a blinding pain as her enormous leg forced a three-inch spike heel into my shoulder. "I *am* a proud black woman, motherfucker, and ain't nobody gonna keep me down!" She launched herself out of the chair directly at me. Her arms were immobilized, but that didn't stop the fact that she could have been a linebacker for a halfway-decent college football team. Chair and I went hurtling back against the wall. She took a step back and I tried to stand.

"You need to sit, ma'am, now!" I said, trying unsuccessfully to exude confidence and authority while scrambling to my feet.

"*You* need to shut the fuck up and take these handcuffs off me," she said, and body slammed me into the back of the door, shattering its full-length mirror.

"Ma'am, you are being destructive."

"You want destructive? You want destructive? I'll show you destructive!"

Another body slam. My hand was bleeding from the broken glass. "Destruct *that*, asshole!" She was in the cuffs, so I couldn't beat her even if I wanted to attempt it. APD finally arrived and opened the door. My face was bloody by this point, and the only reason she had stopped beating the crap out of me was that she got tired.

"Oh, Christ. It's Jasmine," the cop said to his partner over his shoulder. "Listen, you hang tight, Bill. I'm going to call for backup before we move her. Last time she broke the damn door on the squad car."

"Come on, man!" I said, but the door was already closed.

The radio crackled, "Yeah, we got a proud black woman over here at Salty Pete's and we're going to need another unit . . . Roger that."

Eventually, the proud black woman was hauled out by four large officers, two holding her elbows and two holding her knees. It still presented a challenge.

"What the fuck, man!" said Suicide when I walked out of the coat closet.

"Yeah, I'm going to get out of here now," I said. My lip was already swollen and my eye was catching up. "I may be late tomorrow."

"No worries. Patch yourself up. And I'm not gonna say anything about what happened. Because you'll never hear the end of that shit!"

"Yeah, please don't." I thanked him, and hobbled to my car. The cruiser pulled past me, and I saw out of my non-swollen eye a large hand with purple nails pressed against the window, giving me the finger.

CHAPTER 18

★ ★ ★ ★ ★

THE ARREST HEARD 'ROUND THE WORLD

"The media's the most powerful entity on earth. They have the power to make the innocent guilty and to make the guilty innocent, and that's power. Because they control the minds of the masses."

—Malcolm X

My goodwill with Joe Miller paid off, and Drop Zone became "Team Paranoia," the future senator's go-to security force. As the Republican nominee from a red state, Miller seemed headed inevitably for a seat in the United States Senate. I hoped that my history of established trust with him would lead to bigger opportunities in the future. Maybe I could even be an advisor on veterans' issues. It never hurts to be in good with a senator.

Miller's fear and anxiety continued to build throughout the campaign. He was not your typical Randy-Ruedrich-oily-corrupt bastard. Joe Miller was an ideologue. As voters learned more about him and some of his more extreme views, Democrats and moderate Republicans started to become nervous, just as "Tea Party Patriots," libertarians, and the militias flocked to his side. Seeing Democrats' lack of organization, and the hailstorm of criticism pounding Miller, the vanquished incumbent Lisa Murkowski decided to launch a write-in campaign with heavy backing from moneyed interests. Her chance of winning a write-in campaign was a long shot, but it got shorter every day.

Miller accused the Alaska "liberal media" of waging a disinformation campaign against him, focusing on allegations that he had illegally used Fairbanks borough computers in that ill-fated attempt to oust Republican Party Chair Randy Ruedrich. The attack was focused specifically at the *Alaska Dispatch*, a fledgling news website struggling not to be called a blog. The site claimed that Miller was "politicking" on borough computers while working part-time as a Fairbanks North Star Borough attorney. Miller said someone illegally leaked his personnel file to the *Dispatch*, which then decided to sue the Fairbanks Borough for the file. Mixing government work and political campaigns is always taboo. It's what Sarah Palin went after Ruedrich for to get her "anticorruption" credentials. But Miller either didn't learn the lesson or thought he could get away with it.

He had also been accused of hypocrisy by the press. He was always ready to criticize the "entitlement mentality" of society and especially liberals, even as it was shown that he and his wife obtained low-income hunting-and-fishing licenses while he had a $70,000-a-year job and received agricultural subsidies on land he wasn't farming; and that his family of eight children had benefitted from both state and federal low-income medical benefits in the past. Even some of his right-wing support was beginning to have second thoughts.

After an interview with Fox News' Greta Van Susteren, who had come to Alaska to cover his campaign, Miller gathered the press around him to make an announcement. A group of print journalists with little notebooks, local radio stations with headphones and microphones, and TV cameras from small local stations up to Fox News national huddled in. The Alaska media was obsessed with reporting on what Miller considered irrelevant issues, such as his past government benefits. He singled out the *Alaska Dispatch*, whose wealthy new owner had made maximum donations to his opponent Lisa Murkowski's campaign, as the worst offender of "journalistic impropriety" and unfair mudslinging.

"We've drawn a line in the sand," Miller said to the crowd. "You can ask me about background, you can ask me about personal issues—but I'm not going to answer. I'm not. This is about the issues. This is not about continuing the personal attacks, it's not about continuing the diversions based in illegal acts. This is about moving the state forward. And that's our commitment."

The press went insane, most of all the *Alaska Dispatch*. It was trying to prove its legitimacy as a news source, and Miller had gone out of his way to name it as a bunch of irresponsible bloggers. The gloves were off.

This all-out media war became the best entertainment in the state. Long before Alaska was the subject of literally dozens of reality shows, anyone following Alaska politics had a front-row seat to the granddaddy of them all.

It was less than a week after the press was cut off from asking questions that Miller didn't want to answer, that he leased out a school building for a town hall-style event. Questions would be taken from the public. How they or the press were going to be censored was anyone's guess. Bloggers salivated. Democratic operatives plotted how to get in. And the media, which had just been told that Miller was off-limits, was frothing. Out-of-state handlers arrived to try to keep things in line and secure another Tea Party seat in Congress.

Before the Town Hall, I made sure to go over procedure with my security detail for the day. Who knew what kinds of idiots were going to make a ruckus. We needed to be prepared, review the rules, treat this like any other event where we provided security, and not let anything get fucked up. If Joe Miller was happy, everyone was happy, and I wanted everyone happy.

A woman eyeballed my suit and earpiece and asked me who I was.

"I'm security."

"Whose security? Ours? Why do we need security?"

"It's the law, ma'am. This is a public school, and the lease states any event held here has to have security. So, that would be us. Is there a problem of some kind?"

"It's just the suit . . . and the earpiece. It's so . . . Can you try not to *look* like security?"

"Look, ma'am. I can't *not* look like security. When we look like security, it keeps people in line, which is kind of the point of *having* security. We want to be a *deterrent*, not a cleanup crew."

"Well, just don't stand by the candidate. Don't let them get you in the same photo. Just sit and try to blend in as best you can, but be ready to go if there's an incident," she said. "And you did not see me or my organization here, if anyone asks."

"I don't even know who you are or what your organization is."

"Catherine. We're up from California. And we're not here. Got it?"

"Sure. You're Catherine and you're not here."

I had been told by the campaign that there might be people "looking to cause trouble" at the event, and at this point it rang true. It didn't seem like the ol' crazy paranoid Joe I knew at the Republican convention, worrying for nothing. The media was a pack of hyenas, and Miller was a wounded antelope. The masses were getting touchy too, and although I wasn't expecting violence, I didn't put it past a Democrat or a disgruntled Republican to try to start an incident to make Miller look bad.

The election was less than a month away, and every single thing was critical. The last thing anyone needed was another "October surprise." I was to keep the peace, get Miller out of the room the second the event was over, and allow zero hostile contact as he walked through the crowd to leave through a back door to his car. Suicide, Sunshine, and the Big Mexican were my crew for the day—all experienced, all capable. I briefed them on the event and checked the lease paperwork to make sure everything was in order. The campaign had the legal right to exclude or eject anyone from the event for any reason, so if things got tense we could ask the offending party or parties to leave, citing trespass laws. I had done this a hundred times, and had it down to a science. I taught classes on it. I could do it in my sleep.

As the event drew to a close, nothing terrible had happened. He took a few questions after his speech and that was that. Miller nodded to the applause and held up a hand to signal goodbye to the crowd. The place was packed. I was situated close to the podium and began to move to the back of the room. Then I sensed a disturbance in the crowd and turned to see a man pushing toward the candidate against the flow. He had some-thing in his hand, but I couldn't tell what it was. He began shouting, "Joe! Joe! Hey! Over here!" Miller swiveled his head to the shouting and caught my eye over the tops of heads. He had that same scared-rabbit look as when he asked me for body armor on primary night. I struggled through the crowd, calling, "Security, excuse me!" as Suicide signaled he'd seen me and knew what I needed. He closed in from the other side. Sunshine was lost in the sea somewhere near Miller, and the Big Mexican, posted at the door to the back hallway, shoved himself quickly behind Miller as he passed to buffer him from the crowd, but they pushed and followed him down the hallway. This was unraveling fast. The Big Mexican couldn't shut the door on a stream of people who surged after Miller.

I made it to the door as fast as I could. The man was stocky with dark hair and still clutched something as he approached, calling, "Joe! Hey!" I shoved myself through, yelling "Security!" and put myself between the man and Joe, who was full on crazy-eyed by this point.

"Sir, I need to ask you to leave," I said, almost out of breath.

"Who the hell are *you*?"

"I'm security, sir, and I need to ask you to leave the premises. Now."

"I didn't do anything. I don't have to go anywhere. This is public prop-erty," he said, his voice rising.

"Sir, I've given you a warning. You are trespassing at a private event and you need to leave. Do you understand me? If you do not leave, I will have to arrest you."

The crowd pressed in, someone got too close to the man for comfort, and he turned and shoulder-checked the guy right into a bank of lock-ers. It wasn't particularly violent, but physical contact had definitely been made. And once that happened, the rules changed. This had escalated the encounter to another level whether I wanted it or not. This guy needed to be shut down immediately. It was now a question of my own legal liability and that of the candidate. Physical assaults were absolutely not tolerated. No more asking, no more explanations. It was non-negotiable. I had to arrest this idiot and get him isolated and immobilized so no one got hurt.

"Don't touch me! You can't do this to me," he yelled, making sure everyone could hear.

"And yet, I am."

"You can't do this! I'm a journalist!"

"I don't care who you are or what your job is," I said as I zipped a pair of handcuffs on him. "You're not allowed to assault people, and you're going to come over here and sit down quietly while I call the police to report the assault."

"You're hurting me! You can't put handcuffs on me! I'm allowed to ask questions! This is a public event. You cannot do this!"

"Shoving people is not asking questions. And this is a *private* event. You were asked to leave multiple times, and you didn't leave. That means you are trespassing. And you assaulted someone. You shoved someone, and now you're in handcuffs—that's how it works. So now you get to stay. Congratulations. Have a seat."

I guided him by the arm to a seated position on a folding chair, around the corner and out of sight. The object he'd been holding was a tiny video recorder, but he had no badge or identification around his neck indicating he was press. This idiot could be anyone. A small crowd of journalists who had gathered in the hallway stood looking horrified, blocked by the Big Mexican and Sunshine. They held their cameras high and filmed with hand held video cameras, shouting questions, taking pictures, and demanding answers. The idiot in the chair, it turned out, was *Alaska Dispatch* founding editor and reporter Tony Hopfinger. He only had to sit a few minutes until the police arrived. I had worked extensively with the Anchorage Police Department. This procedure was routine.

"Hey, Bill?" said Officer Rod Potter after talking to Hopfinger.

"Hey, Rod. What do I need to sign before you take this guy to the station?"

"About that . . ." he faltered and spoke in a hushed voice. "We're thinking we're just going to release the guy. We don't need to make this any worse than it is."

"Wait, what? Why?"

He gave the side-eye to the crowd of frantic journalists shouting at my guys.

"Oh, great . . . Now *I'm* the one who's going to look like a douchebag?" I said. "This is perfect. *I'm* the asshole."

"Sorry, man. Look, it was a clean arrest, but wrong guy, wrong place. Nobody needs the bad PR, you know what I'm saying? The guy will go peacefully. He's not going to make trouble. It'll be fine. Let's just make this one go away."

Despite Hopfinger's release, and the fact that the arrest was clean, the incident did not "go away." It went *viral* nationally. I discovered that the *Alaska Dispatch* had not one but *five* unmarked journalists at this little town-hall event—I suspected they *wanted* to document some kind of "incident" with Miller after their public shaming. And now they had more than they ever could have hoped for—a first-person account of the arrest of Tony Hopfinger, who became an instant national celebrity journalist to the left. A reporter arrested by a crazy Tea Party Senate candidate from Alaska who had just announced the week before he was taking no more questions from them. Joe Miller vs. the *Alaska Dispatch*. This was pure media and partisan political gold.

And, of course, since I was already known as "Miller's goon" from the Republican convention, and because I did the arrest, as soon as the media connected the dots, I was in the crosshairs—and so was Drop Zone. In the avalanche of articles, TV news stories, blog posts, and radio rants, we were labeled gun dealers, mercenaries, militia members, extreme violent right-wing crazies, racists, fascists, rednecks, neo-Nazis, criminals. Photos of the Obama Joker poster in the window and the Gadsden flag that flew over Drop Zone were posted online as proof that all these things were true. Left-wing bloggers posted anything they could find to back up the narrative in their heads. The blog post from our little community blogger with the Obama poster got shared thousands of times. Phone calls flooded into the store and my house. Stacey answered the first call.

"Is this Mrs. Fulton?"

"Yes, who is this?"

"People like you and your fascist husband don't deserve to breathe air—not in this country. People fought and died for our right to free speech. Sleep with the lights on, bitch."

Stacey hung up the phone like it was red hot and backed away terrified. She stood staring for a few seconds and then broke down crying.

"Is this going to keep happening?" she asked me. "This is crazy. They don't know anything, they don't know you. You need to make this stop! Talk to them. Tell them it was just a job. Tell them we aren't like that!"

She pulled the curtains closed over the kitchen sink.

I couldn't sever my association with the right. If I made some grand announcement to the media disavowing Joe Miller's politics, I'd be cooked. My customers would turn against me, Miller's people would come unglued, and the work I'd done for the FBI would be wasted. I had to stay quiet, but I couldn't tell Stacey that was why. As scary as the threats from the left were, if it were discovered I was working with the government, or if I betrayed Miller to the media and looked like a left-wing sympathizer, it would be worse. They would come after me, after us, with more hatred than the left. If there is one thing people hate more than an enemy, it's betrayal from a friend. I would be a marked man, a turncoat, and we would have to leave Alaska. If I wanted to serve my country, employ those vets, and help get crazy people put away, I had to just let this blow over and let my family suffer. The thought of it made me feel physically sick. Watching Stacey shake in fear and knowing that in her eyes I was choosing not to do anything about it went against every protective instinct I had.

I held her in my arms while she cried. I told her everything would be OK. "I can't do what you want, Stace. It would kill the store if I did that. People will forget. They have short memories. I will protect you, and Emma, and Olivia. I promise. I swear on my life." I kissed her forehead. "Look at me. I swear on my life."

"Daddy! Daddy! You on TV!" Emma squealed from the other room.

". . . Bill Fulton, tonight's 'Worst Person in the World!'" bellowed Keith Olbermann on MSNBC's *Countdown*.

I made sure the doors were locked and all the blinds and curtains were closed. My cellphone buzzed. There was no one I wanted to talk to, but I looked at the screen and answered.

"Hello."

"Am I speaking to the Worst Person in the World?"

It was the Old Man.

"Yeah, I'm a fascist who arrests journalists. And I hate the First Amendment."

"Most people don't even understand what the First Amendment means. It means you get to criticize the government and they don't arrest you. They think it means you should be able to say whatever dumbass thing they think without suffering any consequences for it. Freedom of the press doesn't mean a reporter can go anywhere or do anything he wants on private property. But you know this. More important, how are you doing? How are Stacey and the kids?"

"The kids are OK, but Stacey's not doing well."

"You know, Bill. People's memories are short. In a couple of days they'll be on to something else, and this will be forgotten."

"That's what I just told her."

"Do you believe you did the right thing?"

"I did what I had to do. I did my job."

"Doing your job isn't always easy, and it can lose you friends and gain you enemies. But you have to be able to live with yourself. That's the important thing. 'Woe unto you when all men shall speak well of you.' Even says that in the Bible."

"Yeah, I know."

"Take a deep breath, and go tell your wife you love her, and tell her I said everything will be OK."

The next night, Rachel Maddow had Tony Hopfinger on the show in her New York Studio. *My* Rachel called me a Nazi right on national television. And like I said, the only thing worse than an enemy is the betrayal of a friend. Granted, Rachel Maddow didn't know me from Adam, but it stung.

I was living a nightmare, but the Old Man said everything would be OK, and he'd never been wrong before, so I clung to that. Any port in a storm.

The more the left attacked me, the more the right lionized me.

"If that socialist bitch Rachel Maddow thinks your a Nazi, your alright in my book!" came an email from North Carolina. Hundreds followed.

"I wish I could buy you a beer for arresting that leftist reporter. Totally badass."

"The media has had it out for Joe Miller since the beginning. Glad you put that slimey little lieing bastard journalist in his place. I laughed my ass off!"

But they were far outnumbered.

"I served my country honorably in the U.S. Army. We didn't just march around playing soldier like you weekend warrior assholes. You represent everything we fight against. You hate government so much, move to Somalia."

"You're a piece of shit, the worst kind, who silences journalists. You have no respect for the principles of this country. I don't know who you people think you are but I hope you end up eating cyanide like you're hero, the Fürer. Traitor."

"Dear Nazi Douchecunt, . . ."

That's one I hadn't even heard in the Army. So much for left-wing politics being the nice side.

Everybody wanted Hopfinger to press charges. And of course he never did, because we hadn't done anything wrong. The police investigated the incident, and everything was found to have been done correctly just like I'd said from the beginning. But nobody reported on that. Nobody said, "Hey, remember the Nazi douchecunt? Guess what? He didn't do anything wrong!" The truth wasn't what they wanted to hear. It wasn't sexy. It was much better for the media to have a martyr who could go on a national TV tour and talk about how reporters were unfairly treated by conservative thugs. Tony Hopfinger was like the obnoxious little brother who poked and poked and poked, and then said, "Mom! He pushed me!"

The number of clicks to *Alaska Dispatch* exploded. They were celebrating record popularity, and I was across town accepting the Big Mexican's resignation.

"I really want to stay, boss," he said. "I really like it here, and I need the money, but . . ." But he was active duty military and the publicity had been too much. He was given an order and he had to quit.

There were a couple of near-confrontations in the store with angry people who'd seen the story on TV. Someone gave Sunshine the finger in the grocery store because he was wearing a Drop Zone T-shirt. And it wasn't long before I realized that Drop Zone security was irreparably damaged.

Calls stopped coming in, and even if we'd gotten asked to do a job, I couldn't have put my guys out there like that, running security at events with drunk people when the whole city despised us. I hated having to take jobs from my guys. Everything felt like it was falling apart. I could only imagine what was happening to the Miller campaign.

Alaska Dispatch had its payback.

CHAPTER 19

★ ★ ★ ★ ★

DUMB AND DUMBER

"Our enemies are innovative and resourceful, and so are we. They never stop thinking about new ways to harm our country and our people, and neither do we."
—**George W. Bush**

Schaeffer Cox had told me on the phone to expect a visit from his men, both members of his Alaska Peacemakers Militia, on the day before the militia convention. I could "help them find equipment," he said. I called him to make sure they were still coming.

"You bet. And Bill, I have to say, I'm really proud of you for how you stood your ground for Joe Miller. It took guts."

Schaeffer Cox being "proud of me" about the Hopfinger incident suddenly made me feel even worse.

"Just doing my job, man. So, you're not coming down?"

"No, I wish I could. I'll be with you in spirit," he said. "But my wife's due next week, and I've gotta be around to see Number Two come into the world. I don't want her to wonder where her Daddy is, you know? You have girls, right?"

"Yup, two of 'em now. Best thing in the world, man."

Suicide and I were on the porch having a smoke break when I told him Cox's flunkies were coming to the shop.

"What the fuck do they want?"

"Not sure. Supplies of some kind."

"I don't like this whole thing. Cox makes my alarm bells go off. Don't get sucked in to something you shouldn't. He's bad news."

"OK, Dad," I said, exhaling a stream of smoke.

"Hey, I'm just saying. Someone has to keep you in line, you know. You tempt fate with all this shit. I just get tired of saving your ass from couches and proud black women and the FBI and all your other dumbass stunts."

"Just keeping you on your toes, man. Gotta give you something to do," I said.

"Gee, thanks, butthole." He laughed.

He tossed his cigarette into the giant ashtray bucket as a white Ford Explorer with two men in the front seat came bouncing into the lot followed by a cloud of dust.

"Speak of the devil. I bet this is them. I'll leave you to the circus. Lemme know if you need me," he said as he headed back inside.

From the passenger side, a denim-clad man stepped out—jeans, jacket, the whole thing. He straightened himself upright and postured like a swaggering teenager, thumbs in his belt loops, although he looked to be in his late fifties. He swiped his thinning hair to the side with his fingers, comb-over style, and sized up the surroundings.

"You Fulton?"

"Yes, sir. That's me," I said, taking a drag off my cigarette. "You are . . . ?"

"Lonnie Vernon," he said, wiping his palm on his thigh before extending to shake my hand.

"J. R. Olson," the driver introduced himself as he joined us on the porch. He was younger by twenty years, with a sandy buzz cut and black, thick-framed hipster glasses. "We're friends of Schaeffer Cox, up in Fairbanks."

"I've been expecting you. What can I do for you gentlemen today?" I asked.

"Thing is, Schaeffer's looking to buy some pineapple grenades and thought maybe you might be able to get your hands on some. They ain't easy to come by, you know what I mean?"

"What did you say your name was? Lonnie?"

"Yeah."

"Well, Lonnie, I've known you for five fucking seconds, and I already know you're about as dumb as a bag of dirt. So, why don't you shut the fuck up for another five until we get inside?"

"Jesus, Lonnie . . ." said Olson as he tossed his half-smoked Marlboro into the bucket.

Vernon was a sergeant in Cox's Peacemakers Militia who earned his rank by showing up and doing what he was told. He was from the rural community of Salcha, one of the most conservative in the state, about an hour and a half past Fairbanks into nothing. Vernon had some anger issues with the government, particularly with the IRS, which was taking steps to repossess his house after thirty years of nonpayment of taxes. He was a doomsday prepper, who stored months' worth of food and supplies—pallets of giant canned vegetables and Spam and twenty-four-packs of toilet paper from Costco. He also hoarded ammo. He and his wife, Karen, had illegally retooled a semiautomatic rifle into a fully automatic machine gun to defend their property. In order to obtain grenades for herself and her husband, she was now ready to pawn her family jewelry. Their yard was booby-trapped in case IRS terrorists or any other federal jack-booted thug tried to sneak onto their land.

Olson, from what I could tell, was a grunt. He'd met Schaeffer Cox through a mutual friend from a well-established sovereign citizen group called the Montana Freemen that I knew well from my Montana days. The Freemen wrote the playbook that Cox had been reading. It started with a man named LeRoy Schweitzer, who got into some trouble by not paying his taxes. So he organized an anti-government patriot militia of Christian "sovereigns" who said the federal government had no authority over them. The Montana Freemen under the leadership of Schweitzer went so far as to create a farm commune called "Justus Township" on private land and declared that they were no longer part of the country or subject to the laws of any outside government. They filed all kinds of false liens against public officials, made their own counterfeit checks and money orders. They also conducted mock trials of public officials who they believed had done them wrong. Sound familiar? Pretty much like the Cox trial, only not in a Denny's.

It all ended up where you might think. The FBI conducted a sting, arrested two Freemen for financial crimes in 1996, and the rest of those at the farm ended up in an extended armed standoff with the FBI. After eighty-one days, the Freemen finally surrendered. Schweitzer was convicted of conspiracy, fraud, threats, illegal possession of weapons, and armed robbery of $60,000 worth of camera equipment from an ABC-TV crew on a road near the farm. He died in prison. You'd think that humans would learn from the mistakes of others, but many seem bent on repeating them.

Olson (no relation to Norm) was relatively new to Alaska—an ass-kisser, a bullshit artist—and sounded like he knew more than he did. He was acting like a squirrel on a hot plate, and I didn't like him at all.

While Cox, the soon-to-be new dad, was holed up in Fairbanks, I got stuck with his emissaries—Dumb and Dumber. I brought them into the shop. Suicide had gone into the office and shut the door. He clearly wanted nothing to do with any of this. He was smarter than me.

"So, Lonnie. You just mentioned that grenades were hard to come by. Do you know *why* grenades are hard to come by? Do you know why that is?" I asked.

He stared, frozen, like it was a trick question. I let the question sit until it became awkward.

"Because they're fucking illegal, you dumb shit! Like *really* illegal. Ten-years-in-federal-prison illegal, asshole. You don't just stand on my fucking porch at my place of business and say that shit out to the world. 'HEY! NICE TO MEET YOU. I'D LIKE TO BUY SOME FUCKING GRENADES!' What the hell is that?! And no, *I can't get you any fucking grenades!*" I said loud enough so that Suicide would be sure to hear me through the door. "What the fuck is wrong with you?

"I'll talk to you at the hotel," I said softly as I leaned over to Olson. "And tell this moron to shut the fuck up. You guys were never here, understand?"

Olson nodded, and he and Vernon moved toward the door.

"Now get the fuck out! Tell Schaeffer to go fuck himself!" I yelled.

The truck hadn't even left the lot, when Suicide came out of the office, totally jacked.

"What did I tell you? Huh? Was I right? Grenades! Jesus Christ."

"Yes, Dad."

"Shut the fuck up with that," he laughed. "You know I'm right. Stay the hell away from those guys, or I'll beat your ass and send you to your room."

"Sorry, Dad."

That night around the fire, we were enjoying an especially killer batch of home brew. I had considered asking Suicide not to say anything about Cox's henchmen to the guys, but then thought it wouldn't hurt to keep them on alert for anyone looking to purchase illegal stuff.

"The dude's like, 'Hi, nice to meet you, do you sell grenades?' It was unreal." Laughter of disbelief rose as Suicide told the tale.

"If anybody asks for stuff like that, you let me know," I said. "That shit could get us investigated and I need to know everything you can tell me about who is asking and what they want."

My lecture was interrupted as Sunshine's Jeep roared into the parking lot and skidded across the gravel, dangerously close to my Hummer, raising a huge dust cloud that drifted right over to where we were sitting.

"Hey! Watch the Hummer!" I called over.

Sunshine was oblivious. He didn't even shut the Jeep door. He stood in the light of the fire, breathing hard, pale. Just standing.

"Holy shit, man. What's wrong?" Suicide said.

"Fuck . . . Fuck. FUCK!" Sunshine's hands flew up and he grabbed his head. "I am so fucked. I am so fucking *fucked*."

"Relax, man. It's OK. We got you covered. We got your back, man. Just tell us what happened," Suicide said.

Sunshine looked frantically from face to face, and finally blurted it out: "I slept with Dusti."

The silence was profound and prolonged as the implication of those four words settled into the brains of everyone around the fire.

"Wait. You what?" asked Discount, who thought he hadn't heard right.

"He fucked Gunny's girlfriend," said Clay, chuckling.

Sunshine nodded and covered his face with his hands. "Fuuuuck!"

Despite Suicide's attempt at consolation, this was not going to be OK at all.

"Dude, you know if he wasn't overseas you'd actually be standing here dead right now," said Clay. "Christ, even *I* would never fuck Gunny's girlfriend. That's just . . . wow. You got a death wish, man."

"What do I do?" Sunshine asked me. "What the fuck do I do?"

"You gotta go," I said. It was the truth as much as I didn't want to say it.

"Go? Like I'm fired?"

"Go, like you need to leave the country. You can't be here. When does he get back?"

"I don't know," Sunshine said, rubbing his face. "He just kind of shows up when he's done over there. It could be any time."

"You gotta go *now*. And don't tell any of us where you're going. Nobody."

"What about her?"

"Hey, that's up to you and her, but I'm telling you for your own health and safety you need to get the hell out."

Sherlock offered him a place to stay for a couple of days, but it was universally decided that Sunshine had to get out of Alaska, and out of the country, because if he no longer felt like walking the earth, there was really no better way to make that happen than sleeping with Gunny's girlfriend. We were pretty sure Gunny would bend his "I don't touch people" rule and wring Sunshine's neck with his bare hands until he stopped moving.

The next afternoon, Sunshine and Dusti cleared out of Gunny's apartment, left their car keys on the table, and caught a plane south to LAX where they'd transfer to some small country where they hoped Gunny would never be sent. Actions have consequences, and the more stupid they are, the worse the consequences will be.

CHAPTER 20

★ ★ ★ ★ ★

BAD BOYS

"Power comes from the barrel of a gun."
—**Mao Zedong, Jim Jones, and Schaeffer Cox**

"I'm a radical! I'm a real extremist. I don't want to impeach
judges. I want to impale them!"
—**Michael Schwartz, chief of staff to Sen. Tom Coburn (R-OK), in 2004**

The hotel that hosted the militia conference was right down the road from Drop Zone. Militia leaders from all over the state were in attendance, and I networked like crazy. There were speakers and seminars, and the whole thing had the feel of an actual legit conference. Norm Olson spoke about liberty, and standing up for the next generation, and erosion of freedom.

The FBI had my hotel room ready the day before. They bugged the lamp, and the digital clock that sat on the bar had a tiny hidden video camera inside. It was first-rate spy-thriller stuff. They even changed the clocks in Lonnie Vernon and J. R. Olson's rooms to look the same as my clock, so nobody would be suspicious. I told Sandra Klein they gave Vernon and Olson way too much credit. They were not idiot savants; they were just idiots—lucky to put their pants on forward, never mind noticing that one room had a different model of alarm clock than another and concluding they were under government surveillance. But that wasn't my job. Sandy, Dirk, a US attorney, and two federal marshals occupied the room next door to me, watching Bill TV live from my clock to their screen and listening with headphones. I could hear one of them cough occasionally. The walls were like paper.

The rhetoric and bravado at the conference was thick. A cloud of testosterone hung in the air. Imagine a hotel full of paranoid, drunken gubmint-haters—away from home and feeling emboldened to say what they wanted. Obama and his "unprecedented" overreach of power was a popular topic. At the bar, Vernon was getting shitfaced and hyped up about the IRS and how he would "cure the lead deficiency" of any agents who came to take his house.

"Don't you think I won't do it. My wife and I's serious as a heart attack about this. Them cocksuckers ain't just gonna take my house I worked for. Not my land. I ain't never done nothing wrong. I never took no unemployment, no nothing. I worked hard. I drove a truck, I was a machinist. And I own my own goddam piece of earth. Fuck them little government pricks. I ain't a young man no more. They may get me, but I'll take as many with me as I can."

After a full day of networking, I was getting tired, and the real mission of the day hadn't even started. Brian Beazley, Vernon, and Olson knocked on the door to my room where the beer waited, chilled and ready. *Cops* had just come on TV, so I cranked the volume of the theme song up for Sandy, just to make her laugh on the other side of the paper wall.

Bad boys, bad boys, whatcha gonna do? Whatcha gonna do when they come for you? I mugged into the clock and gave it a thumbs up on the way to the door. It still felt surreal every time it hit me that I was working as a confidential informant for the FBI.

It wasn't long before everyone was drunk. They had a good head start on me from the bar, but I did my best to catch up. The conversation turned, as it always did in this crowd, to a comparison of weapons. Everyone but me was packing. You don't need a permit in Alaska to carry a concealed weapon, so everyone did just on principle, and when they started unholstering and waving pistols around, I realized that the muzzles were about three feet from the heads of federal agents in the next room. And once I started thinking about that, I couldn't stop. An accidental discharge would bring a shit storm of massive proportions.

"I'm going to assume those aren't loaded," I said.

"What the fuck is the point of having a gun with you if it's not loaded?" Brian said. "Excuse me, Mr. Assailant, I have to find my ammo. It's around here somewhere. Just stay right there, please, and don't move."

Everyone but me laughed.

"Seriously? You guys are shitfaced. Not in my room. If any of you motherfuckers kill someone, it'll be bad for my business. Now, put 'em on the bar. And make sure the safeties are on."

They begrudgingly complied and the talk turned to the business at hand, which in this case meant illegal weapons. I was hoping Brian would have left by then, or not come at all, but he looked comfortable, sprawled out on one of the queen-sized beds, an arm behind his head.

"So, what's the deal with the law now? You can have grenade bodies, but the fuses are illegal? So how do you get just fuses then?" Vernon was back at it.

I couldn't let Brian be here for this. He was my friend, and not like these guys. I had to get him out of the room before he said something dumb or potentially incriminating and got caught up in the net. I didn't even know what it would be, but I knew everything was on audio and video. I knew I was taking risks in one way, but at least I knew the FBI wasn't going to arrest me. But Brian had no deal, and one stupid unthinking remark could get him in some major hot water. If the FBI got pissed off at me for ditching Brian, then that's the way it was. I didn't care. I was a volunteer. What were they going to do?

"Where's my fucking lighter, man?" I asked Brian as I patted my pockets, but knowing I'd given it to him earlier.

"You gave it to me, man. You said I could have it. Don't you remember?" He pulled a red Bic out of his front jeans pocket.

"Bullshit. You fucking took it."

"What are you talking about? I didn't take it. You gave it to me, man, like two hours ago. Chill out!"

"You're such a fucking liar, Brian. You *do* that. You just make shit up and then lie about it. I fuckin' hate that shit. Why do you do that? Just give me my fucking lighter."

"Dude! Are you drunk?" he said and tossed it to me. "It's a lighter . . . What the fuck?"

"No, I'm not drunk. You're just covering your ass. Why do you lie about small shit like that? I had it on the bar and you fucking took it. Just get the fuck out of my room. Seriously. Get the fuck out."

This had to be the dumbest argument ever. Barely believable. But in that moment, after drinking all day, and having no other plan, nothing else was coming to me.

"Wow, man. Fine," he said, lingering a little because he still wasn't quite sure I could be serious. "What the fuck is wrong with you? I'll be at the bar." He grabbed his Glock, holstered it, and strode out of the room.

Mission accomplished. I'd apologize the next day. I'd say I had too much to drink. I didn't know what came over me. And he'll thank me some day when these assholes go to prison, I thought. Because they were on the express train right to the Greybar Hotel. I could see it.

Vernon launched off on the IRS again, and insane conspiracy theories about FEMA camps being built to gas people, and kidnapping children to harvest their organs in train cars, and chem trails, and secret societies in the desert, and Muslim terror cells, and lizard people running the government. He never met a conspiracy theory he didn't like. He would have yammered on all night if I'd let him.

"OK, before we get to the fucking moon landing, and the grassy knoll, let's get business done."

"You make fun about the moon landing," Vernon said, "but there's all kinds of information now on YouTube about that. You have to watch it before you say anything."

"No, I don't," I said. "Focus."

I needed to keep the conversation on track and lead Vernon and Olson into the weapons deal. I made sure again that they knew it was illegal and what the consequences were. They wanted to hear none of it. Vernon was right back on his grenades—pineapple grenades, called so because of their bumpy, oblong shape. Could I get "a barrel" of them, Vernon asked. And apparently regular old fragmentation grenades weren't enough.

"Could we make up something different?" he wanted to know. "Have you ever tried phosphorus? I was thinking if you bored out the hole, you could put phosphorus in there."

This guy was unreal. For a total idiot, he was damned dangerous. White phosphorus is a chemical weapon of the most abhorrent kind. It is used in tiny amounts in tracer rounds because it smokes profusely. But phosphorus grenades have a far more sinister use. The defining characteristic of phosphorus is its ability to burn. It will burn through cloth and skin and bones. It will burn through a metal tank. It will burn down buildings. It even burns under water. It incinerates virtually anything it comes in contact with. The damage inflicted on human flesh is horrific. I listened to Lonnie Vernon talk about taking out the IRS agents who would come to seize his house, and how he'd booby-trapped his yard. This wasn't just "boys with their toys" playing militia out in the woods. This was premeditated murder, and what sounded like the intention to use chemical weapons against civilian targets.

"Dude, I throw grenades. I don't make grenades," I said. "I don't even know what you're talking about." He wasn't getting any help from me.

And then, Vernon brought up Schaeffer Cox's plan to kill judges. I had hoped that plan was ancient history, but I was wrong.

"So, Schaeffer's thinking this: If we cut the main electrical lines to a house, then the target is gonna come out to see what's going on, right? And then that's when we snipe him. If we've got a suppressor, then nobody's gonna pay no attention, right, because even if you hear it, it don't sound like a shot. And then, we torch the place. Boards across the doors and windows, real fast, and torch it."

"Whoa," I said. "Just slow the fuck down. This deal we're about to do? It's off if you assholes are killing women or kids."

I hadn't cleared any of this with the FBI, but I didn't care. I'm sure they were cringing on the other side of the wall. They'd rather have had me let him talk and dig his hole deeper. But the FBI isn't magic. They can't stop everything. They could be collecting and analyzing data and strategizing about how to make an airtight case, while someone like Vernon goes off half-cocked and kills people in the meantime. I was involved in this as a volunteer, and I was going to call my own shots. And I wanted Vernon to know that was absolutely not acceptable. Ever.

"Well, obviously that's the last thing ya *want* to do," Vernon said, gauging my agitation. "And it would only happen if . . ."

"No, it wouldn't 'only happen if.' It's not going to happen. If I hear you guys even *talking* about hurting kids, I will fucking kill you myself. Do you understand me?"

"No, no, of course not. We're not going to hurt kids . . . We wouldn't do that. The first round would just be . . ."

"Because that's not what you said five fucking seconds ago. You said 'if' and there is no fucking 'if.' There is no 'second round' with kids in it. *It doesn't fucking happen!*" I felt my face getting hot.

"I get it," he said, nodding.

"Good, because I know you're not the sharpest tool in the shed, after yesterday when you're all like, 'Gee, can I buy some grenades?' but I need you to wrap your fucking pea brains around what I'm saying right now. Both of you."

Vernon and Olson nodded and quickly changed the subject. They went back and forth about purchasing various weaponry including fully automatic machine guns, C4 explosives, sniper rifles, silencers, and the ever-popular pineapple grenades. They settled on two pistols with silencers and fifty grenades if I could get them. Not enough for a respectable arsenal, but all illegal enough to put these clowns behind bars for a very long time.

"So, wait . . . before we finalize, shouldn't we decide if we want silencers or suppressors? What do you think?" Olson asked neither of us in particular. I couldn't believe this guy. There was something seriously wrong with him.

"Silencers *or* suppressors? Dude, they're the same fucking thing. Like *exactly*," I said. "Two different words, same thing."

"Oh, yeah . . . Right, right. No, I know that. I just had a brain fart or something. Totally," he stammered.

"You can get these pistols and the suppressors legally, you know," I pointed out. "You're fucked with the grenades, but you can actually get the others without breaking the law."

"Yeah, legally *if* you get a tax stamp, and *if* you pay $200 to the goddamn feds, and *if* you apply with Alcohol Tobacco and Firearms, and *if* they take your fingerprints, and you tell 'em where you live. No, thanks. These ain't for moose hunting," said Vernon.

These guys would rather commit a felony that could send them to prison for a decade than have to pay a fee to the government and fill out a form. I gave up. Now nobody could say they didn't know when they were on trial for this—which seemed certain if they kept going. It was all on tape.

The final thing on my to-do list was to get confirmation that Schaeffer Cox knew Vernon and Olson were here, doing this business in his name, which would help the prosecutors nail him to the wall and get him somewhere he couldn't hurt people.

Olson said that Cox had been summoned to appear in court the following week, on Valentine's Day, for that misdemeanor weapons charge he received after failing to reveal a concealed weapon to a police officer at the scene of a search. Olson said Cox had decided not to appear, in order to challenge the legitimacy of the court. Failing to appear would immediately make him a fugitive in the eyes of the law. I was extremely familiar with that scenario. He'd be on the run and would regard any act of aggression directed at him by law enforcement (like arrest for jumping bail) as an act of war. As a fugitive-recovery guy by trade, I could see where this was leading and it wasn't good. He would be law enforcement's worst nightmare. Cox wouldn't go easily. He'd make Bobby Ray Watkins look like a Boy Scout. The escalation was about to begin.

I gave Cox a call and put it on speakerphone, recapping the events of the past few days for him.

"Yeah, I wasn't sure about these guys you sent over," I said, shooting a look at Vernon. "One of 'em seemed to have some problems with discretion at my place of business. That was not cool."

"OK, yeah, I heard about that. That was unfortunate, but at this point, let's not dwell on that," said Cox. "What's important right now is that we remember what side we're on. We need to remember we've got the same enemy, right? Lonnie and J. R. know what we need. We talked all about that, so when you deal with them, just pretend like you're talking to me. We know you may not have access to everything, and there's also the matter of our funds. And I'm really sorry I couldn't be there but the timing was just all off."

"Hey, speaking of that, how's Marti? How's that baby doing?" I asked. "I heard down at the bar that you're a dad again."

"Great. They're just great. Mama's resting right now, and I've got the little lady right here in my arms. Right, princess? Who's Daddy's beautiful good girl . . . ?" he said in almost a whisper.

"Well, we're talking about a bag of pineapples and a few other things that fit the budget," I said.

"Yeah. That sounds about right. As many as possible for the money. I know you'll do right by us. You know we'll be back and send folks your way. Lonnie and J. R. know what parameters we've got," he said, and I could hear him making little cooing and kissing sounds.

"Well, for anything that's off the radar, you're looking at a turnaround time of about twelve weeks. You cool with that? I know that's probably longer than you want, but this shit doesn't just happen. There are processes involved, and it takes time."

"Understood. We need to do this carefully and right. But if there's anything you could do to expedite this I'd really appreciate it."

After the call, the setup was complete. Specific illegal weapons had been ordered, these idiots knew that what they wanted was illegal and didn't give a shit, I gave them an opportunity to back out, which they didn't take, and Schaeffer Cox had given his blessing. The agents and the US attorney in the next room had gotten it all on video. And nobody got shot through the wall. It was a good day.

After they collected their guns and left, I collapsed on the bed, which was spinning slightly. I was going to hate myself tomorrow morning. Discount had a cold, and I was opening the shop for him so I had to be up in a few hours.

"G'night, Sandy! G'night, Dirk! G'night Madam US Attorney, and various assorted law enforcemenoff'cers!" I half-slurred toward the spy clock. I heard a little knock come back through the wall as I drifted off.

CHAPTER 21

★ ★ ★ ★ ★

TWO FOR ONE

"We're seeing the fulfillment of the Book of Judges here in
our own time—every man doing that which is right in his
own eyes."
—Michele Bachmann

F UCK!"
It's never good when that's the first thing out of your mouth in
the morning. My phone was dead on the night table, but the Super
Spy Ninja Cam video clock said 9:17 a.m. and the store was supposed to
be open already. I gave the guys such crap about opening late, and now
it was my fault. Good thing the shop was just down the road from the
hotel. I pulled my pants on, slapped some cold water on my face, shoved
my shit in a duffel bag, left a ten-spot for the maid, and flew out the door.

I pulled in the same time as Discount, who had tried to call the store
and then me and got no answer. I remembered his first day on the job when
he showed up three hours late—and now here he was at work, covering my
ass even though he was sick, just because he was being responsible.

"I'm sorry you had to come all the way down here, man. I'll make
you a cup of coffee for the road," I offered as I unlocked the door.

We were met by a wall of stench that made us both recoil.

"Oh my GOD! Jesus CHRIST!" said Discount. "What the FUCK?!" He
staggered backward.

It was like a dead whale after a week in the sun. It was superhuman putrefaction—a smell that made me involuntarily retch. You could practically see it hanging in the air. I pulled over the ashtray bucket to prop the door open, and we stood for a minute looking at each other, wondering what we were going to find.

"Soap is in there, right?"

I nodded.

"You don't think he . . . like . . . died, do you?"

"Everything was fine last night as far as I know. It takes longer than a few hours for a body to stink like that."

We pulled our T-shirts up over our noses and ran in, opening the front door and cranking open windows. We didn't immediately see anything so we ran back out before we had to inhale.

After a few minutes, and turning away a customer because we were "closed due to a yet-to-be-determined issue," we went back in and headed for the office. I braced myself for something horrific, and I wasn't disappointed.

A mound of what appeared to be human flesh occupied the cot where Soap slept. There was also a pile of long tangled brown hair that did not belong to Soap. And there were too many limbs for one person. There was snoring. I turned on the light.

"HEY!" I bellowed. "Wake the fuck up!"

The mound moved and jiggled and it became apparent that despite the tiny size of the cot, there were two people on it, both naked—Soap and a woman three times his size, who apparently shared his philosophy of personal hygiene. The thought of what I'd been breathing in made me want to gag. Discount had already run back outside.

I pointed out the "No wives or girlfriends" sign yet again and the "No fucking in the office" clause beneath it.

"Who the fuck are *you*?" the woman asked, making zero effort to get up or find clothes.

"I'm Bill and this is my fucking office," I said.

"So you're the uptight asshole with the 'list of rules'?" She rolled into an upright position brushing her long stringy hair out of her face.

"Yes. And you're the mouthy, naked bitch in my office who was just leaving."

"Wanda," she said.

"Well, Wanda. You need to put your fucking clothes on and get out of my place of business. Now. Understand?"

She squinted at me.

"Can I have some privacy or are you just going to stand there enjoying the show?"

I got out of there fast and cleansed my lungs with a nice American Spirit on the porch. Discount was sitting on the steps.

"Do you need me, boss? Because if not I think I'm going to go home and go back to bed."

"Get out of here, man. Drink some NyQuil. Forget you ever saw this shit. Or smelled it."

Wanda took her sweet time, and I had to bang on the outside office wall a couple of times to get her ass moving. Eventually, the lovebirds emerged—Wanda leading Soap with a hand around his wrist.

"Francis will be coming to stay with me," she said, as though she was accusing me of something. "I have a place in Wasilla where he's welcome. And there are no stupid-ass rules on the door."

Soap looked at me with a shrug in his eyes, not entirely unhappy that someone seemed to care enough to kidnap him from the office he'd called home for a year now. It was the last time I'd lay eyes on him.

By the next day the worst of the stench was gone, but Soap had been there a long time and it took almost a month before it completely stopped smelling like ass. Soap called once, just to let us know that everything was OK. And then a few weeks later we got some paperwork saying he'd applied for unemployment.

"Unemployment?" Suicide looked at me, bewildered. "We housed him and fed him for an hour's worth of sweeping a week. And did you see this?" He handed me a sticky note.

Shafer called, was scrawled on it. No time, no day, no idea who wrote it.

I didn't know how long it would take to hear from Sandy about my next move, but Cox's court date was looming, and if he didn't show, he'd officially be a fugitive from the law—not that he believed in the law. He was supposed to show up at the Fairbanks Courthouse on Valentine's Day, and he'd somehow gotten the judge assigned to the case, Superior Court Judge Michael McConahy, to agree to let him represent himself. He said he believed Cox could plead his case in a "rational and coherent manner." I wanted to know what was in his Wheaties.

I watched the days on the calendar go by, but as always I was pretty much in the dark. Undercover informants are the low men on the totem pole. As frustrating as I found this, it did make some sense, since, unlike me, the overwhelming majority of informants are criminals and not particularly trustworthy with keeping information confidential or exercising good judgment.

It was February 12, 2011. I tried calling Cox back, but it went straight to voicemail. I didn't know it at the time, but at that moment, his cellphone had its battery removed and was wedged under a couch cushion with three other cellphones, in a gutted-out school bus parked in the woods somewhere outside Fairbanks. The school bus was owned and occupied by a sovereign citizen named Ken Thesing, who had called a meeting there with Schaeffer Cox, J. R. Olson, and Major Coleman Barney of Cox's Peacemakers Militia. Barney was a Mormon, married, father of five, and a well-liked and respected business owner and electrical contractor in Fairbanks. His short dark hair, angular jaw, and close-set eyes made him look more like a fed than a militia member, but if there's one thing I've learned it's that looks can be deceiving.

The meeting was held in order to discuss "the plan." By this point, Cox had made it clear on the record in court that he did not consider the court to be legitimate; he didn't consider himself beholden to the court in any way; and that any man or woman acting against him—either from the court or law enforcement—would be treated "like a criminal," and he would do whatever it took to defend himself and his family from their criminal intent. At one point, he told a trooper at the courthouse that militia members had the Alaska State Troopers "outmanned and outgunned" and "could probably have you all dead in one night." He blathered on about being a peaceful man, but only until any agent of the government tried to do their job. Then all bets were off, and it was "war." And right then, the bus in the woods was the War Room.

"So, Guerrero and Woods who work at the courthouse? They need to dangle together like wind chimes," Cox said as he bent his wrist and wiggled his fingers pointing downwards. "I've got an irrevocable power of attorney that you guys need to keep in a safe place in case I get killed or something, OK?" he went on.

"First of all, there's going to be about fifty or so bodies hit the dirt before that ever happens," said Thesing.

"Good," said Cox. "We can hide out or we can run. The other thing we need to talk about here is Operation One-Forty-One, which is 'one for one,' like a play on words. But what it is, is the Israeli defense strategy, which is—I'm not going to lock my doors. So you can come in the night, and you can kill me, and you can haul me off. I'm there for grabs, but you just know what it's going to cost—one of yours for one of ours. And that's the only defense. I think that's a very, very, very *effective* defense; that's what our code word is—'one forty one.'"

Over the past months, Cox and his militia had amassed weapons and ammunition in secret caches around the Fairbanks area, and plans were made. The signal for the attacks would come from Cox via his Twitter account.

Each man repeated in turn like a chant, "one forty one," "one forty one," "yeah, one forty one . . ."

"Hell, let's make it two for one," said Cox.

"Or five for one!" said Olson.

"Two for one would be the most," Cox said, "and then hopefully the price is so high that they leave people on the shelf. And this is horrifying. Like—this is like the most scary thing for me to talk about. Because, you know . . . this is my *family*."

"Yeah," said Olson, and everyone was silent for a moment.

"But two for one, 'two-forty-one,' that's how we can talk about it on the phone. It's already to the point, and I believe that it is absolutely morally allowable if they were to come and arrest one of us, for the three of us to go kick in the judge's door and the trooper's and arrest two of them. And because it's war, it doesn't even really have to be the ones that did it. Because it's just—it's war. And it's not just a war in fact, it's a war declared by them, explicitly, without mincing any words, and so I think it's absolutely morally allowable that if they arrested Ken or arrested me, to go in and arrest two of them. If they kill one of us, we go kill two of them. If they took one of our houses, we go burn two of their houses. And—and like the philosopher John Locke says, 'It's your duty to make it an ill bargain for those that would aggress you.' And we've just got to make it a bad bargain. Now what's morally allowable and tactically advantageous, that's what we've got to talk about.

"I mean, I think I raise no question that I'd be well within my rights to go drill Judge McConahy in the forehead, and any of these people that are propagating this because they're posing a huge threat to my life and my family. So, the road I'll take is, we're ready and we could have you dead in minutes, but we are long-suffering and we want to be your friends. You've got to stop pushing—we want to be at peace. We're going to continue long-suffering, but not forever."

"And there are things you can do, you know," said Barney, "to get the message through. You go get those little target bull's-eye stickers, and you put them on the back windows of all the cop cars."

Cox nodded, "Yeah. The other thing is, is that even with just, you know, the guerrilla warfare, we definitely could rock this town."

Everyone nodded, each imagining his own scenario of destruction.

CHAPTER 22

★ ★ ★ ★ ★

THE DEAL

"Don't bring a knife to a gunfight."
—Old adage

When Schaeffer Cox returned my message in a panic, saying that he had to have the "supplies" faster than the twelve weeks we agreed to, I called Sandy. I told her he wanted them as soon as possible. It was urgent.

While I'd been giving out bouquets of Valentine flowers—red roses for Stacey, and pink carnations for the girls—Judge McConahy had left his empty courtroom and retired to his chambers, where he'd issued a warrant for Cox's arrest. The "war" was on. Cox had described his terms. Anyone "aggressing" him would be treated like a criminal, and he would be justified in killing in "self-defense." He had given the finger to the court and to law enforcement, and now he was daring them to do something about it. I had a bad feeling about how it was going to end.

A long couple of weeks later, I got the call I had been dreading.

"This is it, Bill. We've got to get ready to move on this thing. Schaeffer is ready to flee the state as soon as he gets the weapons. So, this is the time. Are you ready to do this? We'll need you in Fairbanks."

I'd been shoving this possibility from my mind—that I would have to do something that would expose me. I guess I thought somehow they'd manage the last part without me, and no one would be the wiser. I'm kind of a live-in-the-moment guy, and it always sucked when the price for living in the moment came due. As I processed Sandy's words, their meaning began to register. I would fly to Fairbanks, do the illegal weapons deal, and the arrests would happen. They would happen fast. And Cox and the militias would figure out almost immediately that I was the informant. And from that moment on, there would be a target on my back. And on my family. I knew about this crew's moral boundaries when it came to women and kids, and those boundaries were nonexistent. I would be Enemy Number One and there was no way around it. I'd been used to being hated for "snitching" in the Army and it hadn't gotten to me. Fuck those assholes. But now it wasn't just me that would have to pay the price. I thought about someone torching my house with Stacey and Emma and Olivia inside because "hey, this is war," and my heart began to pound. I was not willing to risk them. And I thought about that happening to the judge's wife and kids or the trooper's wife and kids. I was doing the right thing, I kept telling myself, and I hoped with all my heart that the assholes who thought doing that to people was somehow OK would rot in jail.

"We will get you all out fast, Bill," said Sandy. "I promise. We will keep you safe. All of you. We will handle it. I'm giving you my word."

"Out. Get us out . . . *where*?"

"Remember a while back when you were talking hypothetically about living somewhere else, other than Alaska?"

"Hypothetically, yeah. Hypothetically I said Colorado. Hypothetically. Jesus . . ."

"Colorado Springs. Not hypothetically."

"Fuck."

"So, you've got three days. We'll get all your stuff packed up, so don't worry about that, but whatever papers and documents you need to get together, or safety-deposit boxes you need to empty, this would be the time to do that. You fly to Fairbanks Thursday morning. We'll drop you an email with your ticket information."

It was Monday, and Thursday would be the day my entire life would fall apart. It felt like a hand around my throat.

"And Bill? Not a single word to Stacey. Or anyone. I know this is hard, but not a word. This isn't the time for true confessions. Just be normal, do what you do in the morning, and then get on the plane. We're almost done. We're going to put these guys away for a long time where they can't hurt anybody. You are doing the right thing."

On Thursday morning, I got ready to go to work. The morning was typical for everyone but me. I tried to stay "normal"—feed the dogs, eat a bowl of Frosted Mini-Wheats, fill travel mug with coffee, grab my boots, coat . . .

"Tell Daddy bye-bye!" Stacey prompted.

Olivia was in her busy seat.

"Bye-bye!" I said, and she smiled and bounced up and down.

"Bye, Daddy!" Emma ran around the corner from the living room and hugged my knees. "Have fun at your work! OK? Bye!" Back around the corner she ran.

"OK, Princess. You girls be good for Mommy today, all right? Promise?"

"See you for dinner, right?" Stacey asked as she leaned in for a quick kiss. "And don't forget the milk on the way home. We're totally out now."

"I won't, baby. Have a good day."

I'd become an expert at keeping my life compartmentalized and playing the part I needed to play at any given moment, keeping secrets. But this one was huge. This was real life, the important stuff, and everything was about to come crashing down.

Stacey was looking out the window at the dripping icicles, sipping her coffee from a mug. Today she would know.

"Stace?"

"What?"

"Nothing. I just . . . I love you."

"Aww, I love you too, babe. Have a good day."

My Hummer approached Drop Zone just as the sky started to turn indigo behind the black saw-toothed mountains. Suicide was there already, and I could see the thin, fluorescent light from the office, spilling out into the dark store as I drove past.

"Hey," he answered on the first ring. "'Sup, Boss?"

"I'm going to be out and about today, so I may not be in. If you need something, just leave a message on my phone, OK?"

"Roger that. Talk to you later. Stay outta trouble."

"Later, man. And . . . hey. Thanks for holding down the fort."

"Sure thing."

"And for saving my ass, and being a good friend."

"What the hell is the matter with you, man? You OK?"

"Yeah. Nothing. I'm good. Talk to you later."

I caught the store in my rear view mirror as I turned into one of the winding bends on Spenard Road. I'd never set foot in there again. Never see Suicide again. He'd warned me about this—told me it would all end if I called the FBI. That we'd all be fucked. But this was not the time to think about that. Today, I needed full concentration. Right then, I needed to get to the airport and get on a flight to Fairbanks, and go to the Holiday Inn, room 211. I had to wall off that compartment of my brain, because if I wanted Stacey and the girls to be OK, I had to be fully present in what I was about to do. That was the only thing I could do for them—not fuck it up. Focus. Get to the airport.

"Don't bring a gun," Dirk Ellison had told me the day before. "I'll meet you in the hotel room and give you the pistols and silencers and the grenades, which will all be non-operational."

FBI headquarters in Quantico, Virginia, had been the one to fill Cox's order for illegal weapons. J. R. Olson was to be the bagman on the other end of this transaction, and I didn't trust him as far as I could throw my Hummer. Cox didn't want to deal with me, so he was sending his schizo henchman.

"Tell me you're kidding me, Dirk. No gun?" I had asked. "Seriously, man. You're telling me you want me to be an unarmed illegal arms dealer? That's what you're telling me?"

"Yeah. That's what I'm telling you."

It made no sense. It was dangerous. And I could tell in his voice that he knew he shouldn't be saying it.

There was no way I was going to be totally unarmed. No way in hell. On my short walk from the tiny Fairbanks Airport to the Holiday Inn, I detoured into the Fred Meyer Superstore sportsmen's counter.

And I walked from there to the hotel with a big-ass hunting knife in my pocket.

"Complimentary breakfast is served in the dining room from seven o'clock to ten o'clock, Mr. Fulton, and if you're an early riser, we have a table with coffee and muffins . . ."

"It's fine. I'm only going to be here a couple of hours," I said.

"Oh! I see . . . well, um." The receptionist blushed and smiled. "Enjoy your stay!"

"Thanks." I took the card key in the little envelope and headed to room 211.

Dirk arrived exactly on time. He put three black buckled cases and a soft vinyl bag with a zipper on the bed.

"Hey. Is that a knife in your pocket or are you just happy to see me?" he asked, eyeing my pants.

"I'm just happy to see you, Dirk. Really fuckin' happy."

He smiled and held out his hand. "Give me the knife."

"You know what's going to happen if I give you this knife?"

He thought for a second and spotted the plastic shopping bag on the desk.

"You're going to wait until I leave and walk back to Fred Meyer and buy another one."

"See, man? *This* is why you work for the fucking FBI," I said tapping my finger to my skull. "Nothing gets past you."

"Jesus, Bill . . . Fine. But don't use it."

"Only if I have to."

I popped the latches on the cases and looked at the contents. I couldn't believe what I saw.

"What the fuck is this? This is not what they wanted. These are . . . I don't even know what the fuck these are. Some Eastern bloc Soviet thing? Jesus!"

"It'll be fine," he said.

"You know . . . I'm glad you assholes are sure enough about all this to bet my life on it."

Olson was due to arrive in half an hour.

"He may not have money with him," Dirk said. "And if he doesn't, just give him the guns and tell him you know he's good for it."

"Yeah, because that doesn't look weird. I'm an illegal arms dealer, unarmed, with the wrong fucking guns, and hey, I don't need money, I'll just put it on your tab! What the fuck, Dirk! Are you trying to get me killed?"

"Trust me," he said. "Bill. Trust me. I haven't steered you wrong, ever. Have I?"

"Steered me wrong with what? The taco special? Yeah, you were right, it was great."

"Just trust me," Dirk left, and I spent half an hour pacing until Olson arrived. He looked worse than me, with a damp forehead, and hardly able to stand still.

He eyed the cases on the bed. My heart was pounding, wondering what would happen when he saw the wrong guns. But this was the idiot who thought there was a difference between silencers and suppressors, so maybe it would be OK.

"Well, OK, then . . . Let's see whatcha got."

My palms were sweaty as I snapped open the cases. He looked closely but didn't touch anything. He unzipped the grenade bag and peered inside.

I hadn't even thought about the grenades. They wanted fifty, and that bag was holding maybe a half-dozen. This was really bad. Somebody was going to be pissed.

"I need to use the john," he said. I pointed and he closed the door behind him.

My hand drifted to my pocket. I had looked for signs of a weapon on him but didn't see any. I could have missed it. Did I miss it? If all I had was this knife, I needed to stay close to him. Knives are hard to use from a distance. I stood by the bathroom door. I didn't hear him making a phone call, but he could be texting. A flush. The door opened. He startled when he saw me by the door.

I walked him back to the cases.

"OK, well, everything looks good," he said. "But, there's one thing," he wiped his upper lip on his sleeve, "I, um . . . it's . . . about the money." His voice was tight.

"You don't have the money," I said.

"Not on me right now, no," he looked like he was going to run back to the bathroom. "But I . . ."

"Look, dude. It's not like I don't know where to find you," I said. "The money—that's between me and Schaeffer. It's cool. We'll work it out. I know you need these now. Take 'em. All for the cause, right?" He looked like he'd just been pardoned from the noose.

I held out my hand and shook his. Clammy. This guy was a wreck. As on-edge as I felt, he looked worse and I didn't know why. Scared of me? Worried about a setup? Or about whatever reason he didn't have the money? Maybe he and Cox were setting *me* up.

"OK, well. Thanks, man. So you and Schaeffer work the rest out. I'll see you around." He gathered up the cases and the vinyl bag and headed out the door. I scanned but didn't see anyone in the hall, and Olson strode away.

Doorknob lock, deadbolt, chain. I sat on the desk chair, listening to my heart beating, flipping the knife handle over in my hand, over and over, waiting for the all-clear call from Dirk. Over and over. Over and over.

My cell rang, and I answered without looking.

"Yeah."

"Hey, Bill."

It was the Old Man. It was almost comical at this point.

"Hey . . . What's up?"

"Well, nothing really. I just wanted to check in and find out how you're doing. We haven't talked in a little while. Did I catch you at a bad time?"

"I'm kind of in the middle of something right now, yeah."

"I see." He got quiet. "Bill, will you call me back when you can?"

"It might be a couple of days, is that OK?"

"Yes, that's OK. You hang in there. Everything will be fine."

Ten minutes later, my cell rang again, and it was Dirk giving me the all-clear to head back to the airport. I was done. I wasn't dead. I didn't have to kill anyone. I let the relief come, and it lasted about three seconds before I remembered what would come next.

CHAPTER 23

★ ★ ★ ★ ★

FLASH BANG

"If you see something, say something."
—Department of Homeland Security

FBI Special Agent Michael Thoreson drained the last mouthful of cold coffee from his to-go cup and put it back in the holder on the console. The black Chevy Suburban was parked behind a cluster of spruce trees adjacent to the large, almost-empty parking lot of an abandoned warehouse. He'd been planning the how and where of this arrest for months—down to the last detail. The suspects were known to carry semiautomatic rifles and wear body armor able to stop rounds fired from the handguns normally carried by agents in the field. The armor wouldn't stop an M16 round, though, and he had made sure the teams in play were properly equipped. He'd called in an extra SWAT team from Salt Lake City to assist the teams of eight from the Anchorage FBI. They joined dozens of other officers from the Fairbanks Police Department, the North Pole Police, the Alaska State Troopers, and the US Marshals Service, who were now parked in various vehicles—marked and unmarked—scattered nearby and out of sight. He was not taking any chances. Thoreson had chosen this place to minimize the possibility of innocent bystanders getting caught in a potential shootout or hostage situation, and because it would provide cover for agents and officers.

He had received confirmation that the two inoperable pistols with silencers and several inert grenades had been transferred from the FBI to J. R. Olson in room 211 of the Fairbanks Holiday Inn a short time before. Everything was going according to plan. So far.

Schaeffer Cox and his crew hated the government in general, Thoreson knew, and particularly the FBI. But they had no clue that they themselves had welcomed an undercover informant into their own group with open arms—a criminal informant, who had infiltrated Cox's militia unsuspected. He had been providing information to the FBI for months in exchange for a reduced sentence for a host of crimes he had committed.

J. R. Olson had been a truck driver, and as such he had smuggled large quantities of cocaine in a Fred Meyer grocery store semi-truck all the way up the Al-Can highway from Seattle to Anchorage. He had pulled the truck over into a designated weigh station in Canada, popped the US Customs seal, loaded the heavy plastic bags filled with white powder from a waiting dealer, and stashed them in between pallets of groceries. Then he resealed the rollup door before crossing from Canada to Alaska. He'd also stolen cars and installed seven septic systems in Peter's Creek and Wasilla without a license. Apparently there's a reason you need a license for that, because Olson's slipshod work caused the systems to fail, and floods of raw human sewage backed up into houses and oozed through yards and into neighboring creeks. He was not a popular man.

But right now, the FBI was depending on this inept drug-running con-man-turned-mole to make sure that the arrests went off without a hitch. Special Agent Thoreson took a deep breath.

When I learned later that Olson was a criminal informant, the world suddenly made sense. No wonder Dirk hadn't wanted me to have a gun or a knife at the weapons drop. He didn't want me to put a cap in that squirrely bastard by mistake. Undercover informant wastes undercover informant—the paperwork alone would have been a nightmare. And that's how he knew Olson would accept the wrong guns and not have any money. And Olson didn't know I was an informant, which explained why he was just as nervous about that ridiculous weapons deal as I was. Of course, they could have told us, but the agency works on a need-to-know basis. And technically neither Olson nor I needed to know until it was all over.

Right on schedule, Olson's white Ford Explorer came bouncing into the frozen parking lot over the ruts of gravelly ice, his exhaust making huge plume clouds in the frigid air.

Thoreson watched, every nerve on alert. Special Agent Keith Oberlander sat in the passenger seat next to him, earbud in, monitoring the transmissions from Olson's Explorer, which they had wired the day before. A large box trailer was parked in the lot, and a van with blacked-out windows. Inside both were agents in full riot gear—body armor, shields, helmets, M16s—waiting and listening for the signal to go that would come from Thoreson.

Olson parked midway between the van and the trailer, about thirty yards from each. He got out of the vehicle and looked around, scanning the perimeter, his hands jammed in his pockets, bouncing on the balls of his feet. The mercury was at ten degrees and falling. A few minutes later, an immaculately clean white pickup truck pulled in and parked next to him. Lonnie Vernon stepped out of the driver's side of the gleaming truck, wiping his hand through his hair, smoothing his comb-over. His diminutive, silver-haired wife, Karen, ten years his senior, had a little grey schnauzer in her lap. Another schnauzer stood alert on his hind legs in the back seat, peering out the window. Karen bent over into the front seat as she got out. She wore a blue down coat, a flowered handbag hooked over her forearm. She soothed the dog, kissing it on top of the nose and speaking to it in hushed tones, before she shut the door.

She had pawned her jewelry to buy these grenades. And she had handwritten the little stack of letters explaining to family and friends what was going to happen, and tucked them away in the glove compartment in stamped, addressed envelopes.

The IRS had told the Vernons they owed $118,000 in back taxes, and it was probably more by now, with interest and penalties building by the day. The Vernons had filed a counterclaim. They asserted that they were not citizens of the United States—that they had taken steps and filled out paperwork renouncing their citizenship, and therefore they owed nothing, and the IRS was itself an illegal entity, acting on behalf of a country that wasn't really a country at all. Judge Ralph Beistline, who was assigned to the case, issued an order dismissing the counterclaim as "frivolous" and warned the Vernons of a possible foreclosure sale of their property to satisfy the tax debt. He even suggested they retain counsel for their own good. They didn't. Vernon had not paid taxes in more than thirty years. He had earned his money and decided long ago that it would stay his. But now, the writing was on the wall, and it was only a matter of time before they lost everything. And they'd decided that if there was going to be any justice in the world, then Judge Ralph Beistline and his family would pay for stealing the Vernons' lives with their own.

If you are getting this letter it means we are no longer living . . . said the careful cursive on the folded paper inside the envelopes. *We pray that our deaths will not have been in vain . . . We will not FREELY GIVE our home, land, and personal property to this tyrant, nor will we die cowards, licking their jack-boots. We did not go down without resistance, and standing for our rights, the lead deficiency of those who came to take ours from us, was corrected as best we could.* Vernon had liked that part about correcting the "lead deficiency" of the tyrants.

After climbing into the back of Olson's rig, Karen did as he asked and carefully handed one of the black pelican cases up to him in the front seat. Olson popped the latches, opened the case and passed it to Vernon in the passenger's seat, who took a pistol out of the fitted grey foam insert and examined it.

"This ain't the right gun," Vernon's voice crackled through the hidden microphone.

"You moved up the timetable, man. It's the best they could do. You gotta take what you can get, you know? It'll work, won't it?" Olson sounded on edge. But then, he always sounded on edge.

"Yeah, I guess it'll work," he said, and then after a silence continued, "You don't take what a man has worked for his whole life. You don't do that and expect he won't stand up. I ain't done nothin' to nobody. Sonsabitches started something all right . . ." He handed a roll of bills to Olson.

"Well, it's good doing business with you," Olson said and cleared his throat. That was the signal. It was time.

"OK, we're a go!" Thoreson said into the radio.

The Vernons didn't notice Olson's eyes resting on a spot out the window as the side door of the parked van pushed out and slid open to the width of a pair of shoulders. An agent in full black riot gear threw something that landed a few feet away from the Explorer. A second later, a deafening concussive blast and light equivalent to six million candlepower engulfed the vehicle. A flash-bang grenade.

Motion stopped. The passengers froze. Karen clutched her head and folded over. Vernon's arm flailed reflexively and slammed against the window. Olson, expecting the blast, gripped the wheel and lowered his head. Everything became light and sound. The van and the trailer opened wide. Agents poured onto the ice. A thunder of boots. A stream of black. M16s aimed at the car.

"Don't move! Federal agents! You're under arrest!"

Agents ripped open the doors. They grabbed the Vernons from the vehicle and pushed them face down on the ice. Vernon was stripped of the handgun on his hip. Thoreson ejected the rounds from the chamber. Vernon had been completely disoriented by the blast and had never even reached for the gun.

As the handcuffs zipped onto his wrists, and then his wife's, and his cheek began to get cold and wet from the ice melting beneath it, the situation began to sink in for Vernon.

"Goddamn it. Goddamn it . . . You don't have any authority over me. What jurisdiction do you have? You tell me! You can't tell what jurisdiction because you don't have anything! Nothing!"

Karen quietly sobbed as Happy and Buzzy, the schnauzers, began yapping and frantically clawing at the windows of the truck to get to her, their ears recovered now from the impact of the deafening sound wave.

The Vernons' pockets were emptied, and Thoreson ejected the rounds from the pistol in Karen's flowered purse that was tucked away under the dummy grenades she had just stuffed inside. Oberlander swung open the driver side door of the Explorer where Olson still sat gripping the wheel.

"You're OK. You're all right." He clapped Olson on the shoulder. "Get out for a second and walk around. Clear your head. One more and it's over. You ready to do this again?"

Olson was the color of wood ashes. He took off his black-rimmed glasses, wiped his eyes and forehead of sweat with his shirtsleeve, and looked over to see Vernon's eyes boring holes through the window of the squad car and right into his face—the face of the goddamn rat. Vernon had not seen this betrayal coming. But that had been the point. Awkwardly leaning forward, hands behind their backs, he and his wife were driven to the Fairbanks jail as federal agents tried to calm the dogs and retrieved a pair of loaded semiautomatic rifles from under the seats of the pickup.

There wasn't much time to clear the scene. Schaeffer Cox and his militia Major Coleman Barney would be arriving in a little more than half an hour, and everyone had to repeat the process. Cox had been in hiding after his no-show at his court hearing almost a month before. Shifting from safe house to safe house, he was now ready to flee the state. As soon as he did this gun deal, he was off to meet Mongo, a truck driver who would smuggle him out of Alaska to Montana. He'd hide there until the time was right, and then he'd be back to conduct "guerrilla warfare," he said, against everyone in Fairbanks who had wronged him. But Schaeffer Cox had a problem. Mongo the truck driver didn't exist. He was a figment of the FBI's imagination. J. R. Olson had made the arrangements for "Mongo" to pick Cox up in the parking lot. He would go down today, one way or another. There was no out.

Olson wasn't quite sure how he got his shit together in half an hour, but after he took a prolonged steaming piss into the side of a snow berm, he was back sitting in the driver's seat of the Explorer. And four minutes early, Cox's black Ford pickup pulled in and parked. Riding shotgun was Coleman Barney. Olson tried to smile and nod as they made their way to the Explorer.

The process began again, with Barney taking the role of Karen Vernon, handing a case up for Cox to examine and looking at the other himself.

"What is this?" Cox said, turning one of the pistols over in his hands. "This was supposed to be a Springfield XD9, but . . . what is this, some old Soviet thing? What happened? And where are the rest of the grenades? Seriously, man!"

"Listen, man, you just told me to go get the guns from Bill. And I got the guns from Bill. This is what he gave me, because this is what he had. It's what he could get. He said that you needed this fast. He told you twelve weeks and then you needed it in four. So this is what he gave me." He was like a chipmunk on Adderall.

"Hey!" Barney called from the back seat. "Someone's coming. Who is that? Do you know him?"

Thoreson had already seen the man in the red Jeep pull in to the lot. He'd already established it wasn't one of his own men. And now listening to the conversation in Olson's vehicle, he knew it wasn't one of their guys, either. There was no reason for anyone to be there. Thoreson watched the man in work boots and a dark jacket and baseball cap pull over and get out, approaching Olson.

Cox shut the case quickly, latched it and shoved it under his legs on the floor with the box of grenades as the man approached Olson's window.

"Open it," Cox said in a half-whisper.

Special Agent Oberlander heard the hum of the automatic window roll down through his earpiece.

"Afternoon!" said the man with a wry smile. "I don't know why you boys are here right now, but I think you may have pissed off all the right people. I just thought I'd give you a heads up there's a whole lotta cops parked right up there behind them trees." He pointed with a finger at the ridge.

"Oh, shit!" said Oberlander. They had only seconds.

"Compromise! Compromise! Compromise! Go! Go!" he yelled into the radio.

No time for a stun grenade. Doors flew open. Agents swarmed, M16s aimed at the vehicle. The doors of the Explorer were wrenched open, and Cox and Barney were pulled out and thrown down. On the other side, the random snitch, baseball cap knocked from his head, was prone on the ice and cuffed before he knew what hit him.

Cox and Barney were disarmed, searched, and cuffed. Pockets were emptied, and Barney was relieved of a white envelope containing $5,000 in hundred-dollar bills and a receipt of withdrawal from the bank.

"You have no right to do this to me," Cox said. "This is an illegal arrest. I haven't done anything! I need to make a phone call." His face was flushed as they read him his rights, stood him up, and walked him to the squad car. His eyes darted around madly, taking in the scene as though looking at a dream until they came to rest on Olson, who was leaning against the Explorer, talking to an FBI agent and not wearing handcuffs.

"Son of a bitch," Cox said and let out a half-growl of rage and panic. "You are *not* going to get away with this! You've started it . . . YOU started this. This is all on your head!"

It's impossible to know what was going on in his mind during the ride to police headquarters, but it's safe to say it included his wife and his two kids and what was going to happen to them. He might have believed that he would beat the rap. He might still have been riding high on a wave of self-righteousness and philosophical certainty. He was undoubtedly expecting some kind of bloodshed—someone who would come to his aid, who would set the plan in motion and light the brush fire of liberty. But it had to occur to him, somewhere in the shadows of his thoughts, that maybe no one would put any plan in motion. And that he might not be there to see his children grow up. He might lose everything he held dear. He might spend a very long time in a very small box for ideas and plans and actions that were only his own.

Schaeffer Cox and Coleman Barney didn't speak as they were driven out of the parking lot, leaning forward in the same awkward position as Lonnie and Karen Vernon an hour before. Agents began clearing the scene and bracing themselves for the avalanche of paperwork to come.

"How ya doin'?" Oberlander asked Olson. "Bet you never thought you'd have a day like this, huh? You OK?"

Olson fumbled with a pack of Marlboros. He nodded as he lit one up, the flame trembling in his hand trying to meet the end of the cigarette.

From what I can figure, my plane touched down in Anchorage about the time Cox and Barney pulled into the parking lot to pick up the weapons.

I'd been staring out the window of the plane at the snaking grey rivers and the snow blanketing the mountains and valleys. The world was white and brown and grey. Even the spruce trees seemed colorless from this elevation. I'd been living in the moment until this point, focused on the mission, forcing out all the other thoughts. And now it was over, and it was time for the hard part.

"Honey, I need to talk to you . . ." "Sweetheart, there's something I need to tell you about what I do . . ." I kept running possible scripts in my head, but none of them worked. "Baby, I took an oath once to serve this country, and I've had to do some things . . ." "This might be hard to hear, but everything is going to be OK . . ."

Everything was so not going to be OK. I was going to have to tell this sweet woman who trusted me, who gave me her whole life, and my two daughters, that it was over. The life she knew was gone, and we would have to leave. We were in danger. The one who was supposed to keep everyone safe had put his family at risk, and now we had to go. There was no bargaining. There was no going back. And there was no way to say it. "Guess what, Stace? Our whole life has been a lie. I've been lying to you for a long time. And we're going to Colorado now, so you won't be at work tomorrow, and our dream house is gone, and the kids won't be going to school, and nobody will ever see their friends again. Oh, and I forgot to pick up the milk."

My relentless monologue continued as I paid for parking, drove out of the airport, and slid through the slushy roads. I made the last left turn onto our street and I could see them. Five black SUVs, red-and-blue lights flashing—two in the driveway, three on the street. I was too late.

CHAPTER 24

★ ★ ★ ★ ★

THE UNITED STATES V. SCHAEFFER COX

"I decided to send a message to a government that was
becoming increasingly hostile."
—Timothy McVeigh

"Put a fork in us. We're finished. We're going to default
eventually, and that's why the feds are stockpiling bullets in
case of civil unrest."
—Former Alaska Gov. Sarah Palin

The flight back to Alaska for the trial was long, but not nearly as long
as the "flight of shame" from Anchorage to our new life in Colorado
had been. I don't remember now exactly when it dawned on me that
Stacey would not only have to pick up and leave her life with literally zero
notice, but she'd also have to get on an airplane, and we wouldn't have time
to get a Xanax prescription from her doctor. We'd taken almost three weeks
in the dead of winter to drive to Alaska because of her terror of flying. I sat
in row twenty-four and remembered my beautiful wife, with the snowflakes

on her dark eyelashes and her cheeks red from the bite of the cold, scraping the windows on the U-Haul all those years ago. I drove that damn thing thousands of miles because I didn't want her to be afraid. I wanted her to feel safe with me. To know I'd do anything for her. I remembered her laughing under the long shimmering arc of the Northern Lights, and I looked across the aisle of the plane at this terrified woman, white as paste, gripping the arm rests, with her eyes shut hard, squeezing tears down her cheeks as we started moving down the runway. At one point, I reached across and touched her arm hoping to comfort her. She flinched violently and flashed me a death stare. I think that was the only time we made eye contact during the flight.

Over the course of the following weeks, she went through all the stages of grief for her lost life and lost home—shock, denial, bargaining, anger, depression, and eventually acceptance. She would whipsaw back and forth among all of these stages, but I think anger was her favorite. Ultimately, we settled into a new life. We bought a nice little house, and we liked Colorado. There were big skies and mountains, and the kids loved our road trips to the high desert to see the prairie dogs, and they began to make friends at their new school. And month by month, in tiny increments, Stacey forgave me.

A year will erase a lot of trauma. We passed through all the firsts, like there had been a death. First birthdays, first Halloween, first Thanksgiving, first Christmas, first New Year, the first anniversary *of.* And then it was time to go back. I'd been called as a witness in the *United States v. Schaeffer Cox, Coleman Barney, and Lonnie Vernon.* All three were being tried together for conspiracy to commit murder, kidnapping, and a host of weapons offenses. The Vernons' little side plot to blow up IRS agents trying to repossess their house got its own second trial with husband and wife as codefendants. Everything about my Alaska life came flooding back as my flight out of Denver headed northwest to Seattle, and then north for another three hours to Anchorage. My brain played its own in-flight movie. All the thoughts I'd been pushing out of my head, all the wondering. How was Suicide? Where were Clay and the Big Mexican? Grease, Sherlock, Banana Hammock . . . I even wondered about Sunshine and Dusti and what corner of the world they might have found that was safe from the wrath of Gunny. And Brian. I missed that crazy SOB. He'd been called as a witness for the defense, and I had no idea what he'd say. He'd had a year to think too, and

Brian's brain thinking for a year could have gone anywhere. Stacey forgave me, but I was pretty sure Brian hadn't. I'd had several beers by the time the plane began its descent. We were coming in over Prince William Sound, where Suicide, some of his buddies, and I had gone salmon fishing long ago, and I had learned that you never, ever, ever bring a banana on a fishing boat or you will curse the boat and everyone on it and nobody will catch a fish. And even if you offer to literally shoot the banana and dump its body overboard to get rid of the bad luck, people will still be mad at you.

There would be no sign of civilization until we were within minutes of landing. Nameless mountain peaks, some still snow-capped, cradling river valleys, and the mudflats flanking Cook Inlet. It was June, and the furious greening had begun in the lowlands. I loved Colorado and the Rockies, but there was nowhere like Alaska.

When we landed in Anchorage, I'd be discreetly escorted to a secure floor of the downtown Sheraton. No one without a room or a reason could get to my floor while I waited there to testify.

I'd been watching the Alaska newspapers online and keeping up with the chatter—like a ghost, watching and listening to the echoes of my life, without being seen. The left was shocked. Their most-hated militant right-wing poster boy had been working for the FBI and against Cox? Well then, it must be because he was a criminal. He sold illegal guns, didn't he? He's the guy who arrested the journalist! He turned on his buddies to avoid jail time, I bet. He'd been given a new identity. He left the country. The amount of misinformation was staggering, and I still got no benefit of the doubt.

The right and the militias turned on me harder. Traitor. Turncoat. The worst kind of scum. Norm Olson put out a fake news story on his militia chat board after calling me "the Benedict Arnold of the militia":

FBI paid informant, Bill Fulton, was found dead last night from what sources say appears to be an assassination. His hands were bound and a hood was placed over his head. Militia literature was left near the body with a note scribbled, "Payback's a bitch."

Bill Fulton is very much alive NOW, but he is a man without a country. He was used by the FBI to wreck Joe Miller's bid for the Alaska Senate and has turned traitor to the militia/patriot cause.

And so the conspiracy theories began. It was all about some leftist plot to destroy Joe Miller. It shouldn't have surprised me. Miller lost his shit over someone maybe letting air out of his tires. This would have poured gasoline on the fire of his already out-of-control paranoia.

Norm Olson was quite sure, he said, that when they found my body, the government would blame the militias.

He is of no further use to the FBI EXCEPT FOR THE FACT THAT HIS DEATH WILL BE PINNED ON THE MILITIA AS AN ACT OF REPRISAL. When his miserable carcass is found, the feds will conclude that the militia whacked him. But it won't [investigate] too far.

I would be a false flag. The FBI was going to whack me and make it look like it was the militias so the feds would have an excuse to take them down before they overthrew the government with the Denny's judiciary, a couple of dozen assholes in camo, and a trailer full of ammunition. It was exhausting and surreal, and frankly, I got tired of reading about my own death. Somehow, everyone on both sides had still managed to find a reason to hate me. It was actually going to feel good to testify—to be able to finally have my moment to explain on the record. Because the actual truth of what happened had not yet occurred to anyone.

The Old Man and I had talked a lot. Duty was sometimes an inconvenient thing, he told me. Sometimes we find ourselves in situations that we haven't really chosen, but that have chosen us. All we can do is the best we can in any given situation. Remember what's important and always act with honor. He was like a damn fortune cookie, but I loved that guy, and he always made me feel like somehow things would work out for the best. He was my touchstone, and I needed one.

Several months earlier, an Alaska state judge had ruled that because of Alaska's more stringent privacy laws, the electronic surveillance and the evidence it had revealed were not admissible and were to be suppressed because there had been no warrant issued. Law enforcement officers would have had to obtain a search warrant *before* recording or videotaping, which they had failed to do. As a result, the state was forced to drop many of the most egregious charges, including conspiracy to kidnap and some of the conspiracy-to-commit-murder charges. But the feds operate under a different set of rules from the state's—the United States Constitution—without the strict privacy clause, so the surveillance evidence for the federal charges could be admitted even without a warrant. So now, it would be up to the feds alone to prove a case strong enough to send the three to jail. If they failed, our merry band of whack-jobs could walk free. The new development had already freed one defendant—Michael Anderson, the records keeper and "computer guru" of the militia, as the press was calling him. His offenses had mostly been on a state level, and he'd agreed to testify at the trial.

After I settled in to my hotel room and checked the clock for a tiny camera, I met with Steve Skrocki, the federal prosecutor. He was tall and serious with a Joe Miller–style scruffy beard and small wire-rimmed glasses. He asked me lots of questions. I swore a lot, because that's what I do. He was clearly uncomfortable and as the clock ticked off hours, he began to become more and more of a condescending prick. I didn't like that. It was obvious that all these people were used to lording their power over criminal informants.

"I'm not a fucking criminal," I reminded him. "I did this for you assholes to try to do the right thing. I'm a volunteer, just so you remember. And you fuckers kinda ruined my life a little."

"You know, Mr. Fulton . . . you can't speak like that to the court when you're on the stand," he said.

"Well, no shit. What do you think I am, a fucking moron?"

"I'm not kidding, Bill. If you speak like that in here, that's the way you are going to speak on the stand. I've seen it happen a hundred times."

"Well, you haven't seen me, dude."

"Please don't call me 'dude.' I'm a federal prosecutor. You need to remember that and speak to me appropriately. This is the kind of thing I'm talking about."

"I don't give a shit if you're a federal prosecutor. I can handle myself."

I got a call later from Skrocki.

"I think we'll do fine without your testimony," he said. "We've given it some thought, and that's what the team thinks is best."

So I had traveled all this way for my opportunity to finally get on the record with what had happened, under oath, and all for nothing.

Steve Skrocki, true to his word, did not put me on the witness list. But the team of defense attorneys noticed that omission and couldn't figure it out. No doubt fueled by the rage of Schaeffer Cox, who'd been stewing over my involvement in the sting, they decided to call me to testify for them instead. They figured the prosecution was trying to hide something, to conceal an overzealous undercover informant, to cover up a botched investigation. They thought they had found the smoking gun, and now they just had to make me crack on the stand, to slip up and reveal the incompetence or corruption of the federal investigation. In reality, all the prosecution was trying to cover up was my mouth.

It was a sunny morning, and the federal courthouse was buzzing with media. Two German shepherds trained to sniff explosives stood with ears up and noses twitching in the lobby by the metal detectors. I thought about Charlie and Oscar sniffing out our fugitive Princess under the trailer. Security was everywhere.

In the courtroom, preparations were being made, including a discussion of which defendant would sit where. Two tables sat on floor level before the judge, and there was an elevated dais near a back door where an armed marshal stood.

"Lonnie has to sit at the dais. He *has* to sit at the end by the door. That's non-negotiable. Completely non-negotiable."

"And here are the pens for Lonnie to use during the trial. He has to have these pens. He has to use these with the felt tip. That's non-negotiable. Security purposes."

Nobody wanted to give a guy who threatened to kill judges the chance to lunge at one with a ballpoint pen during his trial. He was lucky he didn't get crayons or chalk.

As the week advanced, the jury was selected, and hundreds of items were entered into evidence—an arsenal of guns, grenade bodies, scanned documents, intercepted texts and emails, body armor, video and audio tape from FBI surveillance, photos, and books.

For the next six weeks, the jury would watch and listen as that evidence and more than seventy witnesses were brought before them.

The defense's argument focused on the informants. They would prove, they said, that the informant J. R. Olson—a criminal himself—was unreliable and that the two-for-one retaliation plan was his idea in the first place. He would do and say whatever he could to reduce his own sentence for crimes committed, and he had pushed Cox and his militia to behave in ways they never would have otherwise. It was entrapment by an overzealous government agency, which sought to demonize the innocent to keep them quiet and stifle their anti-government views.

And me. I was clearly deranged, a drunkard, violent. I was an example of another FBI informant who was out of control. I pulled a knife and threatened to cut a man's throat, they would say; I intimidated and bullied. They were counting on my testimony to back up their assertions. I'd pound the nails into my own coffin just by being on the stand, they thought. I was their best hope for getting their clients off. All their eggs were in my and Olson's basket.

The first major witness was Michael Anderson, the "computer guru." He still wore ill-fitting clothes, but this time it was black pants and a brown belt that had to be six holes too big, shoved through several belt loops and ending at his spine. He wore a lavender shirt with a white collar.

Steve Skrocki showed Anderson a piece of paper projected on a screen:

I am the commanding officer.

    Les and Bill, I would like you to be field officers and start out each in command of a company of 30 men.

    Mike and Dave, I would like you to be in a special tech/indirect warfare team that would probably be in Unit 2.

    Steve, I would like you to stay very low profile and serve mostly as a PR man and also give specialized counter-intelligence training to the men as needed.

    Philip and Isaac, you can be privates in units 3 and 4 respectively.

Josiah, soon you will be old enough to be a part of the militia without the public criticizing us for having members that are too young.

Signed Schaeffer Cox

"Is that you? The Mike?" asked Skrocki.

"Yes, I believe so. Schaeffer was interested in having me build electronic jammers, cellphone and GPS jammers. Tech-warfare stuff. That's what he was interested in. I never answered him."

But he had collected some information for Cox. He had fifteen to twenty names in a database with public information he'd found online about where they lived, property they owned, where they worked. He'd taken one photo of a license plate from a car parked in the driveway of a woman named Wendy Williams from the Office of Children's Services.

"Schaeffer wanted to know where Wendy Williams lived so he could go talk to her," said Anderson. "I told him I hadn't found it yet. He said that he needed to know where she was because 'if she hurt his family, she might get a bullet through her windshield,'" he said.

After the domestic-violence charge against Cox, the judge had ordered him not to have any weapons in his house. Anderson's house became his armory.

"His attorney was there, and I came to his house and picked up his weapons and stored them for him—twenty or twenty-five rifles, handguns, a bunch of ammo, at least one tactical vest, some empty grenade bodies attached to the tactical vest."

Boxes were brought to the witness stand and a white five-gallon bucket full of grenade bodies. Anderson was given rubber gloves to put on. He took a fully automatic machine gun out of the box and identified it as one of the firearms he took from Cox's house.

"Schaeffer said it was a homemade automatic. He said he had built it himself."

Next came a .22-caliber pistol and a silencer.

"There were five to ten grenade bodies attached to a tactical vest. I remember they were attached. I put them all in my tool shed behind my house. There was a .30-caliber 1919—a Browning, and a couple of semiautomatics, some ARs and a couple AKs, and a couple hunting rifles and handguns. They were at my home about two months. Schaeffer came by and picked them up a couple months after I took them from him."

Skrocki went through a long list of people whose names had been found in various places—computer files, notebooks, sticky notes.

"What about Gary Tolop?"

"He's a trooper that lives a few doors down from Schaeffer. He called him 'Trooper Butthole.'"

Cox suppressed a giggle.

"He was giving me some names because I didn't really know how to start the database," Anderson said.

The list of names went on: Alaska State Trooper Burt Barrick; Trooper Ron Wall; Curtis, a DHS border patrol agent; Tom Stedler, DHS; Lawrence Piscoya; Officer Malik Jones; Officer Dave Roener; Officer John Marion; Trina Beauchamp, TSA.

"Cox said Trina was someone he knew. He said, 'She goes to my church. She's a nice lady, but some day she may just follow orders, and she may have to go.'"

As the list began to grow, Anderson started to get cold feet.

"Schaeffer and I had met, and he asked how it was going with the whole database thing and also talked to me about that he thought there was a hit team out to get him. He thought the feds had sent a hit team after him and he wanted to know who they might be and where they might be."

But as Anderson started compiling a "hit list" for federal as well as state employees and law enforcement officers, he started to panic. After being asked by Cox, then by Karen Vernon, and finally by J. R. Olson, to turn over the database, he erased his hard drive. Then he went old school.

"The program was Eraser, I think. I used it to wipe the hard drive. Later on, I smashed it with a hammer. I put it on a concrete floor and I smashed it until little parts of it fell out. Then, I threw it in the dumpster."

"I've been told you save money by getting hard drives out of dumpsters," said Skrocki.

"There are lots of things to be found at the dump. I get 90 percent of my clothes at the dump," he said with a proud smile. The mystery of the giant clothing was solved.

Anderson had spent eight months in prison before the state charges were dropped and he was given immunity in exchange for his testimony.

"I had just been charged with conspiracy to murder someone I thought was Schaeffer's friend and a judge I'd never heard of before. I wondered how I was going to prove my innocence. What was Schaeffer up to? How was I going to get my family through this? I thought they'd be better off if they didn't have to live with this at all."

"Did you try to take your own life while you were in prison?" Skrocki asked.

"I chewed the guard off my glasses," he said, his throat tightening. "In the cell was a bench with a pivot, moving parts, and I squeezed the metal to a sharp point. I sat with my back to the camera, and I started to slit my wrist. It wasn't very sharp. It was more like digging away at chunks of flesh. I did that for several minutes, unsuccessfully. I looked at the blood dripping on the floor. I closed my eyes, and all I saw was a black frame and then flames. And I thought, 'I can't. I'll have to get through this somehow.' "

You had to feel sort of sorry for the guy in a way. Cox had a way of attracting dumbasses who wanted someone to follow. He turned disgruntled people into dangerous ones.

Trina Beauchamp, a TSA employee, had attended Cox's father's church. He'd come to lunch at her house a few times when she hosted home-cooked meals for college kids. Then one day, he showed up for lunch wearing body armor. He asked her if he was on the TSA's no-fly list, and she explained she couldn't help him with that.

She had learned the night before her testimony that her name had appeared with a few others scrawled on a yellow legal pad with a crudely drawn map of her workplace. Beauchamp grabbed a tissue from the box on the witness stand. She mopped her eyes. She was scared, she said. She felt betrayed. It had been only hours since she'd learned her name was on Cox's list, but she'd already purchased a gun.

Cox, who had been smiling and trying to make eye contact with her as she gave testimony, was not smiling any more. He grew flushed and began to cry.

"Trina, I love you! I would never hurt you!" he called from behind the table.

A string of witnesses followed: Cox's mother-in-law, who was afraid for her daughter and said Cox had isolated her from her family; Coleman Barney's sister-in-law, who watched his ideology become more radical under the influence of Cox and knew Cox was hiding out from the authorities in Barney's house. She had seen Cox address a judge in Fairbanks, saying he'd rather see her dead than address her in court. There were several employees of King Jesus North Pole (KJNP) radio who said that Schaeffer Cox had shown up for an on-air interview flanked by an armed detail who intimidated people on the property and that he'd ranted on air of a secret death squad sent by the feds to kill him, his wife, and their child.

And then there was Maria Rensel from the IACC in her red suit and sprayed hair. She and her husband had served as jurors at the Denny's trial. She backed Schaeffer all the way. He was completely innocent of everything, she said. When asked where she got her information about the case, Rensel said, "Newspaper reporters would call me, and I would ask them questions. And from other people who had talked to Schaeffer." Marti Cox never testified at Denny's, nor did the state trooper in the misdemeanor gun charge, who, according to Rensel, "decided not to show up."

Les Zerbe testified immediately before my slot. He evaded questions and sweated a lot. He was asked if something had happened that night at Dark North Tactical.

"Mr. Fulton was not happy with my answer that I had no plan, and he came at me with a knife!" he said, red-faced. "He assaulted me by really raising his voice at me. And he was drinking about ten beers, but I thought he was sane and making believe he was drinking it or something . . ." I had not expected Zerbe to vouch for my ability to hold my alcohol.

"I believed it was a setup. He approached me and came toward me with a weapon."

"What weapon?" Cox's attorney Nelson Traverso asked.

"I was looking in the man's eyes to see how serious he was on harming me. I did not see the weapon, although I was told it was a knife."

Then Skrocki had his turn. "You don't know if Bill Fulton had a knife or not?"

"I looked in his eyes, like a pit bull," Zerbe said. "If a pit bull's coming at you, you look in his eyes."

"You didn't get hurt."

"It felt like I was."

"You had a gun. A .45 in your coat pocket. You think he's coming at you."

"Yes," said Zerbe.

"Under oath, you said you never saw a knife," Skrocki pushed.

"I didn't see it clearly, but it was some kind of weapon. I just saw he had a weapon in one hand. You usually carry your hand differently if you're holding a weapon."

"And you didn't tell a trooper?"

"Nope."

"Because you'd have to tell the troopers where you were and what you were doing."

"I haven't had any luck with the troopers about much of anything," said Zerbe.

Skrocki changed the subject. "You were interviewed by the FBI. You don't like the TSA."

"Most Americans dislike the TSA."

I had to give him that one.

"So, you're speaking for a lot of Americans?"

"We're the statue, and they're the pigeon. It's not a user-friendly situation. It's a 'we must be in control' situation, and it's on the news every day in one form or another. We want our country safe, but the way they're going around it is very adolescent compared to what the Israelis are doing."

Video clips were shown to the jurors of an interview with Cox in the Fairbanks Denny's by a reporter from Vice News. Zerbe sat at the Denny's table the whole time but denied any memory of the interview. He was utterly full of shit. Cox was the only one who talked, and government overreach was his mantra.

"And it will take the men of character and conscience and principle to stand up and say, 'No, that's wrong.' And as a matter of fact, I will shed blood in opposition to that! And that's something that I would do. I would take up arms. I would fire on my own government. I would fire on police officers if they were my own neighbors, if they were party to that. And not because there

was any personal malice, but it's how pure and sacred of a cause liberty is. It's enough to make me reckon with things I don't want to do.

"I've never wanted to hurt anyone. I've never been in a fight. But as a husband, and father, and friend, I've got a responsibility to defend people—to defend my family and to defend freedom. And I can't deny that, even if it's not a very fun task. And so that's something that I'm willing to do. I'm willing to fight, I'm willing to die, I'm willing to oppose a lawless force. I'm willing to defend. And everybody if they think about it will arrive at that point."

The jury was completely silent, and brows were furrowed.

"Can I take it that because you didn't get up and leave, you agreed with Mr. Cox?"

"That means no such thing," said Zerbe who was as red as a lobster, sweating profusely, and somewhat out of breath. I remembered how he sat there in the hotel room at Pike's Lodge, never speaking, letting Cox do all the talking but nodding like a bobblehead even through the worst of it.

"With respect to these video clips, you're Mr. Cox's number-two in command. Never once did you counsel him if what he was saying was a bad idea?" Skrocki asked.

"I don't recall. But we have a command structure. We had all kinds of conversations how many years ago . . . I don't recall."

Skrocki paused and touched the tips of his fingers together.

"You're going to tell me you just listen to your commander. Like what happened at Nuremberg, right?"

"That's mostly correct," said Zerbe.

"I have no more questions."

Now, my turn. Finally. The bailiff motioned for me to enter from the lobby as he held the heavy wooden door open. I strode into the courtroom in my charcoal suit, my white collar starched and pressed, a blue tie, a flag pin, shoes shined, hair in military cut, spine ramrod straight. I gave the side-eye to Skrocki as I walked past. Fuck that dude. I felt like something out of *A Few Good Men*.

Cox's lawyer was first. He tried hard to find the secret reason the prosecution hadn't called me.

No, I was not a member of a militia. No, my store did not sell guns. No, I struck no deal for my testimony.

"Did you understand the Alaska Peacemakers Militia motto? Defend all, aggress none?" he asked.

"I understood the motto, but it had nothing to do with what Schaeffer was about. He was planning on arresting judges, and putting them on trial, and hanging them."

No, I did not express frustration about Cox's not wanting to "go to war" with the feds. The whole point was to keep that from happening.

Yes, I told them I'd get grenades, because I didn't want them getting real ones from someone else. Yes, I was "a good actor" at Dark North Tactical. You would be too if you were trying not to get shot.

No, I didn't make money at this. I was still waiting to get reimbursed for my expenses from the FBI, as a matter of fact. And no, for the last time, I did not have an agreement with the government to get out of prosecution for some crime I'd committed. The concept that I was actually a volunteer, and trying to keep this nut case from killing people because it was wrong, was apparently inconceivable to them.

The courtroom had a heavy media presence—the Associated Press, Reuters, local TV stations from Anchorage, the *Fairbanks Daily News-Miner,* the *Anchorage Daily News,* the *Alaska Dispatch,* of course, and local bloggers. Clicking keyboards, scribbling pens. No cameras allowed, though, in federal court.

Traverso finally ended questioning, a bit baffled. He hadn't found the smoking gun—why I hadn't been called as a witness for the prosecution. Skrocki approached to cross-examine me.

"You were asked a lot of questions about your part at this sale for Dark North Tactical."

"Yes, sir." And by "sir" I meant "asshole" and he knew it. But I looked him in the eye. I had already proved him wrong.

Yes, I was asked by the FBI to listen and participate. Yes, there were firearms; I had a verbal confrontation with Les Zerbe; I made a move toward him. Yes, I was concerned I'd be ferreted out.

"Did you know Zerbe thought you were an informant?"

"Not at the time." I sat straight. "I'm glad I did it, now. Sir."

"You were given information about warrants?"

"Yes, sir."

"You operate a fugitive-recovery business. Did you ever hear of a warrant like the one he wanted you to serve?

"No."

"Did you have concerns on a personal level?"

"Yes. I've learned about the sovereign-citizen ideology now. Here's a guy saying he's gotten together with his friends and created warrants, and he wants us to go arrest judges and others associated with the court. Personally, I was scared."

"Had you ever heard about that before?"

"No, sir."

"Planning arrest warrants and what to do with them afterwards—was that part of the equation? Arrest judges and what to do with them afterwards?"

"I was told they would be tried and fined, or hung, sir."

"Did he mention anything about how you were to treat Vernon and Olson?"

"I was to treat them as I would treat him and they were there with full authority and representation."

I told him how they wanted silencers for XD pistols, grenade bodies, grenade fuses, and that there was some talk of automatic weapons and C4; about how Lonnie Vernon walked into my store asking to purchase grenades.

"That's all I have. Thank you, Mr. Fulton."

Brian Beazley took the stand. We hadn't spoken a word since I left. I was pretty sure he hated me. He didn't know I was working as an FBI informant, he said. But he began to believe my story about Cox and his plan less and less over the course of the day at the fundraiser.

"How did Cox's face look when he was confronted by Mr. Fulton at the meeting about this so-called plan to abduct judges?" Traverso asked.

"Surprised at first, which turned to alarm the more aggressive that Bill got, insisting that he had this 'plan.'"

Brian was covering his ass. I didn't blame him. But I'd considered him a true friend, and this one stung. I knew he'd need to say all kinds of things to keep his business, his reputation, the confidence of his men. I knew he'd have to throw me under the bus. But that was on me. I knew it was coming.

And, finally, the defendants were given the chance to speak. Schaeffer Cox was reined in repeatedly by objections from the prosecution and by stern warnings from the judge. The court was not here to listen to pontificating about political theory. But Traverso managed to have the jury listen, in its entirety, to a presentation Cox gave in Montana that talked about his notion of "creating a second government" and the tyranny of the current one.

"Do you believe in the use of violence against the government?" Traverso asked.

"Yes and no. If your government is breaking the law, if they turn murderous like they did in Syria, then yes. But no, in that by breaking the law and turning murderous they are not the government anymore. They are criminal."

Nothing was ever straightforward with Cox. There was always wiggle room, different ways of interpreting, parsing words, semantics, conditions. If the government was no longer the government, by his definition, then even by acting against them, it technically wasn't aggressing "the government" in his eyes. And I already knew he felt the current United States government was illegitimate, so all bets were off.

"My deepest fear is that our government is not going to hear us until we speak to them in their language, which is force."

By the end of more than an hour of listening to Cox at his charming best speak to his Montana admirers, who clapped and cheered, nobody could say the jury hadn't seen exactly what Cox wanted them to see and heard exactly what he wanted them to hear. He had his shot to convert the dozen members of the audience in the jury box.

Coleman Barney by almost everyone's reckoning had been a good and decent guy who just got mixed up with the wrong kids. His family dutifully came to court every day—his wife, siblings, parents, all holding Bibles. When tapes and videos were played of my interactions with the militia, the women would put their fingers in their ears and rock back and forth every time I used profanity. But Barney was a good wing-man, supportive and dedicated, and he had a good lawyer. He testified in his own defense, and it worked out well for him, although he provided a point of sanity in contrast with Cox, which didn't work out well for the latter.

Lonnie Vernon, wisely, and under the advice of his counsel, did not testify. The more that jackass talked, the worse it got for him. His lawyers spent most of the trial trying to prove he was an idiot and couldn't possibly be capable of much. For Vernon, that was as good a defense as any.

CHAPTER 25

★ ★ ★ ★ ★

WE THE JURY

"There's absolutely no reason to dissolve [the Union],
but if Washington continues to thumb their nose at the
American people, you know, who knows what might come
out of that?"
—Texas Gov. Rick Perry

"The defendant wants to hide the truth because he's
generally guilty. The defense attorney's job is to make sure
the jury does not arrive at that truth."
—Alan Dershowitz

Schaeffer Cox was ashen, wearing a charcoal-grey suit jacket and
white shirt, open at the collar. Coleman Barney's thick brow was
deeply furrowed and he drummed his fingers on the table. Lonnie
Vernon rested his head on his hand, with a hang-dog look, utterly defeated.
The courtroom had been buzzing for weeks, but now it was uncomfortably
silent. After six weeks, anyone who had been watching was deeply invested.
Today there would be no witnesses, no swearing in, no evidence, no testimony. Just waiting. And waiting.

Judge Robert Bryan finally spoke in his usual slow, gravelly tone.

"Well, it's perhaps an art form to know when a jury is deadlocked. This jury has been out for basically two full days, and a little more. I have commented to people that this jury has been one of the most engaged, in a complex trial, that I've seen. They appear to have taken their job seriously and have worked hard during the trial. They appear to be pretty firm in their conclusion that further deliberations would not be productive, and they appear to have only one charge that they have not agreed on. I believe the best practice at this point, based on those considerations, is to accept the verdicts that they have reached and declare a mistrial on whatever it is they can't agree on. That is my judgment." The gavel came down and the jury was fetched.

Barney looked over to Cox, his lips pressed together, and raised eyebrows, as if to say, "Well, this is it."

Cox looked down, the fingertips of one hand pressed against his forehead. His wife had just entered the room and stood in the second row, but he didn't yet know she was there. She spoke to someone, and as he recognized the sound of her voice, he looked up, glassy-eyed. He smiled a sad, grateful smile at her, and she sent one back. They held each other's gaze for a long time. The bravado, the bluster, the bullshit, had all faded away. It seemed, finally, to be perhaps a true moment. And he didn't even have to talk to find it.

I've wondered if he could go back and do it again what he'd do. I had risked losing my wife, my family. But I felt in the end like I'd done the right thing. What was Cox thinking? Would he do things differently? Did he feel justified with his new role as martyr for the cause? Would he have been more careful but done the same stupid shit? Or would he have decided to grow his carpentry business and go to church on Sunday, enjoy his family, and leave the Revolution to some other guy?

The jury filed back into the courtroom and took their seats, many stoic, others downright sullen.

"Do I understand correctly that you have reached a verdict on all except one charge?" asked Bryan.

"Yes, Your Honor."

"Will you hand the verdict form to the bailiff, please?"

The foreman handed a piece of paper to the bailiff, who in turn handed it to the judge.

"There are twenty-one verdicts here," Bryan announced, peering through the glasses that had slid down his nose, and then he read through them one by one. All three defendants had been found guilty of conspiracy to possess unregistered silencers and/or destructive devices. I could vouch for that one. I knew those grenades would get them into trouble from the moment I met Lonnie Vernon. Cox was found guilty of possessing unregistered destructive devices, possession of an unregistered silencer, possession of an unregistered machine gun, illegal possession of a machine gun, and making an unregistered silencer out of PVC pipe and shaving gel. He was found not guilty of carrying firearms during a crime of violence.

Then, the big one.

"We the jury find Francis Schaeffer Cox guilty of conspiracy to commit murder."

In the passage of an instant, Cox's face flushed. His eyes grew wide, his chin went slack, and he began breathing shallow and fast, almost panting. He looked stunned and bewildered, like an animal caught in a trap. His eyes darted around the room as if looking for an explanation for what had just been said to appear somewhere. He didn't snap out of it for a long time and continued to get more and more distraught as Judge Bryan moved on and as the meaning of the verdict began to sink in.

"We the jury find Lonnie Gene Vernon guilty of conspiracy to commit murder."

Vernon closed his eyes.

Coleman Barney's charge of conspiracy to commit murder was the one that had deadlocked the jury. He let out a long exhale. It made the difference between seeing his kids grow up and not.

And, finally, Cox was found guilty of solicitation to commit a crime of violence—the murder of an officer of the United States. This one hit him hard too, before he recovered from the previous news. He would *not* see his kids grow up. He looked at his wife, then, with laser focus, from face to face at each of the jurors—a look demanding some kind of answer. None of them met his gaze.

Then the judge polled the jury one by one, asking if what he had just read represented their findings, and if it represented the finding of the jury as a whole. In turn, one by one, they responded yes—some with confidence, some emotionless, some obviously choked up, eyes wet. Cox licked his lips and swallowed hard, still staring at the jurors.

Lonnie Vernon pushed his chair back against the wall, lips tight, staring up. He'd probably die in jail. He had no wife to look at, because she was in prison awaiting the next trial where she and he would be codefendants—accused of plotting the death of IRS agents. They'd use those stamped goodbye letters they found in his truck as evidence. This was far from over for him.

Cox, still in a state of disbelief, pulled the microphone down to his mouth and stared at it for a long time. "The prosecutors withheld evidence from you guys," he said to the jury, just to say something.

"Mr. Cox . . . please," Bryan said. And Cox never spoke again. He pressed his fingertips together and looked almost like he was in prayer. His wife in the gallery made a gesture with elbows and forearms vertical and touching and palms pointed upward and out with her fingers cupped, giving the effect of a tree or a chalice.

Sentencing would happen in ninety days.

Cox, chin quivering, mouth contorted, took a Kleenex and pressed it to his eyes. Coleman Barney reached over and gave his attorney, Tim Dooley, a hug. Dooley looked relieved and patted his back. The jury stood for the final time and filed out the back door. Three times the metallic zip of handcuffs was the only noise in the courtroom, and one by one the defendants were escorted out.

Marti Cox and Mae Barney, Coleman's mother, hugged each other and cried. I had no doubt in my mind that Marti was going to have a much better life with her husband in jail than she would have with him out.

In the lobby, Tim Dooley stopped to talk to a small group of reporters. He was asked about the conspiracy-to-commit-murder charges that had stuck for Cox and Vernon.

"I didn't see that winning," he said, shaking his head. "That charge came at the last minute. They only levied that charge after we refused to take a deal. And they can do that, but . . ." He shook his head.

The government had offered Barney a plea deal of five to ten years to be decided by a judge, or a straight seven years in prison. He refused the deal, and only after that did the government level the conspiracy-to-commit-murder charge against him, which carries a maximum sentence of life in prison. Dooley said he didn't regret the decision to reject the plea, and for Barney, that gamble had paid off. Lonnie Vernon's counsel and he himself had done as much as they could do, he said.

"The verdicts left Mr. Barney pretty devastated," he went on. "He thinks about letting other people down, not about himself. I don't think I've ever been as blue about a verdict as I am about this one," he said quietly.

Barney hadn't known what was going on with Cox, Dooley told the reporters. "Much of what Cox had done, Barney only learned about when they were both in jail. You never really know who you're friends with—you *think* you know them."

"In light of the way this case went, if you are someone like the defendants, how do you keep from getting in trouble?" asked a reporter. Dooley thought for a moment.

"Shut up and don't express your opinion. About anything. Ever. You know in some ways, these guys are right. The government *has* gone too far . . . If this is what we're doing, we've got a lot of people to lock up in Alaska."

Steve Skrocki rounded the corner into the lobby, and Dooley moved on.

"What do you have to say about the two FBI informants in this trial and how they were used?" asked a reporter.

"That's been part of the investigative process for a long time," Skrocki said, "but in an investigation setting like this, you never just walk someone in without triangulating and firmly asserting the things they say are true. All the informants' testimony was backed up by audio, video, or witness corroboration."

Marti Cox and Bill and Mae Barney walked through doors out of the courtroom and made their way past the reporters. "Not now," said Bill Barney as they approached.

"Schaeffer Cox is different than your typical Fairbanks survivalist libertarian type because of his political beliefs and the very clear pressure Cox was putting on the judicial system in Fairbanks," Skrocki explained. "He was seeking an upwelling of support, and it was not a question of *if* something was going to happen but rather *when* the militia would be strong enough to make it happen. Like, 'We're not ready to do this, but when we are . . . we will,'" he characterized Cox's plan.

"I don't think strong anti-government beliefs are a new comment on the radar screen," he went on, talking about the militia's take on the government and current events. "The concern of a collapse of government is something that is also not new—the Great Depression, the Dust Bowl, Vietnam. We've been there. But right now there seems to be an uptick in that sentiment.

"People think of it as a First Amendment issue," Skrocki wrapped up, "but it's deterrence. That's of primary importance, so nobody gets killed."

For a while the remaining spectators milled around the lobby, talking with reporters and mulling the big issues. What are the limits of the First Amendment? When does speech become conspiracy and when is the time just right to intervene without violating a citizen's constitutional rights? What about the Second Amendment? Should prosecuting crimes involving possession or registration of weapons even be allowed? What about the Fourth Amendment—privacy in a person's personal effects? The Alaska State Constitution and state law had seen a whole host of charges dropped because there were no warrants. Why is the federal Constitution so much more restrictive? These were questions left to the court and law enforcement.

The way I saw it, Cox had crossed the line. I'd rather have people complaining that he'd gone to jail and debating the intent of the drafters of the Constitution than reading about some judge's family burning to death in their beds or a shootout in Fairbanks involving dead officers or civilians. My job was to answer the call to my country. I did my job. Now it was time to move on and get this behind me. Cox had been blessed—blessed to be born in a country where they didn't put him before a firing squad the first time he opened his big mouth. He'd been blessed with a wife he mistreated and kids he didn't deserve. And he could have had a good life, but he fucked it up. My pity only went so far.

Cameras were not allowed in the federal courthouse, so here are some eerily lifelike courtroom sketches by Jeanne Devon. Their inclusion in her daily reports of the trial earned a small cult following. In this one, I'm explaining how much money I got from the FBI to Cox's attorney Nelson Traverso.

J. R. Olson on the stand as the prosecution plays one of the FBI recordings of me talking to Lonnie Vernon. Coleman Barney's Mormon ladies hold their ears and their Bibles to protect them from the barrage of F-bombs.

Les Zerbe, who suddenly had the shittiest memory on the planet, answering exactly zero questions from federal prosecutor Steve Skrocki.

Lonnie and Karen Vernon at sentencing.

Schaeffer Cox testifies, and testifies, and testifies, while Steve Skrocki and Judge Robert Bryan listen.

CHAPTER 26

★ ★ ★ ★ ★

SELF-FULFILLING PARANOIA

> "In this life, we have to make many choices . . . Many of our choices are between good and evil. The choices we make, however, determine to a large extent our happiness or our unhappiness, because we have to live with the consequences of our choices."
> **—James E. Faust**

Well, this proves one thing," veteran Alaska reporter Michael Carey remarked, looking at the crowd in the lobby outside Courtroom Two. "Schaeffer Cox can still draw a crowd."

It was sentencing day. Six months had passed since the verdict.

The day before, Lonnie Vernon had his turn.

"This is no bullshit. I have things to say and it's going to be two hours!" he told his attorney, and the pressure cooker burst.

"I want to know who these people are who have jurisdiction over me! Does the government have jurisdiction to put him over me?" Vernon, red-faced, pointed a finger at Steve Skrocki. "We're going to discuss that today," he said.

"I believe we resolved that before," said Judge Robert Bryan like he was soothing a child.

"Nothing out of disrespect for you, Judge Bryan, but these people have done nothing for me," Vernon said. "If you have no jurisdiction over me, then what does a piece of paper mean? It's just a piece of paper! I see a force of law, forced on me by an unknown entity. I reside in the state of Alaska, not in our government realm. I am sovereign! And who is this clown with his agency?" He pointed at Special Agent Richard Sutherland, who managed the case for the FBI.

"All of us have our appropriate appointments . . ." the judge began.

"Who do you hold your allegiance to? I want to know who these people hold their allegiance to! We owned that land," he said, referring to the couple's home that was under threat of seizure for unresolved tax issues. "They came upon us fraudulently and used those clowns over there. I'm going to stay here and yell until I see it! I don't care about procedure and your 'rule of law' crap."

It was going to be a long hearing. Lonnie Vernon unleashed.

He went on to rail about J. R. Olson, calling him a "$300,000 whore, drug-dealing piece of shit." For once, he had a point. I was still fuming that Olson had been paid handsomely and had charges against him dismissed—and I was still waiting for reimbursement for expenses. No good deed goes unpunished, they say.

"I was born a free man on the land, with all my sovereign rights invoked. I wrote it down and sent it to all of you, and your little whored-out buddy Eric Holder and Hillary Clinton."

It was only a matter of time before he got to chem trails and secret societies, I was sure of it.

"Mr. Vernon, you're ranting about a bunch of stuff that we're not going to get into today."

"This court has no jurisdiction over me and my state. You can turn into George Washington, or you can stay with these paid whores and take it down into the dirt. I am not surrendering to a goddamn bunch of whores!"

"You're ranting about a lot of things that you may *believe* . . ." said Bryan patiently. He had just summed up the whole of Lonnie Vernon's brain in a single sentence.

"What corporation do you work for?" Vernon demanded.

"I don't work for any corporation."

"The United States is a corporation!"

"You can call it what you want . . ."

"I'm making a finding that this court has no jurisdiction over me!" Vernon declared. "You have no authority. You people come here to stir up shit. You paid informants to screw citizens over. We are 'We the People,' not 'We the Bullshit!'"

Those in the courtroom stared rapt. Vernon was a loose cannon, and as the minutes ticked by, it became more and more clear why he was in this position. He was going full-Vernon.

"You scumbag from wherever you're from . . ." He pointed again at Skrocki. "You don't exist in my world. Neither does the slanderous bitch sitting next to you!" indicating Yvonne Lamoureux, assistant federal prosecutor. "You better have a marshal behind you before this day is over."

The irony of threatening officers of the federal court at his own sentencing for threatening federal officers was lost on him. This dumb shit was his own worst enemy, and I knew it from the second he stepped out of his truck and told me he wanted to buy grenades.

"Nobody's going to prove jurisdiction. This court doesn't exist! I move to dismiss!" Vernon called out.

"Motion denied."

"No, it better not be!" said Vernon. "Where is the declaration of war on the state of Alaska from these United States? You people just got me pissed off and wound up. I claim my sovereign rights. This little son of a bitch Sutherland scripted up a story. That's their little drama." He pointed at the prosecutors. "You belong in the shitholes I've been in in the last twenty months, with the doors welded up. You may as well drag me outside and put a bullet in the back of my head. These motherfuckers here started on my wife and me. This is coming from my heart because I am fed up! I drove a truck in this state for twenty-two years. My wife and I bothered no one. We tried to make a place for our home and our kids. We were going to have to be living with them soon because of the worthless son of a bitch that's ruined this country."

He turned back to address the judge.

"If you disrespect me as a sovereign on this land, then you are no better than them. I'm not disrespecting you, don't get me wrong. But I would park a Sherman tank to keep these bastards out of my yard to keep them away from my family."

"I'd like to know if there's anything else you'd like to say about the sentencing," said the judge.

"I am not part of your court."

"I understand you feel that way."

"Nobody ever answered me. You have to prove your jurisdiction in my state. I'm claiming fraud on this whole son of a bitch. It's illegal. It's a sick frickin' bird is all it is. And that's what you are—a bunch of sick frickin' birds."

"What I must do now is determine sentence."

"I want to see a declaration of war! I am not part of this fraud called the United States. I need to see your oath of affirmation. Not in your United Nations or whatever. Not Schaeffer Cox's bullshit. I want to talk man to man with someone who knows his law."

"Mr. Vernon, your position is clear to me. You're making it hard for me to conduct court here. The things that I must consider here, in doing my job, are the nature and circumstances of the offenses. Other than these events that you're here over, you've been a good citizen right up to the point all these things occurred. This is your first criminal offense and I appreciate that. Other than these events, you've lived an exemplary life. I also have to consider the offenses charged, and I've considered these things."

"It's all fraud." Vernon was losing steam.

"The nature of these offenses is most serious, particularly the conspiracy," Bryan went on, plodding slowly ahead.

"It doesn't matter what I say. There was no intent. There was just mouthing it. I popped it off wrong, and I have to apologize. I was pissed. I am born a free man on the land, under God. These son-of-a-whores over here jumped into my life for what—for money? I demand to know who they are before you move one step forward. There's no victim, there's no crime."

"Substantial punishment is appropriate. The court must protect the public from repeat of this crime."

"Dismiss, please dismiss, please dismiss, please! I'm not listening!"

Vernon was like Emma with her fingers in her ears going, "Lalalalalala!" when she didn't want to hear it was bath time. Vernon really believed he'd done nothing wrong—that bluster is bluster and threatening to kill people is all right as long as nobody actually dies. I don't know if he thought much about the fear he'd caused or if he viewed those he opposed as real people. At that moment, he was discovering where the sovereign citizen ideology of "nobody can tell me what to do" led when taken to the end of the road. Urged forward by a charismatic ideologue and a paid FBI informant, he'd thrown himself in front of the train and never realized he was also the one driving it.

"I rule that 310 months is appropriate, with credit for time served."

Twenty-five years and eight months. His attorney had asked for ten, and the prosecution had asked for thirty-five.

"Do you understand?" asked Bryan.

"I understand it's a goddamn lie, and all of you are not of my country. You are from somewhere else."

"I'm sorry your life has come to this . . ."

"I'm sorry people like you run this country, like this son of a whore," Vernon interrupted, pointing at Sutherland. "People come here to get away from pieces of shit. You have no jurisdiction in my state—pieces of dog shit."

"I hope you do easy time," said Bryan.

"You're part of them so I have to disrespect you on that."

"I don't disrespect *you*, and I'm sorry your life has come to this."

And with that, the remaining counts were dismissed, in accordance with a plea deal. And the handcuffs zipped, and Lonnie Vernon was led out.

Karen Vernon's turn had come. As much as Vernon had looked like a raving, delusional nut case, his wife looked like the librarian who does reading circle with kids, or a nice soft-faced old lady who works in a yarn store, or the awesome grandma who bakes snickerdoodles when you come over because she knows they're your favorite. She'd also hocked her family's heirloom jewelry to buy grenades. There was that, too.

Bryan said he'd read everything her attorney had filed about sentencing and he'd reviewed her plea agreement and the events of the trial.

"Ms. Vernon, have you had the opportunity to read the report and presentencing memo?"

A tiny, slow, sad voice answered, "Yes, Your Honor. Yes, we discussed it."

The maximum sentence under the guidelines is 235 months, almost ten years.

Yvonne Lamoureux presented the opinion of the prosecution and started with the reliance on a psychologist's report, which concluded that she posed no risk of violence to the community. Lamoureux said that the psychologist did not have factual evidence about the case that was relevant and did not know what Vernon had admitted.

"Those statements should have been taken into account in determining if she poses a danger to the community. Her own statements demonstrate the serious nature of offense—statements about killing federal officials." She talked about the letters found in Vernon's truck that said, *We need to cure the lead deficiency of judges*, and the fact that she'd said of the grenades they obtained, "These will do the job."

There was a plan, a map to Judge Beistline's residence with the route highlighted. She had given J. R. Olson a Post-it note with the information and talked about how they would murder family members. There were plans in the works that were interrupted when they were arrested.

Lamoureux conceded, "She worked hard and was a good member of society. Since she was incarcerated, she's been a contributing member of the prison society." Taking that and her age into consideration, Lamoureux asked for at least 188 months.

Karen Vernon's attorney, Darrel Gardner, was next and referenced numerous letters of support for her.

"Look at her as an individual—five decades of lack of criminal history. And the letters also indicate 'the current case does appear to be a significant exception to her usual way of functioning.'" Her problems, the report said, came about in part because of the "functions of the dynamics of a long-term relationship with Lonnie Vernon. It's clear from evidence that she was not a willing participant and was assisting her husband to acquire grenades . . ."

"She's been married to Lonnie Vernon for thirty years," Gardner said and asked the court to imagine what that must have been like. I couldn't even imagine it. I could barely stand five minutes with the guy.

"She maintained that relationship, loved and was devoted to him. When you have a strong personality like Mr. Vernon, you join them, or leave them. She went along to the point where she willfully participated in making these plans. In her mind, she never thought this would actually happen. Lonnie Vernon had lots of weapons, a machine gun, as lots of people in Fairbanks and the country do. Would she have gone through with it, or been involved at all except for Mr. Vernon?"

That was the question. Gardner recommended five years. "The chances of anything like this happening in the future are practically nonexistent."

Then it was Karen's chance to address the court. Judge Bryan asked if she had something to say.

"I wrote me some notes, because it was easier," she practically whispered. "I would like to offer a sincere apology to this court and . . ." She faltered and tried to stifle a cry. ". . . anyone who may have felt my words or actions were meant to cause harm to anyone. I also apologize to my family and friends for the shame and embarrassment this has caused. And I mean that, sir, I truly do."

Bryan looked like he believed that.

"Where is your mind regarding this whole income-tax issue regarding Judge Beistline?" he asked.

"It's out of his hands. They sent it to another judge. It went to the Ninth Circuit. I'm doing it the lawful way like I'd been doing all along. It's up to them. I'm trying to do everything the lawful way."

Bryan, looked at her, head in hand. He appeared to be struggling with the schism between her demeanor and her husband's—between who she appeared to be and what she actually did and said.

"You can't escape responsibility because it may have been your husband's idea. Why didn't you say no upfront?"

"I did say no, and no, and no, and no. Over and over! 'Don't say things. Don't say things that are threatening, that someone else will think is threatening.' I said no to the grenades. We can't afford 'em. We don't need 'em . . . and I just finally gave in. And when I'm with him sometimes my mouth overruns my thought process. That happens with a lot of people . . . or maybe it doesn't. I didn't want him to feel . . . The guy was offering him work, and I didn't want to stand in the way, and cause him to say, 'You lost me that job.' "

"Who was going to give him work?" asked Bryan.

"J. R. Olson." Her voice got dark as she spoke the name of the FBI informant her husband had just called "a $300,000 whore, drug-dealing piece of shit."

"Your husband remains very angry. How do you feel about this court system and this whole thing?"

"I know I made a mistake in who I associated with. Not my husband—no! I love him. I don't agree with what he says, and the way he says it, but I still try to get along. And I know there's corruptness in the court—anyone who tries to deny it is blind. There's corruptness in everything. I try to do things in the way that's lawful, and I think the way some of this was done is wrong, but that's my personal opinion. It isn't something I can just make a change and do anything about. I think I still have the right to disagree with how some things are done."

"Well, the law tells us to look at the nature of the offense and the history of the defendant and her characteristics. Let me talk about that latter thing for a minute," said Bryan. "Before this all came up, Ms. Vernon was the salt of the earth. You couldn't find a better person or a harder-working person, as far as the case and the letters indicate. Since this happened, the nature has come out with what she has done in the prison helping the other inmates. It looks like what we have here is a good person who did a very bad thing. And that leads to the seriousness of this offense. This was a *most* serious offense, and it was a conspiracy that I'm afraid was well on the way to possible conclusion, with horrible results. It may have been more your husband's fault than yours, but that does not excuse you, and I guess in these days of women's liberation, women are expected to speak with their own voice and not get dragged into things because of some guy, no matter how they feel about that guy. In light of her age, there should be some modification of the guidelines, but not much. This is a situation where there are a lot of people in the community who think the prosecution should never have happened. But these things are part of our law, and what we recognize as important to live in an ordered society, so we don't hurt each other. This offense was serious.

"I'm not sure it's of concern to deter Ms. Vernon from further offenses, but certainly any sentence should be sufficient to deter *others* from thinking they could somehow win by doing away with public officials whom they disagree with. Ms. Vernon is not likely to commit any further crimes, let alone a crime like this . . . but the seriousness of this crime keeps coming back. When the smoke clears, a sentence of twelve years is sufficient. Twelve years from when you were first arrested will get you to your mid-seventies. I'm past that myself. There's a lot of life to be led, even after such a lengthy sentence. I think it's appropriate for the seriousness, but also considering all the other things in your life you've done so well."

"Twelve years from when I was first arrested?" Karen Vernon asked quietly.

"Ten, less good time. And I think you'll be able to use your prison sentence to be of service to others. We had Mr. Vernon in court this morning. He was very angry, and I guess you understand that. I told him that I was sorry that his life had come to this, and I'm sorry your life has come to this. I hope you do easy time, and that you continue to serve the other women in the prison system. You're looking at a long, hard time ahead, but it's not the end, and it's something you can live through and come through the other side, and be a better person than you were during this period of time."

Everyone stood as the judge left the courtroom. Karen Vernon looked up at her attorney with big eyes, gave his hand a squeeze, and whispered, "Thank you."

Her husband's problem was thinking nobody could tell him what to do. Hers was letting someone do just that. Sometimes going along to get along to keep the peace does just the opposite. He didn't know when to shut up, and she didn't know when to speak up.

There was no conversation in the courtroom when Cox's turn came. A few sniffles, the scratch of a sketch artist's pencil, and a very occasional soft whisper. Schaeffer Cox, out of his suit and tie and now in a yellow prison jumpsuit, scanned the crowd with intensity, his eyes landing on a familiar face here or there.

"All rise." Flip up seats clattered as Judge Bryan entered and took his seat.

Cox had fired his attorney, Nelson Traverso, after the verdicts, and his new one, Peter Camiel, had for the first time provided the court with a psychologist's report. Shockingly, this had not been done before. According to the report, Cox suffered from paranoid schizophrenia, paranoid personality disorder, and delusional personality disorder.

Skrocki blew past the eleventh-hour diagnosis.

"The report has the audacity to say he's not intelligent, not a leader, not capable of doing the things he's done. It's frankly audacious. This person is intelligent. The one who wants to 'leave the state' and blame everyone else is not someone you should be lenient with. He's blaming the government, Bill Fulton, Brian Beazley, J. R. Olson. The excuses he's giving you in the report, do you ever hear him say, 'I'm leaving the state, I'm worried about Fulton, I'm worried about Beazley, I'm worried about these guys coming to kill me'? There's none of that. He said that after his plan to leave the state, he would come back and 'wage guerrilla warfare.'

"He's a master manipulator you've got here, that will change his argument to fit any circumstance. The jury's conviction washes all that away. They sat twelve feet away and disregarded these excuses. More excuses just came up now in this report. We're asking you for a long sentence. For some, it may be shocking and disturbing. But we made this recommendation with a lot of deliberation. We're not asking for life but a long sentence . . . Mr. Cox is predisposed to have grenades and silencers. He sent Lonnie Vernon and J. R. Olson down to go to a militia convention to obtain hand grenades. What did he say? 'I know how to make them.' He didn't get this info from anyone but himself—the DVDs, his own computer searches. What did we find him looking for on YouTube? Ammonium nitrate bombs and fuses! There is no entrapment here. This was not him being led by the nose by the government."

He talked about audio from FBI surveillance tapes in which Coleman Barney and Schaeffer Cox talk about how it takes longer to die if you're shot by a .22-caliber gun and that the shooter has to "get in close" to do it.

"These are not the recordings of a man who says, 'I really want to get my family out of Alaska.' This is someone who wants to take a human life. The bravado with which he talks about taking human life is chilling. When he talks about other people he doesn't even know—a clerk in a courthouse in Fairbanks needs to die and 'dangle like a wind chime of liberty'? It's dangerous, and it makes him a dangerous man."

I was not a fan of Steve Skrocki, but I agreed with everything he said. Skrocki recommended a sentence of thirty-five years.

Peter Camiel stood to address the court. Balding, in a grey suit, he explained that he'd had a lot of work to do in the six months between the verdict and the sentencing to catch up on the case.

"Steve Skrocki can be very persuasive, and he describes Cox as a master manipulator, and you should put him away for thirty-five years because he is a danger. But there is more about him, and what he was going through, than what was shown in trial. It's not an excuse, but it is a fact. When I came into this case, I did not have the benefit of sitting through the trial. But I met with him every week over the last six months. As I first started meeting with him, I thought he's a young guy, only twenty-eight. By his early twenties, he was married, starting a family, had a home, was starting a business. He was never in trouble as a juvenile or teenager—no criminal history. And I'm confronted with this young man convicted of serious charges. How did he get from there to where he is right now? And as I listened to him talk, read speeches, listened to recordings—something's not right. There's a disconnect. He's not seeing how he comes across to others. So I asked for an evaluation by an expert.

"We provided her with a good deal of material. I wanted to make sure she got government's opening and closing statements, the whole presentencing report that listed in detail all he was convicted of doing and all it shows at trial—letters, news articles, etc. She got a good dose of the kinds of things he was saying and did. She was well aware of what he was accused of. She didn't meet with him just once. She also gave him the standard MMPI test, which is scored by computer, and she came out with the report and diagnosis, including meetings and observations:

> *Mr. Cox has, for some time, been suffering from some serious mental illnesses to include paranoid schizophrenia, paranoid personality disorder, and delusional personality disorder.*

They forgot pathological narcissism and being annoying as shit.

"She issued opinions about that," Camiel continued. "I can appreciate that the government didn't get this report until late, but it took a while to get it done. Mr. Cox was reluctant to participate at first, but he did participate. When we got results, he was reluctant to accept the diagnosis at first, but he talked to his wife and parents and other family members. They began to say, 'It explains a lot of what was going on, and we wish we had known sooner so we could have intervened and helped.'

"He said terrible things. He was going down a dangerous path, no dispute. It's not an excuse for behavior, but there were things going on that enhanced his already paranoid view of the world. You had the child protective services attempt to interview his son—because of paranoia, it got blown out of proportion to such a degree that he and his wife and son were seeking asylum and protection at Fort Wainwright Army base. He's got in his mind that there's a team of federal assassins out to kill him and his family. How can you look back and say, 'This is just an angry guy, with anti-government sentiment'? This was a paranoia taking over his life. By the day of his arrest, he's abandoned his home and friends and is making plans to leave Alaska. What was pending was a misdemeanor firearms charge. There was no rational reason for doing what he was doing. He was being controlled by this paranoia."

Cox's wife and parents leaned slightly forward in their chairs, nodding.

"His wife didn't know what to do. She sees him obsessed with this. And his parents. A lot of people wrote it off to youthful arrogance or enthusiasm about his views. It was much more than that. This is something that can be dealt with. Counseling and medication is something he would be amenable to.

"Yes, he got involved with silencers and grenades. Won't argue. They were made available . . . But what if he *had* left the state? What if instead of trying to put grenades and silencers in his hands, we let him leave? It's clear he was trying to leave. There's such a stark distinction between what was going on with Cox and Vernon. Vernon had already written out these suicide notes. The government interrupted Vernon's plans to commit this horrible act. What was interrupted with Mr. Cox was his plan to leave the state. Whether he would have had the will or intent to carry out what he was talking about is speculation. He talked in ways that are chilling, but he never harmed anyone. For all these weapons he collected or put together, he didn't point a gun at anyone, and it isn't clear, even with paranoia, that's the direction he would be going.

"Mr. Cox completely lacked ability to see how others saw him and how his words sounded to other people. I'm not sure he appreciated at all how threatening he sounded. I don't think he understood when he was approaching someone in a particular way that they felt threatened by his words and his conduct. It's going to take some time to deal with that.

"I'd never argue these are not serious. How much time is necessary to remove him from society, get him the help he needs, and get him out on supervision? He has a strong support system of family and friends who now appreciate what was going on. There are people out there who will help him to stay on the right path."

And then, Cox got his turn to speak. He began softly and deliberately, and halfway through the first sentence he began choking up.

"I put myself here with my own words, and I feel horrible about that. And I hurt my family, and that's who's really paying, and I feel horrible about that. And this is devastating to my life, and my wife is in a position of pain and uncertainty, and I know that that is my fault. And my children, who I love with all my heart, they lost their family as a result of this, and the thing that they need the most is their parents and their home there for them while they're growing up. And that was the most important thing in the world to me, and I was so scared that something would jeopardize that, that I wound up running into the very thing I was running away from. I hurt my family first and foremost, and I put a lot of people in fear by the things that I said, and some of the crazy stuff that was coming out of my mouth, and I see that, and I sounded horrible. I couldn't have sounded any worse if I tried, and the more scared I got, the crazier things I started saying. And I wasn't thinking, I was panicking, and I lost all of my composure, and created a horrible mess."

He paused to wipe his eyes and blow his nose.

"You know, if I was the FBI, I would investigate me too. I don't blame them for that. I don't blame anybody but myself for starting this. But for all the crazy things I said, at the end of the day, I knew what I needed to take care of myself, and that was to remove myself from the situation and aggravating circumstances, and that's what I was trying to do. I was obsessed with that. I was terrified and living in a nightmare I couldn't wake up from . . . and it still is. It's gotten even more now . . . sitting here, waiting to get sentenced is even worse. But I felt it, and they saw it, and they didn't know what it was, and I didn't know what it was, but it was there. But one thing that I really, really want you to know is that I had no intention of hurting anybody. I had no desire to hurt anybody. I don't think I could have hurt anybody. I didn't have anger that would drive me to lash out; I had fear that drove me to run away. And I know I said a lot of scary, intimidating things, and when I listen to those now, I realize how serious some of the stuff I said was. But that was emotional, fear-driven bluff. And I've never been in a fight in my life. I've gone two years in jail now without getting into a fight, and that's unusual. I'll bluff and run.

"All I wanted was to leave, walk away from the situation, get away from the danger and the agitating factors and regain composure. I knew I lost all composure and was doing extreme things to try to get away. I am not a danger to anybody. And I want to apologize to the people I scared."

He still remembered how to talk.

"And that brings me to my children. I have a two-year-old and a four-year-old, and my little girl was born just a couple days before Marti and I decided to move to a different country, and . . . My little boy is my best friend in the world, and I've had some really good friends who have lost children, and I will never ever understand the pain a parent goes through when that happens, but I know that it's got to be really devastating for my children to be losing their parents and their home. There's nothing more that I want than to be there for them during their young formative years. There's nothing I can think of that's worse to lose in this life than that, and I feel like I've lost it no matter how this goes. I would just ask you to have mercy on me, and my family, and sentence me in a way that allows me to be there for my children while they are still children. I read the psychiatrist's report, and like I told Peter, I didn't want to do that. I didn't want to talk to her, I dismissed that, I was skeptical, and then I didn't want to accept results of what her diagnosis was. But after thinking about it, and after talking to family, mother, father, wife, and some people who know me real well, and who I know love me and care about me . . . and they're saying, 'Yeah, we see that and it makes sense, and you need to accept that, and it makes sense of things that didn't make sense before.' I agree there's something there and I want to listen to the people who love me. And I will do whatever I need to do to get better because life has been a horrifying nightmare for the last few years. And that's all I have to say. But I know I put myself here and I still am saying I didn't have any intention or plans to kill anyone or hurt anyone in any way, but I could have prevented this whole thing from happening and I didn't. That's my fault."

When he finished, the courtroom was absolutely silent but was broken in a few seconds by Judge Bryan.

"I need fifteen minutes," he said brusquely and left as the courtroom stood again to the clanging of chair seats flipping up.

When he returned, he was all business.

"Under the guidelines that were mandatory up until the last couple years, Mr. Cox would be getting life in prison without question, and I would not have the legal discretion to do anything other than that.

"It's interesting that the probation officer, the government, and of course, the defense, have all recommended a sentence below the guidelines. The sentencing guidelines have fallen into some disrepute, but they must be considered in sentencing.

"It's important to understand this. This is not a case about free speech or the government trying to shut somebody up. It's a criminal case about criminal acts. It started with speechmaking, and in part the speech in Montana included in it confession to crimes and possession of mines and bombs and machine guns. It's not surprising it got the government's attention. Mr. Cox started the investigation not because of the nature of his political philosophy but of the nature of criminal acts. We prize free speech in this country and that's simply not what this is about. We welcome those who have differing opinions.

"I keep reading in the paper about this 'militia,' but it never amounted to a militia. There was no militia. There was a group of guys who wanted to form a militia but never did. This group was never trained for military service, it never actually formed, and was not a true militia."

True militia or not, whatever Schaeffer Cox and anyone else he could round up were prepared to do could have caused horrible damage. All it takes is paying attention to the news to see what one crazy person with a gun is capable of.

"I want to address the psychological study and a little bit about Mr. Cox's mental status. At the end of the trial, I made some notes about Mr. Cox, after hearing all the evidence and his testimony. And I wrote down some words that are psychological in nature, but I'm not qualified to make a diagnosis, but these are what I observed about Mr. Cox."

He read from his notes.

"'Paranoia, grandiosity, narcissism, egocentricity, pathological lying.' Pathological lying is lying as a result of a disease rather than as a result of an intent to lie. I believe Mr. Cox lies without knowing that he's lying."

Even the judge nailed the narcissism part.

"The events of the trial led me to the conclusion that while Mr. Cox is reasonably or very intelligent, he is naïve, he lacks wisdom, he lacks understanding, he was raised in an insular environment, and I think part of the problem that led him into this is a failure to understand other people, the institutions of government, and the ability to understand himself. We've heard about this diagnosis; assuming that it's correct, it may supply some reasons for what Mr. Cox did, but it did not provide excuses. There's no showing he should be found not guilty by reason of insanity, or anything of the like. But it's part of him, to some extent, that he has to live with. He has never been so ill that he's not had followers and been able to convince people to follow him.

"On the letters of support I've received—I've read every one and there is a theme that goes through them. The first theme is that he is a good man, before this came up, a good family man, good worker, nice person, good neighbor in all ways. I think that is basically true, although he may have made mistakes, before this came up he was a good man with a bright future.

"The second theme, particularly from members of the church his father is the pastor of, is that his family needs him, and one of the sad things about sentencing is that there are victims of crimes far beyond the specific victims. Criminals are victims of their own crimes, and their families are. How does that play into sentencing? I can tell you what the sentencing guideline says about family: 'Family ties and responsibilities are not ordinarily relevant.' One cannot help but have a great deal of sympathy for Mrs. Cox and her children, but the fix she finds herself in is exactly what happens when the breadwinner of a house commits crimes.

"The third theme is that he didn't do it and he isn't guilty. In letter after letter that idea was expressed. Well, you know, folks, *he did do it*. He *did* commit these crimes. The jury decided that. Some will never accept it, but the law is the law. They came to court and sat for day after day. They made the decision, and he is guilty as charged. I would also say that some say the government maliciously made up this whole thing—those letters are based in large part on information that came from Mr. Cox. He said in a letter he wrote that is in wide circulation now, written on August fourth of this year, he was still saying, 'The government manufactured a case against me and told lies.'"

I had a sick feeling in my gut that there were enough true believers left in Fairbanks that this was now going to become a "thing." I could see the chat boards now—Schaeffer Cox is a patriot! He was framed!

"I don't blame people for believing that Mr. Cox wasn't guilty, or that there was another reason for his conviction. But what led to that was from Mr. Cox, and Mr. Cox is not a reliable person when it comes to telling the truth about these events, or just about anything else.

"This idea that the government made this all up was that the government somehow entrapped Mr. Cox. Entrapment in the law is a particular thing, and there was no showing of any entrapment in this case. Certainly, Mr. Olson provided the opportunity for Mr. Cox to commit the crimes, but they did not entrap him into committing the crime. And there is no sentencing entrapment—where the government simply piles it on to get a higher sentence. When there is a claim that the government has overreached, the court watches closely to see if there is some indication of overreaching or unfair prosecution. We're actually here to stand *between* the government and the defendant. I saw no indication of overreaching of the government. They operated entirely within the proper and ethical expectations of the public."

I was betting that wouldn't have been the conclusion at Denny's. Just a guess.

"We see rather typically that government tends to make things sound worse than they are, and overstate—and the defense seems to understate, and make it sound not so bad. What the court has to do is look at the offenses of conviction and go from that, rather than the rhetoric of counsel. I don't suggest either were inappropriate. You can't make it worse, or not so bad, by argument," he observed.

"We know from the convictions that he was a danger to the public in the past. We also know, despite his statements, we can have no confidence that he would not be a danger in the future. It's obviously difficult to anticipate, but Mr. Cox's personality and mental status indicates to me that the public needs to be protected from him.

"If we are to believe the results, Mr. Cox needs continuing long-term medical care, and I'm not convinced he'd get that outside a condition of incarceration. The court must also consider guidelines, which suggest a longer sentence than I'm prepared to give him. In this situation—the sentence given to Mr. Vernon yesterday—it seems to me very similar to what Mr. Cox should receive. Mr. Vernon was a different problem, presented different issues, and was perhaps much closer to carrying out the murder of a public official. But he was also a follower of Mr. Cox, and I can't help but wonder how much Mr. Cox's influence over Mr. Vernon may have lent some impetus to Mr. Vernon's desire to kill a federal judge.

"All things being considered and the issues I've discussed indicate 310 months (twenty-five years and eight months) in custody, total. That's a long time, same as Mr. Vernon, but we have the most serious offenses here, and it is very substantially below the guideline range."

Bryan looked at Cox, who seemed resigned to his fate, and said that the sentencing on all the charges was to be served concurrently, with five years' supervised release and no fine. He also said he had the right to appeal.

"Do you understand everything I've just said?"

And with a numb, "Yes, Your Honor," Schaeffer August Francis Cox was cuffed and out the back door, headed for processing into the "Communications Management Unit" in the federal prison in Marion, Illinois, where his communications with the outside world would be severely restricted. There, he'd shack up with the terrorists who'd tried and failed to blow up the World Trade Center in New York City back in 1996, Mafia bosses, drug kingpins, prisoners convicted of international and domestic terrorism who tried to recruit or radicalize others, and those who abused their communications privileges in prison by harassing victims, judges, and prosecutors. Home sweet home. And nobody put him there but himself.

CHAPTER 27

★ ★ ★ ★ ★

THE CALL

"I think there is one higher office than president and I
would call that patriot."

—Gary Hart, former US senator from Colorado

Back home in the high desert, Stacey and Emma and Olivia were creating a beautiful new life. I felt lucky every day that I was a part of it. The trauma of that night in March two years before was ebbing for them. I could tell in little ways. Emma had stopped asking when we could go "real home." Stacey had stopped staring daggers at me at random times when a thought unknown to me passed through her mind. She had stopped jumping every time the doorbell rang. And everyone started finding things they liked about Colorado—the mountains, the flowers, new friends.

I missed the guys, and thoughts of them and the fire pit in the parking lot, no matter how happy, made my stomach cramp and shrivel up. I believed with all my heart I'd done the right thing, but that didn't change the fact I'd hurt the people who meant the most to me. All of them. I wish I could have had time to explain everything, but even that wouldn't have guaranteed they'd understand or forgive me. Suicide probably wanted to kill me. No doubt he thought back on our last conversation when I called him as I drove to the airport and realized why I thanked him for everything. Because it was a goodbye call. Poor Jesus would have been in shock. Discount would feel lost. His world was finally coming together, becoming stable and predictable, and now he was in the middle of a storm again where nothing made sense. Brian, most of all, would be furious and feel betrayed. I knew him well enough to know that. He stuck his neck out for me and never knew the full story. He'd feel played, and he didn't like feeling played.

I had to force myself to think of the people who were living their normal lives now, and didn't have to worry that Schaeffer Cox "had them outmanned and outgunned," and could sleep at night without having their houses torched. Because they were the whole reason for this. The reason I would never have my friends back, the reason my wife would never really trust me the same way again, the reason I lost what I'd built. And I was still waiting for a reimbursement check for expenses from the FBI. Bastards. I'd stopped holding my breath a long time ago for that.

And for my own part, I missed belonging to something, being useful, grabbing a gun and going on a mission, planning the tactics, getting the adrenaline rush, doing bad things to bad people.

When Stacey was at the sink a few nights earlier rinsing carrots, I'd thought for a second about saying, "So, I was thinking about joining a militia down here." It was a joke, a bad one, but there was an elemental truth to the impulse. The same primal driving force that leads some to the military, that led my guys to Drop Zone, and led me to work for the FBI, was the same force that drove others to the militia and other patriot groups—duty, responsibility, belonging, camaraderie, purpose, honor, loyalty, service, patriotism, doing the right thing. The only difference is who you think are the bad guys and what you believe *is* the right thing.

If a man says he's a fisherman, or a farmer, or an artist, there is an understanding. These aren't "jobs"; they are identities. If you take a fisherman away from the sea, he will find a way back—he's got the sea in his blood. A farmer will grow things; an artist will create. If not, they'll lose their minds.

But when you say you're a soldier, people don't understand. It isn't romantic, or politically correct. It doesn't sound like a "calling." But warriors have been around as long as fishermen. And if you stop being one, they think you can be something else—like the manager of Best Buy, or a carpenter, or some guy who lands a desk job with the state. The truth is that being a soldier is more who you are than what you do. You will always seek a way to protect and defend, to scan the perimeter for danger, to feel your purpose, to band with your brothers. And if you don't, something in you will never be right.

"I'm gonna run and pick up some beer. You need anything while I'm out?"

"Just milk," Stacey said.

As my Jeep headed down the road to town, an optical illusion from the heat made the asphalt look like water. My pocket buzzed. I fumbled for the phone. "Yeah, babe? You need something else?"

"How about a dozen eggs!" a woman's voice said on the other end, but it wasn't Stacey. Nobody ever called me but her anymore. I looked at the phone. *SK.*

"Oh, God, no. It's you," I said.

"Nice greeting. Great to hear your voice, too," Sandy laughed. "I just wanted to touch base and find out how everything is going with you guys. How are you doing? How are Stacey and the girls?"

"I'd be doing better if I got a goddamn check in the mail, now that you mention it. When are you guys cutting me a reimbursement?"

"We're working on it. I'll give another nudge."

"Yeah, right."

"Was that your horn? Are you driving?"

"Yeah. Goddamn roadrunners. Seriously. I didn't even know they were real. They just run right out in front of your fucking car."

"Other than that, how's Colorado? Are you bored?"

"Girls are fine. Stacey's fine. She's speaking to me again, no thanks to you assholes. So that's good. It's quiet. I've started gardening. I have chickens. I make beer. Other than that, there's not much going on."

"Well, there may be more going on in your neck of the woods than chickens and beer," she said.

"What do you mean? What . . . Oh, no. No."

"Bill . . ."

"Don't you fucking do this to me, Sandy. Do NOT. No."

"You know me pretty well, right?"

"I'm not listening to you."

"And you know I would never dream of asking you unless I knew it was really important. Especially after all you've been through."

"No! I can't do this again, Sandy. Seriously. Please don't ask me."

"Bill . . . people could get killed."

EPILOGUE

"Abuse of words has been the great instrument of sophistry
and chicanery, of party, faction, and division of society."
—John Adams

"We must learn to live together as brothers or perish
together as fools."
—Martin Luther King Jr.

The Drop Zone was family—stronger than family. We put our lives in each other's hands without hesitation. We trusted each other. But the day I stepped onto that plane and left Alaska, Drop Zone died. It didn't die because I was any more important than any of the others, or because I did more, or cared more. My job just happened to be the hub of the wheel, and when the hub came off, the spokes flew and the rim splintered. The point of connection was lost, and everything broke apart. I still wake up every day knowing I destroyed the most positive influence in the lives of people I loved. I betrayed the trust of my family—my blood family and my band of brothers. I'd like to think I did it for the right reasons—the greater good. I can justify it to myself by saying that innocent people didn't die, but even though that's true, "the greater good" can feel like cold comfort to someone who has been hurt.

The political right wing has built a mythology: In order to be a patriot and a good American, you must embrace the military-industrial complex that has become our government and the clusterfuck of foreign policy it

271

has created. The Republicans say if you don't support everything we do militarily, then you aren't a true patriot. "Patriot" has become a code word for conservatism, and the fear of being labeled as "unpatriotic" has driven support for bad policy and unjustified war.

Patriotism does not mean conservatism or unconditional support for military action. Patriotism is more than a bumper sticker on your car or drinking a Budweiser and waving a flag. That's easy and hollow. True patriotism means serving—actually *doing something* for your country and the people in it because it's the right thing to do.

America is the best place on Earth. It's my country and I'd give my life for it, but it's not infallible. Our founding principles demand that we question ourselves, demand that we grow, that we make ourselves better. To do that, we must take a hard look at what America does and how it does it. It's not always pretty.

The "my country right or wrong" attitude is just as misguided as unconditionally hating the government. Do I hate the government sometimes? Fuck, yes. The FBI still owes me a bunch of money for relocation costs and expenses I'll never see; some douchebag at the TSA thinks it's OK to grope my junk, and a good chunk of the money in my April 15th IRS check goes to shit I don't support. But in the big picture, we are the ones who have voted the people who run the government into office, and we have done this over many generations. We have the government we made. Just because I don't agree with it sometimes doesn't mean I have the right to opt out. I cannot just exempt myself from the laws of my country, however misguided I may personally find them, because we are the government and the government is us. It's not some bogeyman out there in the dark of night. We created it, we voted for it, and we allow it to exist. You can't hate the government without hating yourself.

So, if you're angry, take a hard look in the mirror and figure out where you screwed up. The blame is ours, and if we don't wake up and demand the government we want, the system as it sits will not be able to function much longer.

I can put people in jail all day long, but it won't fix the problem. A fix will require grown-up conversations about big issues. Because right now, I'm here to tell you that there are a lot of pissed-off people out there, and some of them are batshit crazy. And if the right one hears some inflammatory rhetoric, it may not take much to leap from angry thought to violent action. When it's just a couple of people, we can deal with it, and I believe that the FBI has done a decent job of keeping threats in check. But when craziness becomes the new normal, then we're fucked. And craziness is becoming more and more normal all the time. Just watch the news.

There's a rise in extremism, and with extremism, innocent people die. It will be up to the right to acknowledge that other patriots exist. It will be up to the left to stop vilifying the word, and reclaim it with its true meaning. And if we don't work together, and talk, and remember that we are all Americans, Schaeffer Cox's war may come after all. For the great American experiment to survive, we will require patriots—real patriots.

ACKNOWLEDGMENTS

This book is dedicated to the men and women of the FBI, who work tirelessly to keep us safe every day; my brothers at Drop Zone, who saved me just as much as I saved them; Ken Blaylock and Russell Mims, who both shaped me into the man I am today. And lastly, but most importantly, to my wife, who has stood by me while I do what I do. Without her, none of this would have been possible.

—Bill Fulton

Deep gratitude to Bill Fulton for having faith in me to use his voice and tell his story; to my wonderful children for putting up with a mom who lives behind a screen much of the time; to my sister who has always been my rock; to Mudflatters everywhere for your loyal support; and to David for expanding my mind and my heart and showing them both new worlds.

—Jeanne Devon

ABOUT THE AUTHORS

Bill Fulton is an Army veteran with extensive and ongoing training in areas including anti-terrorism; nuclear, biological, and chemical weapons; surveillance and operations; and law enforcement and military justice. He is also an adrenaline junkie who owned and operated a fugitive recovery service in Anchorage, Alaska, that took more than 400 criminals off the streets. During his career, he has worked with the Army Criminal Investigation Division, the FBI, and other governmental agencies, while working undercover to apprehend domestic terrorists.

He currently works as an undercover operative with the FBI and other federal and state agencies and serves as a subject matter expert on right-wing domestic terrorism. Bill lives in an undisclosed location with his wife, two children, and assorted pets. When he is not assisting governmental agencies in combating domestic terrorism, he enjoys organic gardening, permaculture, reading, being a dad, and fine wine.

Jeanne Devon is a *New York Times* best-selling co-author of *Blind Allegiance to Sarah Palin* (with Frank Bailey and Ken Morris), widely praised as the ultimate tell-all and the most thoughtful and complex analysis of Palin's personality and early political career. Devon is also a political writer and the founding editor of the multiple-award winning Alaska political blog *The*

Mudflats. She catapulted to national attention when Sarah Palin was nominated as the Republican candidate for vice president, and *The Mudflats* became one of America's primary sources of information for all things Palin. Devon went on to cover Senate candidate Joe Miller in 2010, and won an Alaska Press Club Award for her coverage of Alaska militias.

A New Jersey native, she moved to Alaska more than two decades ago seeking adventure, and it found her.